CBI Insider Speaks

Birlas to Sheila Dikshit

Attention Authors

'We Convert Fighters into Writers'. That's the motto of Manas Publications since more than four decades. Our message to the world is that India can win the battle not only by the bullet but also by the pen. There is no dearth of intellectuals in our country, but their knowledge is confined to them only. No sincere effort has been made by any other publisher to channelise their knowledge in national interest. That is why the talent of a large number of intellectuals remains latent. An author transforms his knowledge into a manuscript, and it is our job to spread his/her knowledge by converting it into a beautiful book. For over four decades, Manas has been motivating the intellectuals by publishing their manuscripts and would like to publish your manuscript too. If you or your colleagues have any manuscript ready for publication or are working on it, kindly contact us with detailed synopsis and list of contents. We will transform your work into a valuable publication. If you wish, we can also suggest you the suitable subjects for writing the books related to your area of expertise. Manas is known for its publishing quality and commitments. We take utmost care in production and give wide publicity to the book as well as its author through our national and international distribution network.

CBI
Insider Speaks

Birlas to Sheila Dikshit

Shantonu Sen

Former
Joint Director: CBI
OSD to Lt Governor-Delhi

Manas Publications
(We Convert Fighters into Writers)
New Delhi-110002 (INDIA)

MANAS PUBLICATIONS
(We Convert Fighters into Writers)
(Publishers, Library Suppliers, Importers & Exporters)
4402/5-A, Ansari Road (Opp. HDFC Bank)
Darya Ganj, New Delhi-110 002 (India)
Off. 23260783, 23265523, Fax: 011-23272766
E-mail: manaspublications@gmail.com
manaspublications@yahoo.com

ISBN 978-81-7049-503-1

₹ 795/-

Designed at
Manas Publications

Printed in India at
RK Print Services, Delhi
and Published by Mrs Suman Lata for
Manas Publications, 4402/5-A, Ansari Road
Darya Ganj, New Delhi-110 002 (INDIA)

Contents

Preface

For all the apparent all-pervasive corruption in society that one is accustomed to hearing about in modern times, crime is not an aberration that homo-sapiens are guilty of at all times. Arguably, modern day pressure to perform or simply the need to keep up with societal demands may tempt the ordinary individual to throw convention to the winds and literally hit out at norms established by society. Committing a crime on the other hand, is disobedience of the statute, the society has encoded for its own protection, development and growth. Often sheer greed – irrespective of its specific character, motivated by wealth or power, or need – propels crime. At the upper echelons of the moneyed society, men in positions of authority become prone to it, in tune with Lord Acton's famous aphorism "Power corrupts and absolute power corrupts absolutely."

It would not be unfair to belabour the point that the Indian socio-political order, under the systems governing society, politicians and public servants are most comfortably placed to bestow unto themselves absolute power. It would again be no exaggeration to say that these two segments of society have by and large been the fountainhead of crime. Their abomination knows no bounds as they commit crimes, venal and horrendous and they do it all the time, afflicting both civic society and those ordained to preserve law and order alike. The Indian Police is accused of being a cesspool of corruption and among the varied and variegated groups of public servants in the subcontinent they alone enjoy the power to arrest without warrant, something that they have used to singular distinction to catapult themselves to frontline positions in the business of abuse of power.

Paradoxically, the only group of public servants that has retained a modicum of credibility; some fame and name as the scimitar against all that is corrupt in India is a group of policemen that goes by the acronym of CBI - the Central Bureau of Investigation. That this group could give a better account of itself—as most of us could is not in question. The point is that, despite the limitations imposed on it and not withstanding its failures, this group has served as the country's iron fist in its battle against corruption and crime.

Where does a CBI officer find himself in this scenario; and one is talking of an officer who believes in the rule of the law and considers himself as a vital tool in the process. Clearly punishment is not his domain. Investigation of a crime and the trial of the criminal definitely is. This is the background that provides a scenario to introduce my personal experience of a lifetime spent with the CBI, to the reader. Clearly, a CBI officer must first compel himself to close his eyes to the doings of judges, their judgements and their findings and focus clearly on investigating by the book. Whatever the pressures on the officer—and one does not deny that they have increased over the years—investigation and trial by and large are responsibilities of the investigating officer. What about interference? Things were certainly straight when I first joined the CBI, though matters may have become sticky in 1967, when the CBI was asked to do the Birla's in but certainly after 1977 interference in the areas of investigation and trial began to be quite frequent. By 1986, almost all high-profile cases of corruption were being interfered with and the pages that follow provide examples of the nature of interference.

The bottom line is that interference exists and will continue. Nevertheless, there is a role for a thorough investigation and complete monitoring of trial of cases sent up to court, which is still the responsibility of the investigating officer. This is also a responsibility that he can discharge, irrespective of interference of any kind that he may have to put up with. There is really no need to be helpless in these two areas—the areas of investigation and trial.

I spent nearly 34 years in the CBI and have often felt that certain experiences, certain decisions, certain views and insights need to be put down on paper, if for nothing else, to share what I have experienced. The battle-ravaged Golden Temple was a heart-wrenching sight (among the many cases that were for me to investigate) and one that continues to haunt me. How did it all happen and what did I see? I believed, that I must share my experience with those who might want to know about it and who should have a chance to see and feel what I saw and felt in June 1984. Similarly, there are other areas that might be of some curiosity as well.

Coming back to the question of interference in the CBI which, I am sure, bothers young officers and the lay public alike: What happens when a high-profile case is under investigation? This question has been asked of me so many times that I feel that it deserves to be answered. I have tried to answer it in this book.

The CBI as an investigating agency is one of the finest institutions created in the post-Independence era. Even today, there is nothing structurally wrong with the institution; despite its many slippages. Truth to tell, whenever it has slipped, it had been bad and servile leadership that had caused it. Vir Sanghvi, Editor, *Hindustan Times,* described CBI as poodle of Narasimha Rao. In an article he wrote in his paper on Sunday, 1st October, 2000-- to quote his exact words—"under Vijay Rama Rao's malign leadership, the CBI functioned as Narasimha's Rao poodle." On 4th May, 2001 on BBC Question Time, in the presence of the just then retired Director of CBI, RK Raghvan, he described Vijay Rama Rao as Narasimha Rao's poodle. The latter did not protest. This is the first basic truth. It is not the CBI that should be condemned but the leadership of the organization that is in command when a particular incidence takes place that leaves a question mark on the ability of the CBI. It is the truth that none of us can shy away from.

There is also a fundamental appreciation of crime and punishment that the lay public should be equipped with. All what the judiciary does is not based on a strict determination of issues before it. Often times, there are extraneous factors leading to a judgement or a conclusion. Sometimes, the best investigated cases get thrown out for reasons outside the pale of legal logic. The Hawala cases were a prime example of how not to proceed with the investigation which as everyone knows was directed by the Supreme Court and it finally also hammered the final nail in its coffin. Equally pathetic was the manner in which the conviction of Kalpnath Rai and Vincent George's brother-in-law, Saboo Chackoo and the BJP Member of Parliament, Brij Bhusan Saran, were set aside by the highest court of the land even while others were convicted with enhanced sentences*[1]. No less agonizing was the manner in which all the three courts—the trial court, the High Court and the Supreme Court—rejected the CBI's well-investigated case that recommended that Ameeta Singh and her paramour Sanjay Singh be tried for the murder of Syed Modi, the badminton star, to whom Ameeta was hitched in bizarre circumstances. The nation has watched in dismay as the top in the Prime Minister's Office (PMO) have been protected in the Urea Scam. The weak are good fodder for prosecution; the powerful seldom. This is the increasingly raucous refrain of the Indian criminal justice system. It is within these restrictive parameters that the CBI must perform.

This brings up the question of sanctity of judicial process and of members of the judiciary. Reports that some judges are suspected of having mafia connections are spine chilling. Political interference can be countered but the court's interference, especially under corrupt judges, will be akin to dynamite, destroying everything that is sacred about the Indian polity. This may be a very simplistic comment on the judiciary in India, otherwise a very respected institution. The fact remains that in high-profile cases, the judiciary often tends to procrastinate, plays to the gallery and comes up with a decision—based on extraneous factors. A word of cheer at this moment, may appear hypocritical. Even if it is so, in many instances it's not the end of the world. As democracy and democratic practices take root such deviations will face exposure and this exposure will bleach them white and hasten their demise. This is also a compelling reason behind this book. Finally, what is it that connects these separate and unconnected episodes? In one word, investigation. The nuances that make up a criminal investigation are very many and some of them are exposed for those who wish to read, assess, perhaps weigh and also judge.

Shantonu Sen

Acknowledgement

The incentive to put down on paper a little of what is the Central Bureau of Investigation (CBI) has come from the great team that publishes *Seminar*. Malvika, Tejbir also known as Jugnu and Harsh, years my junior in school must receive the credit or the discredit for getting me pepped up to write. I first wrote for them. Two issues of *Seminar* were my brain child. *Seminar* issues have shaped my convictions and my thoughts here will find their echoes there. So thank you Mala Jugnu and Harsh.

Aditi Roy Ghatak, Kolkata formerly of *The Statesman* Kolkata and now a freelancer went through the entire manuscript when I wrote it first. Though it has under gone many revisions most of what she edited has remained. She is a loyal devoted friend with fluent command over the English language and I cannot thank her enough.

In its publication CBI Bulletin encouraged me to write. Some of the chapters here reflect my earlier writings in the Bulletin. One officer of the CBI, MP Singh who retired as a DIG years after I superannuated, has from the days of his probation impressed me and many more in the organization with his ability to detect and find evidence where the odds often looked insurmountable. The Chapters on Sikand Murder and Assassination of General AS Vaidya reflect his acumen at some length. There are many officers in the CBI with his ability, perhaps to a slightly lesser degree. I thank him and others unnamed whose work will be credited to me just because I wrote it. Where there is a good word I share it with all of them. Where its panned the blame is mine. Lastly I am quite thankful to Manas Publications for motivating me to write this book so long after the events have taken place.

Dedication

CBI INSIDER SPEAKS is dedicated to my teachers (1942-1959), my school where I received my moral grounding and to my parents Girija Nath Sen and Leela Sen nee Mazumdar who are shining examples of integrity, discipline and affection.

Chapter-1

Big Money
The Birlas have the Last Laugh

"It is an affront. This is entirely unexpected." Mr BK Birla, the third son of the great "GD" looked pained; his aide, RC Maheshwari, furious and Suresh Chandra Roy, acutely embarrassed. I had made the remark in 1975, in Calcutta, at the New Road, Alipore, residence of Mr Roy. The angry retort of an idealistic officer, no more than ten years with the Central Bureau of Investigation.

The Birla Textile Group was an empire that had steadily grown under the patriarch, GD. It had factories in Delhi, Gwalior, Ahmedabad, Calcutta, Bombay and Bhiwani with a liaison office in Bombay. The seeds of this episode lay in 1967. I had completed brief stints at Calcutta and Lucknow and had just received a Delhi posting when I came across this interesting case of the Bureau alleging a conspiracy, involving all Birla Textile operations, to breach textile laws for a massive evasion of excise duty. All factories, offices, liaison offices of the company were simultaneously searched on the basis of these allegations reproduced on a first information report dated June 13, 1967. I had arrived in Delhi in September 1967 and was assigned to the CBI team investigating the case.

The investigation was hardly a smooth affair. The Bureau had been let loose on this empire, deliberately. The Director of Revenue Intelligence, in the Ministry of Finance, had pinpointed the areas of evasion sometime earlier. The easiest thing to do was to recover the arrears. Perhaps, the scions of the Birla empire propping up the Swatantra Party was a bit too much for the then Prime Minister, Indira Gandhi who, aided by information collected by the then "Young Turk", Chandrasekhar, first directed the DRI and later, the CBI to launch an investigation. The Birlas challenged the investigation and within a few years succeeded in getting the Supreme Court to hold the entire search illegal. All that had been seized was ordered to be returned. The search being extensive, much of the seizures was redundant and the investigators had little problem returning the documents. The evasion aspect, however, continued to be investigated based on such documents as were available from official sources and those could be easily connected with references from the premises of the Birla factories and offices.

In February 1973, I shifted to Calcutta and assumed charge as Superintendent of Police, Economic Offences Wing (EDW), Calcutta. The Birla cases were behind me, I had hoped. Most cases against most mills had been closed and the CBI had lost them in trial courts. Save one mill: the New Swadeshi and Manjushri Textile Mill. Under a pugnacious executive, it had stoutly resisted parting with a single paper once the CBI had been compelled to return the documents. CBI persisted in various courts seeking custody of such documents that were connected with crimes under investigation. The ding-dong battle continued till 1974 when the Supreme Court ordered that related documents be handed over to the CBI. I was ordered to start the investigation and also to continue to run the Economic Offences Wing in Calcutta. It was an imposition no doubt, as the official papers were in my former office in Delhi, which I had left in 1972. The mill documents were in Ahmedabad and I was in Calcutta. The most anguishing part was that the West Indies-India Test match was to take place at Eden Gardens and I had tickets for all five days. No way was I going to miss the match. To cut a long story short, I manipulated my way to Calcutta-Ahmedabad air ticket and saved myself the long train journey. I saw the Test match and witnessed Chandrasekhar demolishing the mighty Clive Lloyd's team and then dashed to Ahmedabad. MD Agarkar, a Deputy Superintendent of Police, joined me and John Lobo later, to distinguish himself as Director CBI, then a Deputy Inspector General from Delhi, whose leave had been cut short, came from Goa to oversee our work. We put in long hours and had to call for many more documents from the mill as investigations revealed much more that was shady. The mills refused to go beyond the letter of the court order and we felt that the spirit of the order required them to part with all such documents, that we could establish, as part of evidence of even new offences that came to light.

What we found was that a plan had been hatched, initiated from the very top, to gyp the central excise authorities, and it had been under way since 1964. Here was no case of mere infraction of textile orders, but this large textile house was plain and simply cheating. What its executives had done was to misrelate huge amount of yarn as producing a controlled variety of cloth when considering its quality it was not and paid lesser, much lesser. Excise in taxes then, they should have really paid. In one glaring instance in three years, 1964 to 1967, they avoided paying taxes to the tune of slightly more than Rs. two lakhs, no measly sum in the late sixties. Similarly, there were various other offences and taxes avoided. The data strongly suggested the filling of the coffers was operated from the Managing Director, Mr SN Hada's chair and others followed him without any protest .

We dragged the mills to the Ahmedabad High Court and won. They went to the Supreme Court and had Ashok Sen appealing that beyond the documents given the Birlas would part with no more. We pointed out that indications of crime had surfaced and it was CBI's statutory duty to investigate the new angle. The Supreme Court accepted this argument and the CBI gradually regained the ground lost on account of "illegal" search. All that had been returned had been listed and as we found the need to see them, we would seek the court's order and obtain the right, to see and, if required, retain them. Hada was obviously most upset at this turn of events. He alone had challenged the legality of the search, and it had been his victory in the Supreme Court, holding the search irregular and illegal that had helped other mills to get back their documents and nullify the investigation of the CBI to that extent. He fought back ferociously and we encountered enormous problems at every step. With the Courts seeing the transparency of material collected and submitted each time by affidavit under my own name on our side, however, we got every document that we wanted from what we had been compelled to return. The end result was a satisfactory investigation where the 'big-wigs' of the mills were held culpable. BK Birla and Hada topped the list of persons whom we sought to arraign in court. The first hint that all was not well was when the name of BK Birla was dropped from the list on legal advice. The rest, Hada included, were summoned by court to face trial. I came back to Calcutta and took over the Economic Offence Wing.

Coming back to the beginning of this story; one day, SC Roy, a former Sheriff and a leading citizen of Calcutta, whose office was in the same building as mine, came to my chamber. After some hemming and hawing, he said that BK Birla was very anxious to meet me once. I had met him in my chambers in Calcutta, about a year ago, during the investigation of the case, to seek clarifications on offences which his mill had committed. There was no occasion at all to see him again. The trial had not yet started; I was reluctant; but Mr Roy was very persuasive. The venue was his house and he himself would be present. Frankly, I did not want to meet them. The CBI Director, Devinder Sen, was against such bonhomie with members on the other side. Although, he had overruled the view of **Agarkar** and myself, supported by two of my immediate superiors, and dropped BK Birla from the list to be prosecuted on legal advice, he could question such a meeting. I recalled how he had chided me when, in a mix-up caused by the common surname, their lawyer from Ahmedabad had rung him up instead of me. He had sternly asked me why "Birla was in touch with me." I made inquiries and explained later, why the call had been made, and I knew that he was most unhappy about such meetings.

Nevertheless, I was persuaded to meet the industrialist. After office, I drove to his New Road residence. BK Birla and Maheswari were already in. Tea and snacks were on the table. We got talking. Soon, BK Birla got to the point. He knew that I had wanted to prosecute him, but had not succeeded. His question, framed in a nice, round aboutway was, whether I was making a second attempt to pin him down. I met his question dead on and told him, that I wanted to prosecute him but, my superiors had decided otherwise. There was no question of anyone again seeking and then ensuring his trial. I was not in this game. Then he went a bit too far; asking whether it was not possible to drop Hada from the list of those facing trial. That was when that I lashed out. Maheswari said that I was using strong language, but Mr Birla was more conciliatory and matters rested there. Hada has had the last laugh though. I retired in 1996. His trial never commenced in my time. Briefly, in 1993-1994, I was superior to the Superintendent of Police in charge of the case and both of us made a special effort to start the trial. The matter had been repeatedly mentioned in the Supreme Court but the records had been mislaid and thus matters slowed down till I retired in 1996. I have now (2014) learnt that this case was withdrawn by the Government of India, from trial on 30.03.2009 on the ground that it was an old case and that most of the accused had died.

Chapter-2

The Line is not for Toeing!

Is influence exercised on investigation? Is CBI susceptible to political influence? Such questions are often tossed at CBI officers. Most CBI officers, including myself, would normally respond in a manner that would convey an impression that influence does not really come in the way of CBI investigation. It may be there, at some level, but the investigating officer is seldom bothered by it. The CBI investigates about 1,200 fresh cases every year. Political interference or influence or directions cannot, and do not, affect all of them. That, however, is not enough of an explanation. Some cases do receive political attention, the persistent skeptic would insist. Is there interference? The accounts of experiences that follow tell their own tale, some of the most fascinating interference coming during the investigations into the Punjab terrorist cases. Interference came in various shapes: from what strategy to follow, to instructions about who would be prosecuted even without a preliminary enquiry. Did I do anything about it all? Dealing with this problematic aspect of my career has been fascinating.

I, personally, never succumbed to any kind of interference, direct or indirect; I may have had to go around interfering directives through acceptable subterfuge though. With a year to go for retirement in early 1995, I sat down and discussed my perception of all this with the then executive editor, *The Times of India*, Mr Gautam Adhikary. There were many others, both in and outside the CBI, to whom I mentioned these issues and expressed my apprehension that since, many within the organization were succumbing to this pernicious evil, this premier investigating organization—already hamstrung by Rajiv Gandhi's Single Directive—would soon become a department of the Government of India. Incidentally, this notification barred the CBI from commencing any enquiry, let alone investigation, against any official either in the Government or the Public Sector, if he occupied any post that was equivalent in rank of a Joint Secretary, in the Government of India, without a formal approval of the Government. It was Adhikary, who suggested that I write a paper on my perception, which *The Times of India* would be happy to publish. He, of course, warned me to take prior permission of the authorities before writing on such a sensitive subject. I decided to write, but also decided not to ask for specific permission.

In a CBI conference held a few months ago, I had suggested that as we were receiving a bad press, we should be permitted to write about our methods and investigations and the trials that followed in the national press. This had been agreed to. Therefore, the permission to write existed in principle. On April 17, 1995, I sent my piece that was carried on the Open page of *The Times of India*, in all its editions on April 25, 1995. Expectedly, it raised a bit of a storm. *The Navbharat Times* (April 26, 1995) addressed an editorial to this article on April 26, 1995, Calcutta's *Ananda Bazar Patrika* took this article for a report. It expressed surprise, that a serving public servant could write in this vein, and put the Government on the mat, by suggesting that civil servants are in nexus with the crime syndicates that comprise most of the political masters of today. That, there is an incestuous relationship with their political masters and they are active abettors with the crime syndicate. That, they not only earn protection, but also rewards in the shape of cushy promotions, postings, extensions, gubernatorial appointments, out of turn assignments, unimaginable clout and, of course, unimaginable lucre. I received a few complimentary letters, too. One by R K Khandelwal, formerly Chairman, Joint Intelligence Commission and Secretary in the Cabinet Secretariat, written on April 25, 1995 itself, was particularly gratifying. He had been terribly upset with me in 1992, when his nephew, Mohan

Khandelwal, a Harshad Mehta, power of attorney holder, was arrested under my instructions. Mohan Khandelwal had spilled the beans on Harshad Mehta's links with V Krisnamurthy, his carrying the suitcase to the Prime Minister's Race Course residence and then accompanying Harshad to the Congress Party treasurer's house the same afternoon and Sita Ram Kesri's role in keeping the same and many other deals with the public sector banks and companies, all of which helped in cementing the evidence against Harshad. The difference in my perception and him was that he saw himself as a honourable witness for the prosecution and I saw his as an approver only (which he ultimately did become) and therefore, taking him under custody was a step forward in the investigation. This upset his uncle and he often spoke of me in that upset vein and hence, his letter was quite bracing.

The Government did call for a written explanation from me for expressing my views on corruption in *The Times of India*. However, when I explained that my piece was written by prior permission and it was actually a study of corruption in the civil services from the British days to the present times, the chapter was closed. That more serious action was contemplated and ultimately not taken came to my knowledge from a little item published in *The Telegraph*.

I, also developed a strategy to avoid being interfered with. That was used in getting the 'waging of war' charges dropped in the Bombay blast cases without giving a hint to those who would have definitely prevented me from doing so. In a subsequent case, involving the members of the underworld and politicians such as Kalpanath Rai, I avoided confrontation and manoeuvred the investigation to ensure that only on directions of the court action would be initiated against the politicians.

I did not file a chargesheet either against Kalpanath Rai or the other politician, Brij Bhushan Saran Singh a BJP MP or even Saboo V Chako, brother-in-law of V George, Rajiv Gandhi's secretary, who was the regional manager, East West Airlines, New Delhi. Kalpanath Rai was the Union Minister for Power. He had ordered that a guest house of the National Thermal Power in Delhi be reserved for months for two criminals who were then wanted by Maharashtra police for murder and several heinous crimes. They had close links with Dawood Ibrahim. The entire expenditure for their stay/food was borne by the Public Sector Undertaking for about two at the express, oral and written instruction of the staff of the honourable Minister. Brij Bhusan Saran Singh was their associate. Saboo, as Regional Manager, East West Airlines, Delhi, provided monetary assistance and hotel accommodation to Dawood's men. The CBI did not even arrest them. Kalpanath Rai refused even to be questioned and every time he was contacted, he turned abusive. Every word of what he said to the CBI officer was recorded in the case diary of the CBI which the court perused during the trial. The strategy was to put the entire evidence against them in the material before the court yet, not charge sheet them on the plea that investigation was still continuing. While the earlier judges trying the case did not take note of this material, Mr Justice SN Dhingra, who finally tried the case, read the evidence and slammed the CBI for not laying chargesheets against Kalpanath Rai, Brij Bhushan Saran Singh and SV Chako. It was then, that the CBI was able to go ahead and lay the chargesheet against all the three accused. Kalpanath Rai was arrested and produced in court and remanded to judicial custody for the entire period of the trial. Interference had been avoided by not arresting him earlier though at a cost of earning a severe reprimand from Justice Dhingra. I had succeeded in lulling them into the belief that they would not be prosecuted and, therefore, their political clout did not come into play.

Journalists have been interesting as sources in a two-way traffic: they part with information to receive information. Soumya Ghosh, of *Hindustan Times*, was a source in that sense. He provided me with substantial information on the behavioural patterns of some high-profile persons under investigation. He was not the only journalist I had used but, he was certainly the most useful. In return, I shared with him information on cases under investigation, and enquiry much of which appeared under his by-line. Chandan Mitra was his editor who was aware of this relationship. In his book on corruption, Chandan Mitra, without mentioning names, has suggested that the journalist who befriended Krishnamurthy when under investigation was allegedly the beneficiary of Krishnamurthy's largesse, and this was apparently for the investigating officer's benefit. There is obviously then a danger involved in running a source network. However, merely because Krishnamurthy made allegations to Chandan Mitra, suggesting that despite gratifying the journalist, the charges against him were not dropped, one does not have to forego this useful source network. It is of advantage both to the journalist in question and to the investigating officer if used intelligently. I might add here, that while this operation was on, the journalist in question had reported to me the various attempts by Krishnamurthy to stall the enquiries and I had personally verified some of them and found them to be correct. Not only in the case of Krishnamurthy, in a few others as well, notably the one involving the East West Airlines, where Kalpanath Rai was very much an accused, the same journalist had tipped me off as to how attempts were being made to stall the investigation. All this had enabled me to take some counter measures which I have mentioned in some detail elsewhere in the book. Chandan Mitra himself possibly did not believe the charge of gratification made by Krishnamurthy, as he continued with the same journalist not only in *Hindustan Times* but, with *The Pioneer* as well. Why he chose to mention the story in his book may intrigue me but Chandan must have a practical valid reason for writing what he did.

In my last year, I was a pariah with the top in the CBI and the government, and an attempt was made to put me on the mat for renting out my Jaipur house to the CBI. Inquiries were initiated through the Central Vigilance Commissioner and this information was leaked to the media. Of course, nothing followed as they found that while the CPWD assessment of the house rent was Rs 7,500 per month, the CBI Jaipur had suggested that I take only Rs 4,500 per month as that was within the powers of the CBI Director. I had informed both the administrative divisions of the CBI, which had processed the case and fixed the rent within the powers of the Director, CBI and also the policy division which is CBI's internal vigilance as required under the conduct rules of the Government of India. They, however, found a flaw and the reprimand that I received suggested that the regional office CBI, Jaipur, had been under my charge when I was a DIG (though at the time of renting I was not DIG CBI Jaipur) and, therefore, I should have taken prior permission of the Director, CBI, before he actually agreed to take it on rent from me. The logic escaped me but since the communication held no threat of punishment, it had also avoided asking for my comments before communicating the advice , a standard procedure, and was only advisory in nature, I did not take up the issue further.

Mr T V S Shenoy gave me an inside story on this episode after I had retired.. It appears that the special assistant to Mrs. Margaret Alva, then the CBI Minister, was jubilant and told him that "we have finally got Sen. He has rented his house to CBI at an exorbitant rent. We will now get him." The same special assistant was crestfallen a few days later when he found that the rent was even less than the CPWD assessment. Years later, I learnt from a former Director of CBI that when Mr Vijay Karan was the Director of CBI in 1992, a complaint from the Government had been sent on the rent issue and as Add. Director he had made enquiries and finding everything regular he had reported that the complaint was without foundation. This report was sent to the Government, and hence, Krishnan was disappointed. So, how come I was reprimanded by Mr Vijaya Rama Rao on a file that was closed by his predecessor when I was a DIG, and that too in 1995 when I was a Joint Director CBI for the last three years and on a charge that had been dropped in 1992?

The crime syndicate in Government continues to be powerful. The Government of India's failure to extradite Anis Ibrahim, Dawood's brother, in the Bombay blast case from Bahrain, despite his having been arrested there on an Interpol alert issued on the CBI's request, only showed the power of the Syndicate. There was a price to be paid for choosing to be different, of course. Interpol Lyons had selected me for an assignment and a sponsorship from the Government of India could have ensured, that I joined this organization. The Government sponsorship was denied. The Department of Personnel was prepared to consider my case for promotion to the next rank but, the CBI Director refused to sponsor my name. The Health Ministry under Mr AR Antulay was prepared to create a post of Director of Intelligence but, this too was denied. After retirement, I joined the National Fertiliser Limited as a consultant in May 1996 for a period of six months. However, as soon as the urea scam came to light, partly because of my efforts, Mr Vijay Rama Rao, Director, CBI, had the Joint Director, Mr Gopal Achari, to write to the Managing Director, NFL, to relieve me of the assignment. This was in June 1996 and the MD actually showed me the letter. This letter was also made available to Mr Prabhu Chawla of *The Financial Express* who reported that I would soon cease to be a consultant with this public sector. I left at the end of August, three months before my term expired, without waiting to be terminated.

In January 1997, I joined as consultant to the Lieutenant Governor, Delhi. I met Mr Vijay Rama Rao at a dinner given to Interpol delegates by the CBI in early 1998. Mr Rao walked up to me and said that he had learnt that I had joined as one of the advisors to the Lieutenant Governor of Delhi, and he thought that I was eminently qualified for the job. A professional to his fingertips and a budding politician to boot, he found a position as a minister in the Cabinet of Chandrababu Naidu. As for myself, I faced a departmental enquiry for renting out my house at Jaipur to the CBI. I was denied a promotion, I was denied a chance to seek assignment outside the CBI. I was sacked as a consultant to National Fertiliser – all during Mr Vijay Rama Rao's tenure. It could have been worse.

Chapter-3

Urea Stinks; so does the Cover-Up

The urea scam surfaced in the last days of the Narasimha Rao government, around October 1995. The not so happy denouement is that at least three senior members of the *dramatis personae* have managed to elude trial. This is by no means to suggest that they were guilty. This is only to point out that they were not even brought to trial. The three were Mr Prabhakar Rao, son of the former Prime Minister, Mr Narasimha Rao, Mr Surendra Singh, Cabinet Secretary, the man who chaired the group of secretaries that decided that National Fertiliser Limited would be an additional canalising agency to purchase urea from the international market and the late Mr AN Verma, the Principal Secretary to the Prime Minister who to all intents and purposes was supporting the entry of NFL - that saw itself fall into the trap of doing business with Karson Danismanlik Turizm Sanayi Ticaret Ltd of Turkey and ending up a victim of a Rs 133-crore fraud. This is not to conclude that their intent was malafide. It is to emphasize the fact that their role in inducting NFL into the urea import business deserved a legal scrutiny that did not happen.

To get back to the story of the scam, by March 1996, the feeling that a crime had taken place was getting into the minds of both the National Fertilisers Limited and the Ministry of Fertilisers.

In fact, in the last week of April, 1996, Mr Indrajit Chowdhury, Secretary, Fertilisers, wrote to the Director, CBI, Mr Vijay Rama Rao, suggesting that the CBI should look into the transaction that had taken place between the NFL Ltd and Karsons for supply of urea. Though advanced payment of Rs 133 crores had been made, not a gram of urea had been supplied.

When Mr Chowdhury asked me to join the NFL Ltd as a consultant, I had just retired from the CBI. He specifically wanted me to look into the urea deal and suggest how the situation could be retrieved even at this late stage. I joined in the beginning of May 1996 and within a few days was convinced that here was a scam and a crime of proportions yet unheard of. NFL had been conned into paying Rs 133 crores in advance for urea from the international market - an area in which it had no prior experience, fertiliser imports hitherto being canalised through the Minerals and Metals Trading Corporation. There was not even a ghost of a chance of any of the urea being supplied.

I, therefore, recommended that NFL, as the victim of the fraud, should name the insiders in NFL who had connived with Karsons along with those private persons who were party of the crime and, request the CBI to treat that reference as a First Information Report. This was done on May 19, 1996. By May 23, I was receiving signals that Mr Vijay Rama Rao, an appointee of Mr Narasimha Rao, was reluctant to order a criminal investigation, as one of the accused was Sambasiva Rao, a resident of Hyderabad and a kinsman of Mr Narasimha Rao. He was a part of the fraud. The 13-day Vajpayee Government was in the chair by then. Mr Narasimha Rao had vacated office, and I decided to be pro-active, and requested Mr TVS Shenoy, a member of the BJP think-tank to join me for breakfast on May 24, 1996. I narrated to him the full story of the urea scam as it appeared to me from documents that I had seen in the NFL office and the discussions that I had held with all those who were concerned in NFL in the Ministry of Fertiliser and in the legal branch of the Government of India.

Mr Shenoy heard me, and said that he would carry on from my residence to the house of the BJP president, Mr LK Advani, and fully brief him in the matter. I had personally met Mr Murli Manohar Joshi, then Home Minister and briefed him on the matter. The very next day, Mr Indrajit, Chowdhury received instructions from Mr Bishan Tandon, Secretary to the Prime Minister, to send the urea case for the Prime Minister's perusal and orders. It was done and within a day or two, the Prime Minister's Office prevailed upon

Mr Vijay Rama Rao, the CBI Director, to register the case. Though the FIR sent by NFL and the earlier report sent by the Ministry of Fertilisers, were not used by the CBI to start the investigation, they did start the investigation on the basis of a report the CBI had prepared on its own. Soon after, the Vajpayee government fell. With the new Prime Minister, Mr HD Devegowda—in chair with the blessings of the Congress Party—my days as consultant to NFL were clearly numbered.

In fact, the first person to tip me off about Mr Surendra Singh was Mrs Achala Moulik, then an Additional Secretary with the Government of India who had been passed over as Secretary to the Government and was in the room of the Cabinet Secretary to discuss her loss of rank. In her presence, Mr Singh received a call when he was apparently informed that a certain Sen was investigating the urea scam case as a consultant for NFL. A visibly disturbed Surendra Singh barked out: how had Sen got involved and asked the caller, what were Sen's credentials to investigate such a case. The reply apparently shook him further, because he said, he would deal with the matter later, obviously having realised that he had a visitor with him.

How had Mr Surendra Singh dealt with the matter? His colleague in the Cabinet Secretariat wrote to Mr Indrajit Chowdhury questioning the appointment of Shantonu Sen. In a curious twist of circumstances, Mr AR Antulay, took over as Chairman of the Parliamentary Committee on Chemicals and Petroleum. It so happened that chemicals included fertilisers, and Mr Antulay decided to investigate the urea scam. He was in the know of things and had apparently no reason to protect any of those suspected to have been involved at that stage. The initial report was explosive and made available to the media. *The Times of India* reported on September 11, 1996: "Ex-Cabinet Secretary (Mr Surendra Singh) is responsible for urea scam." Whatever be the reason - it is suspected that Mr Narasimha Rao got to Mr Antulay and definitely Mr AN Verma met him - the report was never officially written but the reports on the inquiries found their way to the large sections of the media. Mr Antulay's formal position was that he had ceased to be Chairman of the Parliamentary Committee, as the next elections had been announced, and it was for the next Chairman of the Committee to prepare the report.

Whatever the games the politicians were playing, nine persons were chargesheeted in December 1997 and neither Mr Singh nor Mr Verma were among them.

Two persons from Switzerland, Alankus and Karanci, senior officials with Karsons and Pinto and one of the agents involved in the deal from London has since been extradited. They are undergoing trial. The others facing trial are the former Managing Director, NFL, Mr CF Ramakrishnan, Mr D S Kanwar, Executive Director, NFL, Mr Sambasiva Rao, the Indian agent for Karsons going under the name of Sai Krishna Impex, Mr Sanjeeva Rao, brother-in-law of Mr Prabhkar Rao, son of the former Prime Minister, Mr PV Narasimha Rao, Mr Prakash Yadav, son of Mr Ram Lakhan Yadav, the Union Minister for Fertilisers. The notable exception was Mr Prabhakar Rao himself.

Why was Mr Prabhakar Rao suspected to be involved? This brings us to the core of the story. For starters, the partners in crime realised, that import of urea could be fertile land for scam, provided, of course, one could break the stranglehold of the MMTC, that was the sole canalising agency. The simplest solution was to introduce another public sector company that could be manipulated by the powers that be. The powers that be in this case were in the Prime Minister's Office and, therefore, it was not difficult to get NFL into the canalising act with its Managing Director and Executive Director agreeing to toe the PMO's line. Why was the PMO interested? The major players inside NFL were suddenly part of the supporting cast in this crime and several Raos began to emerge as main players: Sambasiva Rao, a mere BSc Agriculture from Baptala Agriculture College, who started his life as a sales representative, was the Karson agent with Sai Krishna Impex on his letterhead. Sanjeeva Rao, who had married into the Narasimha Rao family, was his college friend. Even though NFL received not a kilo of urea against the advance paid, Karsons did pay back in part! Only the money was routed back through two Hyderabad businessmen, Dharmesh Yadav and Rajinder Babbani, who were associated with a Dubai firm, Edible Foodstuffs, to the bank accounts of Mr Prabhakar Rao, Sambasiva Rao and Mr Sanjeeva Rao.

The kickback reported to be $4 million went in a very major way to these three Raos. The other politician's son, Mr Prakash Yadav, son of the Fertiliser Minister, Mr Ram Lakhan Yadav, was not entirely left out either. A sum of $2,000 was sent to Rhea Brothers in New York, a firm owned by Prakash Yadav. Of the $38 million (Rs 133 crores) paid to Karsons, what returned as kickback was probably more than $4 million and made to others too. But, even Mr Prabhakar Rao has not so far been prosecuted.

Chapter-4

Bolt from the Blue Star

The Golden Temple, Amritsar, was the scene of a bloody battle fought by 350 Infantry Brigade against the terrorist Jarnail Singh Bhindranwale, dismissed Major General Sahbeg Singh and others. Between the afternoon of June 5, 1984 and June 10, 1984, the operation saw a large number killed, many arrested and large quantities of arms and ammunition recovered by the Army. Several officers (JCOs) and other ranks (OR) were killed and 1,592 were captured in the Army operation in and around the Golden Temple.

The Defence Ministry was adamant that all men arrested should be prosecuted as terrorists. Its statements to us described them as terrorists confronting the army. Mr KP Singh Deo, Minister of State for Defence, went along with the Army version. Our sources and subsequent investigations, however, told us a different story. Not all were actually fighting the Army on this operation. Indeed, interference had been built into the case even before the CBI had entered. The fact remained that a large numbers were pilgrims with no terrorist background. Some were students and ordinary folk who had come on a pilgrimage for Guru Arjun Dev's Martyrdom Day, observed just a few days ago. The Army produced much evidence, but our investigations convinced us that while many who fought as terrorists had been killed, only a small number out of the 1,592 had actually confronted the Army. At the end of it all, we had our way that only 379 persons were actually terrorists and prosecuted them. The rest were all freed from judicial custody. When Siddhartha Shankar Ray was the Governor of Punjab, cases against them were withdrawn and they were all set at liberty.

Of import, from the point of view of the investigators, was the enormous socio-political significance of the fact, that a terrorist movement had grouted itself in a place of worship, and an Army operation was required to crush it. Any attempt to prejudge the issue or any facet of it by the administration would, therefore, sit very heavily on the minds of the investigating officers. It was clear to me, when I was investigating, many of those rounded up by the army as persons waging war. The look of sheer terror in otherwise simple faces was a giveaway. They were devotees who had gone to seek divine blessings, and did not deserve to be condemned on a charge that meant a death penalty. I was quite vehement in opposing the Army position.

It would be interesting to go through the evidence, as the CBI gathered it from day 2, after the Golden Temple complex had been freed of militants in "Operation Blue Star" though it had been ravaged. The back of the militants was broken, but they were not to give up. They took their time to regroup and take revenge. Among their most important victims was General AS Vaidya, Commander-in-Chief of the Indian Army at the time of the Operation Blue Star. General Vaidya was killed in Pune on June 10, 1986, around 11.50 a.m. He was returning from the market with his wife in his white Maruti car DIB 1437. That too, was a case, that was placed under my charge on August 16, 1986.

To go back in time, as the CBI stepped in, step by step: Brigadier DV Rao, Commander 350 Infantry Brigade, then stationed in Amritsar, launched an Army action on June 5, 1984 in and around the Golden Temple complex. It was an action that continued till June 10, 1984. The Army, acting on the request of the Civil power to aid it under the Armed Forces (Punjab and Chandigarh) Special Powers Act, 1983, was required to deal with the situation wherein banned organisations – All India Sikh Students Federation, Dal Khalsa and other terrorist groups, led by Sant Jarnail Singh Bhindranwale, had collected arms, ammunition, explosives and men within the temple complex, to wage war against the Government of India.

The 350 Infantry Brigade was under the overall command of a charismatic Major General, KS Brar, AVSM, Veer Chakra,

General Officer Commanding, 9 Infantry Division, Meerut. Before launching the operation, both Brigadier Rao and Major General Brar had studied the situation in and around the Golden Temple Complex. They found:

- The main entrance in the north fully fortified from its east end to the west end;
- All the openings in the arches and the main entrance sealed with brick leaving a few holes for a view in;
- Bunkers constructed at a number of places;
- Streets leading to the temple effectively covered, and movement across them inviting fire from these positions;
- Hotel Temple View, Braham Boota Akhara, Sindhi Hotel and other dominating buildings in front of the main entrance fortified, and fire being brought down from the positions;
- The Parikrama dominating the Akal Takht area on the western side, and all the dominating buildings to the west of the Akal Takht fortified. So, was the entire length of the western Parikrama;
- The openings in the arches on the south temple wall sealed with brick walls and bunkers constructed on the top of the roof;
- All the high rise buildings, south of the above portion of the Parikrama occupied and controlling all the lanes leading to the temple;
- Baba Atal Gurudwara, on the western side, fortified;
- The buildings of the Guru Nanak Niwas SGPC office, Guru Ram Das Langar, towers at the roof tops of Derababa Kharak Singh fortified with bunkers. The wall tower on the east of Guru Ram Das Sarai fortified and occupied;
- Construction work still continuing on some of the bunkers in the entire complex.

Very clearly, this was a war like preparation and *prima facie* there was every justification in asking the CBI to investigate a case where terrorists had planned to commit a criminal offence, "waging of war" under the Indian Penal Code that would invite the death sentence if the charges were proved. The fact that Brig Rao had under his command a substantial force to start with, and had to draw on the entire reserves was testimony to the kind of opposition the Army faced. The Brigadier had para military forces comprising BSF and CRPC; 9 Kumaon; 12 Bihar; 26 Madras; 9 Garhwal; 10 Guards; 10 Dogras; 15 Kumaon; S. F. F.; 1 Para Company; 1 Squadron 16 Cavalry; 1 Company 5 Mech; and Elements of 60 Engineer Regiment. A description of the operation as we gathered from a detailed Army briefing told us the tale with graphic clarity and it was clear that the proposed operation, to be commenced on the afternoon of June 5 and concluded by the following day, would be far more elaborate and gruesome. Operation Bluestar, in fact, continued till June 10, 1984; snipers remained active beyond this time and even took pot shots when the then President of India, Giani Zail Singh, visited the temple after the operation was officially declared as over. The operation was conducted fiercely on both sides. The detailed account of the Army deployment would go to establish the extent of the terrorist preparation. Yet, it would be clear to the CBI investigators that not all of those caught in the crossfire were terrorists. All units under Brigadier Rao suffered heavy casualties; 26 Madras had been assigned the task of entering the temple from the eastern gate, clearing the area towards the southern Parikrama and the rooms up to the Atta Mandi Gate. It was also to seize illicit arms and ammunition, and apprehend the terrorists in its area of operation. Lt Col R MG Panniar commanded 26 Madras which moved into Jallianwala Bagh on June 5, 1984 at 21.30 hours. Within half an hour, it commenced advancing towards the southern Parikrama and drew heavy and effective fire from the Sindhi Hotel, Langar Sahib and all other buildings, almost all of which were fortified. The Company moved ahead suffering heavy casualty and finally entered the Temple at 01.30 hours on June 6, 1984. As it moved on establishing a firm base on the southern side of the earlier gate, it was fired with LMGs, automatic rifles, pistols and hand grenades. It also drew heavy fire from the Harmandir Sahib but, as per instructions, did not return the fire towards Harmandir Sahib. One of its Companies attacked the Akal Takht and suffered casualties. A wounded JCO entered the Akal Takht and got captured, whereafter he was blown up with the explosives. Though beseiged, after heavy fighting, 26 Madras captured 83 terrorists together with their arms and ammunition. They were able to enter the Akal Takht only on June 7, 1984. In the basement was found the bodies of the dismissed Maj Gen Sahbeg Singh and

Jarnail Singh Bhindranwale. The operation continued even on June 8, 1984; 26 Madras lost one officer, two JCOs and 12 other ranks. Among the wounded were 12 other ranks and among the wounded were one wounded and 50 other ranks.

One of the most important operations was mounted by 10 Guards under the overall command of Lt Col Israr Khan and his Deputy, Major IS Sethi. This battalion was engaged in seizing illicit arms and flushing out terrorists from the northern wing of the Golden Temple complex. They had further orders from their Commander, Brig DV Rao to maintain the sanctity of religious places, not to fire on Harmandir Sahib and Akal Takht and not to use high trajectory weapons. They moved in at 22.00 hours on June 5, 1984 and were under orders to complete their assignment by 01.00 hours on June 6, 1984. The northern wing was heavily and intensely fortified. A large number of bunkers had been constructed on the top floor, with the help of sand bags, and bricks. There were many loopholes strategically opening to all the roads leading to the Golden Temple complex. They entered the temple through the Ghanta Ghar Chowk area. They were led by mechanised forces who faced heavy volley of fire from small automatic firearms, single shot as well as hand grenades. So heavy was the firing, that it was impossible to proceed and the mechanised forces were forced to seek cover of protective firing. They were halted, and leading elements in the Columns earmarked to capture right, and left halves of the northern wing were ordered to clear the main entrance by lobbing hand grenades and spraying it with automatic fire. As the Column moved on to the stairs, they were fired upon from the ventilators of the basement which dominated the stairs. The troops mainly received injuries below the knee level and progress was slowed down due to heavy casualties caused by fire from all directions.

The 10 Guards Columns finally managed to clear the left half of the ground floor at 23.30 hours on June 5, 1984 and the right half at 01.00 hours on June 6, 1984. The Column Commanders then erected aluminium ladders and climbed the first floor. There they established a foothold, and moved ahead to clear the room, one by one. While this was in progress, militants suddenly appeared from the basement and inflicted heavy casualties on the troops. A total of 19 officers, men and other ranks were killed that night and 52 were wounded and disabled. The situation was controlled to some extent on June 7 when 50 of the captured militants were handed over to the Provost Unit of the 9 Infantry Division to be lodged in custody. After exhausting the earmarked forces, Brig DV Rao went to the reserve troops. 15 Kumaon under Lt Col NC Pant was in reserve awaiting instructions since 23.00 hours of June 5. At 01.30 hours of June 6, it was ordered to move towards the Atta Mandi Gate of the Golden Temple complex and report there by 03.15 hours. It moved accordingly and reached Atta Mandi Gate at 02.45 hours. There it was directed by the commander to enter the Golden Temple complex and clear the Akal Takht. As it moved through the covered portions of the Parikrama, it met with heavy firing of automatic weapons, grenades and rifles. There was shooting from all directions—windows in the covered portion, rooftops and other fortifications constructed all round inside the complex—slowing down its progress. By the time it was near the water tank, the 15 Kumaon was facing anti-tank weapons from the rooftops and eight of its men were already seriously wounded. It was only at 05.30 hours that it could make its first move to enter the Akal Takht and it drew a very heavy volume of fire from all sides; from the Akal Takht as well. It lost one officer and six other ranks in the battle to enter the Akal Takht. Time and again, it mounted assaults to enter, only to be repulsed, suffering 15 more deaths. 15 Kumaon used an APC to provide covering fire from the western corner of the Parikrama but, even that was shot by anti-tank weapons and destroyed at the western gate itself. Troops inside the APC suffered heavy casualties, and Infantry weapons failed to neutralise the complex, including the Akal Takht, the red building and the Nissan Sahib complex. Brig Rao sought permission to induct tanks into the Parikrama. General Sundarji spoke to Rajiv Gandhi in the early hours of June 6. He and Arun Singh were in the control room in the Prime Minister's House. Without consulting the Prime Minister, the army was allowed to induct tanks. Mrs Gandhi heard about it later, and was reportedly shocked and stunned. She had been told that the Army operation would be swift, short and decisive with minimum loss of lives. She is reported to have clapped her hand on her forehead and announced that her death was now almost inevitable.

The tanks entered the Parikrama on the morning of June 6. As they engaged the Akal Takht, a big explosion took place inside the Akal Takht. A huge fire started and dark and deep columns of smoke and flames spread high and wide. So intense was the heat, that the troops had to be pulled back. Much later they advanced, and took positions on the northern corner of the temple complex, up to Nissan Sahib and the major portion of the southern Parikrama. The militants, though without hope now, continued to hold positions in the rooms and continued to fire on the troops. The clearing action, therefore, continued till June 10 and for some time thereafter. At the end of the operation, the Army had rounded off 1,592 persons in their operations inside and outside the temple complex. This included 433 it had arrested during the battle to rid the complex of the militants. That this list was of 433 persons only was clear from the log kept by individual commanders of the number of persons who had surrendered to them, and the quality and quantity of weapons that they had captured from the battle area, and from the individuals they had captured. Barring the later lot, the others had raised neither Khalistan slogans nor taken up arms against the Indian Army. They had, of course, violated the curfew announced and repeatedly proclaimed effective from June 3, 1985.

There were repeated announcements for pilgrims to leave the temple. What was the announcement "PYARE SADA SANGATJEE,

VAHE GURUJI KA KHALSA, VAHE GURUJI KA FATEH

AAP JEE NU VINTI KITI JANDI HAI KI HUN TON 5.30 VAJE DE DARMIAN SECURITY FORCE NE FIRING BAND KAR DITTI HAI ISS DAURAN SARRE SADH SANGAT NU VINTI HAI KI OH DARSHINI DEORI CHOWK GHANTA GHAR VAIEPSION BAHAAR AAKE SIDDHE KOTWALI AAJAN. ISS DAURAN JE KISSE NUMAINDA GAL KARNE HOVE TAN VE KOTWALI AA JAN. VINTI HAI KI SIDDHE KOTWALI AAJAN. SAJJE KHABBE JAH WALE DI JAAN NU KHATRA HO SAKHDA HAI." Many chose to do so, risking the wrath of militants, while many stayed behind. To the army it meant staying behind to provide, if nothing else, moral support to the militants. Yet, there was the very probable explanation that they believed, that the walls of the temple would provide greater security, than risking their lives in any attempt to leave the temple. Fear would have been the key for them. The militants fought without giving any quarter, took the Army by surprise and inflicted heavy casualties. On June 5, there were 56 dead officers and men. On June 7, 22 officers and men died, and on June 9, another five lost their lives. Another, 252 Army personnel lost their limbs or were otherwise disabled. Weapons of assault were unlimited—Army weapons, ammunitions and explosives. The militants not only had light machine guns, SLRs, rifles and carbines, they also had sten guns, anti-tank guns and Chinese assault rifles. A factory equipped to manufacture small arms and ammunition was located inside the temple complex and was found in a running condition. The Punjab Intelligence had actually warned the Army about the extent of preparedness of the militants, which was not ready to buy the accuracy of the information. The Army paid a bitter price for its skepticism and reacted with a position that all the 1,592 rounded up during battle and from the vicinity of the temple were militants; should face prosecution and, if convicted, hanged. Senior officials of the Ministry of Defence were also keen that the Army view should prevail. The argument was that, the prosecution does not mean conviction and, therefore, there was no harm in prosecuting all the persons that the Army held in custody. I was not ready to prosecute except those, whom the evidence showed had *prima facie* committed the criminal offence of waging of war. According to my evidence, many were pilgrims caught in the crossfire. They had no weapons and were fear crazed, having found themselves in custody. Some of them may have been sympathetic to the cause but that by itself was not sufficient material to consider them offenders under the Waging of War Act as defined in the Indian Penal Code. This tug of war continued for a while at the initial stage of investigation, and it was only after a few months of commencement of investigation that we succeeded in releasing from custody all but 433 individuals. This figure of 433 was staring at us from the commencement of investigation, as that total was arrived at when the individual situation reports (stirrups) of the fighting units were perused and their numbers of those captured by them within the Temple Complex after emerging victors were totalled. What finally, convinced Brig DV Rao and his senior colleagues that all those apprehended, 1592, could not be terrorists was our firm determination, that unless these 433 were identified, we had no case against any one, let alone the entire 1592, the army and para military people had captured and held. No one would be sent up for trial just because they were held by the army authorities. It was then, the production of prison camp registers of prison 1 and 2 maintained by the two prison commanders who received the captured militants on different dates between the night of 5-6-84 to the late hours of 10-6-84 saved the day. They were captured with their arms on these dates by the fighting units of 12 Bihar, 9 Kumaon, 10 Guards, 9 Garhwal. 10 Dogras, 26 Madras, other para military formations who had joined the war, etc. The OC Provost Unit 9 Infantry Division had received the captured men and he had the men and transport to transfer them to the prison camps, where their full personal particulars were noted in registers, by the two prison commanders. They themselves had separated the militants, and terrorists from the others, who neither had arms nor raised slogans in favour of an independent Khalistan. They had correctly taken down the particulars of only those that were captured as a consequence of actual exchange of arms immediately, and the remaining numbers were lumped together for questioning separately and at leisure when their details were, also noted. Those that were captured, were 433 of them including two women and the investigation was confined to them only. In the heat of the battle, this register was forgotten and finally, when all this surfaced quite late in the day after days of CBI investigations, it cooled temperature all round. The battle for the capture of the Golden Temple complex had lasted 4/5 days, and fighting had been fierce indeed. (Photographs)

At the end, I had found insufficient evidence even against all of these 433 and sought court's permission to discharge 54 of them, who the investigation showed, though captured by Army units during the battle, had neither confronted the Army with arms, nor raised any slogans in favour of Khalistan. The men and officers who made them surrender said so, in as many words, and their only fault was that they were inside the temple when the battle was being fought. The remaining 379 were those who were caught with arms of destruction, and were also heard raising slogans in favour of Khalistan at the time of their capture. Finally, it was this lot that was held in custody during investigation and trial, which came to an end when in an overall Punjab Settlement in 1986, they were freed and charges dropped against them. But, the bolt from the blue star, struck two deadly blows and the victims were, Mrs. Indira Gandhi on 31st October, 1984 and General AS Vaidya on 10th August, 1986.

Chapter-5

Catching the Vaidya Killers

The battle for the Golden Temple was not quite over – never mind, that the militants had been flushed out. Those that survived, bid their time to reorganize. One primary mission was to take the life of General AS Vaidya, which they successfully did. I was asked to handle the case on August 16, 1986. If the investigation into the role of the militants and non-militants at the Golden Temple complex was confronted by interference, the investigation into the assassination of General Vaidya presented an even more difficult obstacle that, indeed, found me at the receiving end of the investigation.

The investigation was directed under me by the CBI. The Pune police joined the team's efforts at detection and arrest with zeal, with both public and media cooperating at every step. I had learnt that 'careful' working with the media was useful and continued to call upon their resources, as long as I was associated with terrorist cases. Some senior officers held a different view. After the arrests of Sukhdev and Nirmal Singh – the former riding the Indu Suzuki motorcycle (MFK-7548 with Jinda, the assassin, the pillion rider) and the latter, an accomplice, on September 7, 1986 – the Director General of Bombay Police, Mr SS Jog, shot off a vociferous protest to Mr MG Katre, CBI Director, on September 10, 1986, about my taking the press into confidence, against his explicit advice. He considered it professionally immature and inappropriate to give out any details, and even suggested that I be removed from the investigation.

There were two errors in Mr Jog's missile: He had overlooked the fact, that the story of the arrest of Sukhdev and Nirmal Singh had appeared before my Press Conference and, in any event, Mr Katre had agreed with me, that certain selected leaks to the media would only help our case and put the terrorists under pressure. Mr Katre's response of September 30 to Mr Jog was very categorical on both these points: "As you know, about a week after the assassination, as a result of the request made by the investigating teams, there was hardly any publicity about the progress of the investigation about this case. Perhaps, this lack of publicity induced the criminals to believe that the pressure had eased and they could safely visit Pune and take away the weapons and the motorcycle. Co-operation of the Press can be sought by releasing information about the investigation and, if necessary also requesting them not to publish certain details. Total lack of official communication can also result in undesirable publicity, which is evident from the fact that even the names of witnesses who identified the killers have now appeared in the Press. This has exposed these witnesses to a considerable danger. I feel, if the Press had been taken into confidence, these details could have been kept away from the newspapers."

For ample measure, Mr Katre added: "Even if there can be a difference of opinion between us and about this issue, I do not think this calls for the taking away of the supervision of the investigation of this case from Sen, who is one of my very able officers and has been associated for more than two years with the investigation of crime committed by terrorists." Thus, it was that I continued, with the support of Mr Katre, and reiterated the need to cooperate with the media [Facsimile of letters on Page 52-59.]. That was the end of this attempt to derail me, and I continued investigations.

On 10.08.86 General AS Vaidya (retd) was shot dead on Veer Abhimanyu Marg, Pune, at about 11:50 am. He was driving a Maruti car DIB 1437. His wife, Bhanumati Vaidya sat by his side and a lone security guard, Head Constable, Khirsagar, sat on the rear seat behind his wife. I took over the investigation from Pune police on 6.08.86. Within one month, on 07.09.86 the killer was nabbed in dramatic circumstances on the Pune Mumbai highway near Pimpri. His associate was caught in Delhi, a well laid trap organized by the IB. CBI, Pune Police and IB worked in close coordination at the ground level. Those who arrested the killer, who had his killer revolver and tried to shoot his way out were honoured with President Police Medal of Gallantry. At all levels in all three organizations, the team work was swift and it delivered results in a manner that is something to be cherished. The Director CBI, informed the Government in September 1986 itself that with these arrests the "participation of 8 other terrorists in 20 other crimes committed by this gang in Delhi, Ahmedabad, Bombay, Pune, Ludhiana and Nainital "has been revealed." Both the killers, after trial, were sentenced to death and were hanged in Yerwada Jail, Pune.

SECRET:
MOST IMMEDIATE.

DO No.SB/XIII/199/1986.
Old Council Hall,
S.Bhagatsingh Marg,
Bombay 400 039,
Dated 10th Sept.1986.

S. S. PUG
DIRECTOR GENERAL
& I. G. OF POLICE

My dear Katre,

I was shocked to read the flash news in all the newspapers today regarding the details about the results of interrogation of Sukhdev Singh and Nirmal Singh who were arrested in Pune by Pimpri Police in an Arms Act case on Sunday, the 7th Sept.1986 and have been in police custody since then in the case.

2. I had very clear directives from the Chief Minister that details should not be publicised till all consequential action following interrogation, such as raids of hideouts, contacts, etc. were fully ascertained, established and verified. I had accordingly not only passed these instructions to the Commissioner of Police, Pune but to all other officers NOT to disclose anything arising out of the interrogation for public consumption till all matters are verified. Secrecy of action was also professionally necessary because the investigation and raids were expected to be carried out in different parts of the country and when suspects or accomplices would not be on guard.

3. I have reasons to believe that their complicity in General Vaidya's case was also leaked out to the press on the day their remand was obtained. You must be aware that we had, as a result of interrogation, known about the likely complicity of Sukhdev Singh in the assassination almost on the first day of the arrest, i.e. Sunday (7-9-86) night. We had therefore conscientiously decided to keep it to our heart till the details were cross checked and verified. The Union Home Secretary was also of the same view that this information should be kept a closely guarded affair when we spoke on phone on Monday (8-9-86) and he had so expected of me.

4. Yesterday (9-9-86) morning Commissioner of Police, Pune, Misar, mentioned to me that DIG CBI, Sen, who had come from Delhi the previous evening was keen to meet the press, take them into confidence, and give them photographs of some 19 accused! I had therefore asked Misar to inform Sen that he should NOT

-2-

meet the press at this time or give out any information regarding the course of interrogation and I have been apprised that the Commissioner of Police, Pune did pass on this advice to Sen.

5. You will also recollect that when we met yesterday (9-9-86) evening in my office along with Commissioner of Police,Bombay, Shri Soman and I.G.P.(Law & Order),Ramachandran, this was also discussed and it was decided that it would be professionally immature and inappropriate to give out any details at this stage. You were prompt enough to call sen on telephone and ask him not to do so, but it appears that Sen had already collected the members of the Press in the Police Commissioner's Office ! Even so, he was advised not to give any details.

6. When the first leak appeared in papers here on Monday, naturally I was asked for my comments by almost every newspaper man in Bombay, and I had to parry all queries almost to the point of denial as investigation was in progress and the so called confession needed verification.

7. Late last night, I was put in a very embarrassing position by the members of the press when they told me that the DIG CBI has already given all the details. I had therefore no comments to offer till I got confirmation from Misar that this was in fact so.

8. I feel that it was most indiscreet on the part of Sen to have rushed to the press to give details of interrogation and particularly so when he was accordingly advised by us. I do agree that the case of assassination of General Vaidya stands transferred to the CBI and we can have no grudge if the CBI were to make all information available to the press regarding this case, but you will also agree that the interrogation has revealed the complicity of the individuals in other important bank robberies in Bombay and Pune with which are directly concerned and we feel that by this premature release of information to the press, valuable clues are likely to be lost.

9. I also feel that interrogation has not really led us to the complete story, e.g. what was proposed to be done with the weapons that they were carrying; their hideouts; contacts, etc. They are also following the standard practice of disclosing

-3-

only enough facts that would cause "minimum damage" to their cause. One man is quite willing and quick to accept responsibility for several offences obviously to parry any further questioning about complicity of other persons. As we know, it had been the practice of these extremists to deliver weapons whenever a plan of an action is hatched and quite likely these weapons might have been transported for the next plan of action, and premature disclosure has, I am sure, caused a loss to us in preventing any other major strike by these extremists.

10. I am constrained to mention to you that this behaviour of your DIG has created serious problems of cooperation between the State Police and C.B.I. You are aware that we have been, as it should be, rendering all out assistance to C.B.I. in connection with this case and will continue to do so in future also. Under the circumstances, I leave it to you to decide whether Sen should continue to head this investigation team in Maharashtra.

11. If it was only to share the glory of success, we would have been too happy to give this exclusive privilege to the DIG CBI ! Incidentally, nothing prevented us from making these disclosures earlier on our own particularly when the initial arrest and initial break through was done by Pune Police, but we had purposefully and in the interest of investigation refrained from doing so.

12. I am endorsing copies of this letter to the Government of Maharashtra and to the Union Home Secretary also.

With regards,

Yours sincerely,

Sd/-

(S.S.Jog)

Shri M.G.Katre,
Director, C.B.I.,MHA,Govt.of India,
North Block, New Delhi 110 001.

CENTRAL BUREAU OF INVESTIGATION
SPECIAL INVESTIGATION CELL(P)
NEW DELHI.

Subject: Press Publicity in Gen. Vaidya Murder Case

Press cuttings of the following papers are enclosed:-

(1) Tarun Bharat dt. 8.9.86
(2) Sakal dt. 8.9.86
(3) Prabhat dt. 8.9.86
(4) Sakal dt. 9.9.86
(5) Indian Express 9.9.86
(6) Free Press Journal dt. 8.9.86
(7) Maharashtra Times dt. 9.9.86
(8) Nav Shakti dt. 9.9.86
(9) Maharashtra Herald dt. 9.9.86

2. From the cuttings it will be clear that the news items pertaining to the apprehension of Sukhdev Singh and Nirmal Singh appeared in a big way in the press on 8.9.86 and 9.9.86 even before 10.9.86. The details of the names of the arrested accused, number of the Indo-Suzuki motor cycle used by them and the weapons recovered from them were known to the public on 8.9.86 and 9.9.86. What appeared on 10.9.86 did not go beyond the basic essentials already published while confirming that at least one of them was wanted by the CBI. Watever cover up the other members of gang would resort to would have been set in motion with the details published on 8.9.86 and 9.9.86.

R put up on 25/9 along with DO letter of DG Maharashtra
23/9

3. In my opinion, the approach in investigation and tackling of terrorists crimes has to be different from that adopted in other conventional crimes. In the latter case, a criminal has committed one single act and is hiding to escape detection. So, necessarily, the police has to be circumpect. Terrorist criminal will continue commiting series of terrorist crimes. He has to be kept under pressure so that either he will be low or will commit mistakes leading to his detection. The activities of this gang bring home this point. Despite a string of bank robberies, murders, car thefts since February, 1986 and the police raid on the Antop Hill Flat on 3rd May, 1986 by the Bombay Police, the gang continued to operate in Bombay. Possibly, also, stay there off and on, too. A vehicle was robbed at gun point on 9.6.86 at about 0900 Hrs and the same vehicle was used to loot the bank on 9.6.86 at 1200 Hrs. A member of the gang who had suffered injuries got himself admitted to a hospital in Bombay and stayed there for weeks together after 16.4.86

Sr PA
DO of DG Maharashtra is placed below please
R Bajpai 25/9
DCBI

and fully recovered. The gang was never under pressure and moved on to Pune and committed a bank dacoity killing a guard on 13.6.86 and then assassinated Gen. A.S. Vaidya on 10.8.86. Utter silence and ban on publicity did not lead either to apprehension of any member of the gang or finding their hide outs or even locating the hospital. The police and public remained lax (witness incident of 9.6.86). The needs of secrecy was preserved to such an extent that knowledge was not shared with Delhi Police with disastrous consequences. Result was that there was no pressure on the gang from Feb. 1986 and it succeeded in its terrorist operationsin Maharashtra till 10th August, 1986.

4. In Gen. Vaidya case, the CBI after taking over the investigation used the press and other sources of publicity to bring about a three fold action. (i) Create pressure on the suspects by letting them know that they were wanted and a nation wide search had been launched (ii) Alert the public regarding the activities of this gang and then obtain information from them as well. (iii) Putx the general police on a state of high alert.

5. The suspects had left their weapons and Indo-Suzuki Motor cycle in their hide-outs in Pune. Because of series of reports indicating that CBI was in search for them in Pune and was trying to locate their hide-outs the suspects felt that the CBI might find their hide-outs and then locate their weapons and the Motor-cycle. When on our request a blanket ban on publicity was imposed they assumed that pressure was easing and despatched the two persons whose photographs had not been published to reach Poona and fetch the weapons and the Indo-Suzuki Motor bike. The two persons did not have the courage to stay in Pune for more than a couple of hours. They arrived, picked up the weapons and Motor-cycle and left in such a tearing hurry that it resulted in an accident. They were under pressure. Even then they could have escaped but the alert public fed by the press and the alert police kept on a state of high alert by constant goading to look for hideouts and find their local contact, prevented them. That publicity through media and other sources played an important part in the break through cannot be doubted.

6. Publicity regarding the names and aliasm of the members of the gang, their photographs together with the details of crimes which they are suspected to have committed if published will help in putting on pressure not only on the member of the gang but also on those who are inclined to give them shelter.

-: 3 :-

This publicity will ensure such pressure on them that they are bound to commit some mistakes which would help us to locate and apprehend them. No Police officer will share information with the press that will hamper investigation, but publicity of the type suggested above will help the investigation. It will make the members of the public aware of the crimes of these members of the ~~public~~ gang, certainly help in keeping the terrorists under constant pressure, will help to slow down their terrorists activities and it will also help to ensure that their relations and friends who have been freely giving them shelter not being able to take the plea that they did not know about the crimes of the persons whom they have been sheltering. No one State police, far be the CBI, without the assistance of the public and press will succeed in laying hands on the members of this dreadful gang. I would even now urge action as proposed under para six be taken."

Sd/- 20/9/86
(S. SEN)
DIG SIC(P) CBI NEW DELHI.

DCBI NEW DELHI
UO NO. 410 RC 6/86/SIU-III/FX/SECRET DATED 2?.9.1986.

SECRET

D.O.No. /NB/DCBI/86
Date: the 30th September, 1986

My dear Jog,

Please refer to your d.o. letter No.SB/XIII/199/1986 dated the 10th September, 1986 regarding publicity in the press about the release of the interrogations of Sukhdev Singh and Nirmal Singh.

2. When the information regarding the arrest of two criminals who may be involved in the assassination case received by me on 7th instant at Delhi, I had also issued instructions that these arrests should not be given any publicity immediately. However, on 9th September, I was surprised to read the names of the two persons arrested at Pune on 7th, with the number of motor cycle which was attached from them. These details appeared in the Indian Express, Free Press Journal and Maharashtera Herald of 9th September and number of marathi newspapers. On the basis of the disclosures made by these criminals raids had already been carried out on 7th and 8th September in Punjab, Delhi and some other places. With the publication of the details about their arrests, which the CBI officers did not release, any advantage which was likely to be gained by keeping their arrests secret was already lost. It was, therefore, felt that instead of allowing unauthorised leakages to appear in the press fueling more speculation it would be better to release limited information to the press. This is what was done by Sen.

3. As you know, about a week after the assassination as a result of the request made by the Investigating Teams there was hardly any publicity about the progress of investigation of this case. Perhaps this lack of publicity induced the criminals to believe that the pressure had eased and they could

-2-

safely visit Pune and take away the weapons and the motorcycle. Cooperation of the press can be sought by releasing information about the investigation and if necessary also requesting them not to publish certain details. Total lack of official communication can also result in undesirable publicity which is evident from the fact that even the names of witnesses who identified the killers have now appeared in the press. This has exposed these witnesses to a considerable danger, I feel if the press had been taken into confidence, these details could have been kept away from the newspapers.

4. Even if there can be a difference of opinion between us about this issue, I do not think this calls for taking away the supervision of the investigation of this case from Sen, who is one of my very able officers and has been associated for more than two years with the investigation of crimes committed by terrorists.

5. You very well know, how wrong reports in the newspapers about CBI sending a team of officers to assist Pune Police, resulted finally in the CBI being asked to take over the investigation of this case. CBI has given full credit for the arrest of the accused in this case to the Pune Police. CBI does not have to bask in glory by 'Sharing' the success of others.

Yours sincerely,

(M.G.KATRE)

Sh.S.S.Jog,
Director General of Police,
Maharashtra, Bombay.

Copy to:
1) The Chief Secretary, Govt. of Maharashtara, Bombay.
2) The Home Secretary, Govt. of India, New Delhi.

(M.G.KATRE)
DIRECTOR. C.B.I.

Chapter-6

Loot & Scoot : Terrorists as Brigands

The terrorists had turned to looting banks by the mid-eighties. Such banditry had peaked by 1988 and was indeed, the main source of funds for some terrorists. On February 12, 1987, the director CBI, Mr MG Katre, sent a brief note communicating the Ministry of Home Affair's decision that the CBI should immediately take over the investigation from the Punjab Police of the looting of the Punjab National Bank, Industrial Area Branch, Ludhiana, by suspected terrorists, 12 in number and dressed as policemen, who were believed to have taken away about Rs 7 crores.

A special aircraft had been ordered and, my unit was to proceed to Ludhiana, immediately to take over the investigation. The dacoits had left no one in any doubt about their identity and their intentions. Investigating this case was a joy because there was no interference here. Instead, there was cooperation from every quarter and accolades at the end of the day. The significance of this investigation lay in the fact that it resulted in breaking the back of this group of terrorists. The critical import of this case was recognized by the then Director General of Punjab Police, Mr Julio Ribeiro, midway through the investigation.

The terrorists had seized the entire currency chest in the bank. It was suspected, the group had got away with 19 other such crimes, prior to the Punjab National Bank looting. This spree had actually started in 1984 and had lasted till 1987 and included a number of bank dacoities and looting of jewellers shops, apart from murders and attempt to murder. The group had hideouts in Jalandhar, Chandigarh and even in about six places in Delhi. They had committed terrorist acts in Chandigarh, Punjab, Delhi and in Kasaoli in Himachal Pradesh, in the Terai area of Uttar Pradesh, in Sri Ganganagar in Udaipur and in other border areas in Rajasthan, Ahmedabad, Baroda along with the border areas of Pakistan. This network extended to Bombay, Pune, Durg, Bhilai, Raipur, Calcutta and Tatanagar.

There were at least two dozen top terrorists, who were functioning from these places with their lieutenants. They had collected arms and ammunition in huge quantities, purchased two steel-plated trucks with concealed cabins where these arms were stored. The crores that they had looted from various banks were distributed among the associates, including the Damdami Taksal, where Rs 3 crores was stocked. They were ready to launch almost a blitzkrieg to give a tremendous fillip to the Punjab Terrorist Movement. Only, they met their nemesis at the Punjab National Bank.

Prior to looting the bank, the terrorists had hired an accommodation at 81, Field Gunj, Ludhiana, in December 1986. Jinda (the killer of General Vaidya) and his associates had surveyed some banks and had selected the Punjab National Bank, Industrial Area Branch, as the one to loot. To keep surveillance over the bank and gather information about the location and the strength of the guards, they did their morning exercises, running in track suits, in and around the area in which the bank was located. Once they were ready to strike, they stole three vehicles, a Maruti van, a Fiat car and a Toyota truck. Arms were brought from Jalandhar.

About 22 persons actively participated in the crime. At 9 am., four of them, disguised as policemen, entered the bank, one dressed as inspector, one as head constable and two as constables. They carried small arms – a sten gun, a .303 rifle, four of them had pistols, one had a .30 special sten carbine and one had a .455 revolver. Those who stayed out and kept watch also had one AK 47 among them. One of the persons who entered, was deliberately not given a weapon, as he was in the habit of opening fire on the slightest of provocation. The four that entered, quickly overpowered the police guard, while the other 18 provided vigil from outside the bank and from other vantage points. On investigation, Rs 5.70 crores was found to have been taken. Of this, Rs 5.55 crores was from the currency chest and Rs 15.21 lakhs from the strong room.

The cracking of the case required resources as well as informants, close coordination between the Punjab Police, CBI, the media and more selected sources, including those who worked as spotters, enabled us to crack the case and name 18 culprits and as many as 25, who though associates, could not be prosecuted for lack of proof acceptable in court. The cooperation led to raids and operations, which slowed down terrorist activity in Punjab. The first breakthrough came in the shape of the seizure of the Maruti car, involved in the crime. Eyewitnesses had seen the car that the terrorists had abandoned after the crime. What they had left behind was a fake driving licence, which, however, gave away the address: Khud da Mohalla. When the address was raided, the investigators found one army deserter by the name of Balbir Singh staying there. From the house was recovered arms, ammunition, locker keys, cash worth Rs 1,96,750 with the Punjab National Bank, Ludhiana, marking along with a number of documents, which suggested that properties and vehicles had been acquired in fictitious names by the terrorists of this group.

The arrest and interrogation of Balbir Singh, army deserter, from April 27, 1984, gave us the necessary openings to blast open the case. From one man we reached another, from one hideout we found another, and over some days, 18 top terrorists had been nabbed and another 25 associates identified. The chain of breakthrough started in April 1987 and carried on, reaching its peak in end-June, 1987. Another 25 were identified along with their hideouts. With investigators hot on their heels, the terrorists had to flee and left behind tell-tale signs and, that included negatives of photographs of some members of the group. With the photographs, tracking and arrests became easier and over a period of time, the investigators painstakingly collected arms and ammunition and their vehicles. With hideouts identified and transportation and money seized, the terrorists were set back by several years. This is what the Punjab DGP acknowledged.

Mr Ribeiro, on his own, wrote to the CBI director, Mr MG Katre, on June 26, 1987, praising our efforts: "...I wish to place on record, my sincere gratitude to the officers of the CBI who have been entrusted with the difficult job of investigating the Ludhiana Bank

Dacoity case. Shri S Sen, DIG, Shri Murari, SP and other officers who worked very hard and, with the help of uniformed police raided the various hideouts of the extremists, captured arms and culprits.

"If they had a little more help, they could have done much better. I strongly recommend that at least three more DSPs and three more inspectors should be deputed to help this team, if they are to consolidate their gains. It will be realised that the gains of the team will also be to the advantage of the Punjab Police and all those who are fighting terrorism in this State..."

I recalled the occasion, when Mr Jog had slammed me. Mr Ribeiro now put in some adrenaline into my system. I carried on in the area of terrorism till 1988, before asking the director to relieve me and, give me some other posting. To my delight, after a few months he sent me to head a CBI training centre, where I spent about a year before getting back into the interrogation stream.

The accused, sent up for trial in July 1988, were tried in the Terrorist and Disruptive Act Court in Ludhiana. The trial continued till 2012 and on 20.11.2012, all 12 who faced prosecution were convicted and sentenced to 10 years' rigorous imprisonment.

Copy of the Letter

J.F. Ribeiro, IPS

DO No. ____/Cr.I___
Director General of Police
Punjab
Dated Chandigarh, the 26th June 87

My dear,

I wish to place on record my sincere gratitude to the officers of the C.B.I. who have been entrusted with the difficult job of investigating the Ludhiana Bank Dacoity Case. Shri S. Sen, DIG, Shri Murari. SP and other officers have worked very hard and with the help of uniformed men raided the various hide-outs of the extremists, captured arms and culprits.

2. If they had a little more help, they would have done much better. I strongly recommend that about three more DSPs and three more Inspectors should be deputed to help this team if they are to consolidate their gains. It will be realised that the gains of the team will also be to the advantage of the Punjab Police and all those who are fighiting terrorism in this State.

Yours Sincerely,
Sd/XXX
(J.P. Ribeiro)

Shri M.G. Katre,
Director, C.B.I., Govt. of India,
CGO Complex, Lodi Road,
New Delhi.

No. SS671-73/Cr-I dt. 26th June, 1987
Copy of the above is forwarded demi-official to the following for information:-

1. **Smt. P.P. Trivedi, Secy, Personnel (MHA), Govt. of India, New Delhi.**
2. **Sh. C.G. Somiah, Union Home Secy. Govt of India, New Delhi.**
3. **Sh. S. Sen, Dy. Inspr. General, C.B.I., c/o Punjab National Bank, Ludhiana.**

Sd/XXX
Director General of Police,
Punjab, 26.6.87.

Chapter-7

Shuttlecock Investigation Syed Modi Murder Case

Among the most fascinating cases of political interference, changing the course of law was the Syed Modi murder case in Lucknow, in the winter of 1988. The celebrated badminton player had been done to death and, the friendship of his wife, Ameeta Modi and Mr Sanjay Singh was a matter of public knowledge. Not that such friendship should automatically lead to murderous motivation, but the case aroused intense political interest. The CBI suspected, on the basis of sound evidence, involvement of Sanjay Singh, of the then Jan Morcha, and arrested him. The suspicions were further supported by revelations following the arrest of Akhilesh Singh.

Akhilesh Singh had actually organised the murder of Syed Modi. He had just broken up with the Congress and had joined VP Singh's Jan Morcha along with Mr Arun Nehru and others. Mr Rajiv Gandhi and the Home Minister, Mr P Chidambaram, knew him personally. Mr Arun Mukherjee, Additional Director, CBI, time and again cautioned me to ensure that the investigation did not look like a vendetta against a person who had ditched Rajiv Gandhi to join VP Singh. When Akhilesh named Sanjay Singh, as the man behind the crime, it was necessary for us to arrest Sanjay Singh, search his residential and other premises, and also collect evidence against Ameeta, Syed Modi's widow. While Mr Mukherjee was reluctant to approve these operations, Mr Mohan Katre, who joined the investigations later, on his return from an overseas visit, agreed with my proposed line of action. Sanjay Singh was arrested and all necessary actions were carried out. The Jan Morcha and its party members surrounded the CBI office on Naval Kishore Road, Lucknow, and shouted slogans opposing investigations against Sanjay Singh. We, however, proceeded with the investigations and Mr Arun Mukherjee also informed Mr Chidambaram that if he was not happy with the manner in which the investigation was being conducted, I could be withdrawn from the investigations along with my team. Mr Chidambaram backed off. But, he was upset and has remained displeased with me. Sanjay Singh was an old friend, a former member of the "Sanjay Gandhi Brigade." He was known to have expressed the view that by Sen's "actions against Sanjay Singh, Sen was giving the opposition a handle to attack the Congress Party, with the charge that Sanjay Singh was the target only because he had deserted the Congress Party for VP Singh." This anger manifested itself years later, when as Home Minister of India, he told the LG Delhi, Tejendra Khanna that he should dispense with my services. Till the Sanjay Singh episode, as Minister for State, in charge of Internal Security, in the Ministry of Home Affairs(MHA), he often sought me out. Only a year before this incident, he had, while giving a statement on the Rajghat attack on Rajiv Gandhi, stated before Parliament that they had the best organization, (CBI) investigating the case, and within the CBI, they had the best people handling the matter. I was in charge of that investigation.

The facts of the case were straightforward enough. Syed Modi was shot dead on July 23, 1988 at about 7.45 pm. as he set off on his scooter from KD Babu Stadium, Lucknow, after a regular badminton practice session. Amar Bahadur Singh and Bhagwati Singh pumped five bullets into his body. Four spent bullets were recovered from the spot and, according to a subsequent ballistic report, they were fired from a .38 bore revolver. Balai Singh and driver Jitendra Singh waited in a Maruti van - HYG 1959 - parked nearby. After firing, the killers jumped into the van and drove away. The number had been noted even as the killers were fleeing the spot. The van was spotted in Lucknow and after it was seized it was only a matter of time before the hired killers and the brains behind the murder were nabbed. Investigations subsequently showed, the hired killers were associated with Akhilesh Singh, who had implicated his friend Sanjay Singh in his statement to the CBI. Then, there were Ameeta Modi's celebrated tell-tale diaries and love letters (extracts pages 69-71) which provided ground material to investigate her and Sanjay Singh.

Back to the politics surrounding the case. There was a change in the centre that saw VP Singh, a close relative of Sanjay Singh, as the Prime Minister. There was intense pressure on the CBI now to go slow on the Sanjay Singh case. The first casualty was AP Mukherjee, then director, CBI, who as additional director, CBI, had supervised the investigations. The next man, R. Shekhar, was under pressure to drop the prosecutor, SG Samant of Bombay. Unable to get R. Shekhar, Director, to drop the special public prosecutor, the VP Singh government did the unthinkable. Most government departments with the concurrence of the Ministry of Law engaged special public prosecutors, when they had to prosecute a person. Apart from the CBI, special public prosecutors are appointed by Customs and Excise, Railways, Enforcement Directorate, Company Law Board and even by the Ministry of Law. In a sweeping order, all, *repeat all*, special prosecutors, appointed by the previous government were dispensed with. From the date of order, these departments had no public prosecutor to conduct their cases in courts. This order also relieved CBI public prosecutor, Mr SG Samant. This decision would put back the trial of case by years but getting rid of Samant was important enough for the VP Singh government to accept such a delay.

Selection of new prosecutors takes months. It would first require obtaining the consent of the person concerned. This would be followed by a verification of his antecedents and, then the meticulous procedure adopted to set in motion the actual appointment. Ironically, Samant had to be reappointed immediately as the media —thanks to some internal briefing done by me—exposed the story of his dismissal. VP Singh immediately claimed that the entire episode was without his knowledge and concurrence and forced the Law Ministry to reappoint Samant. A very disturbed senior criminal lawyer came back to the hustings but, clearly his heart was no longer in the case. A few months later, the new government struck again. The additional district judge, seized of the case long before the commencement of the trial from the investigation stage itself, was removed after he had heard the entire arguments for framing of charges against Sanjay Singh, Ameeta Modi and five others. The new judge had to rehear the entire argument and the public prosecutor, Samant, had to go over the case again. His order pronounced Sanjay Singh and Ameeta Modi, as not guilty of the charges, but held that the remaining five were *prima facie* guilty of charges and must face a trial.

As on date, those whom the CBI accused of masterminding the crime, Akhilesh Singh, Sanjay Singh and Ameeta are free. Akhilesh moved the High Court at Lucknow, eight years after he was charged for the conspiracy to murder Syed Modi, some time after Supreme Court set Ameeta and Sanjay free and this Bench freed him of the charge of this heinous murder. Sanjay Singh divorced his wife, Garima, niece of the former Prime Minister, VP Singh, and married Ameeta Modi. He represents the BJP in Amethi and his new wife, Ameeta, is the sarpanch in village Amethi. Akhilesh Singh is a senior member of the Congress Party in the Uttar Pradesh legislature. All the four hired killers are on trial but two of them Amar Bahadur Singh and Balai Singh were killed when they came out of the jail on parole. Ameeta Modi has never tired of accusing CBI of torturing her, quite regardless of the motives that she provided to the CBI through her diaries and her love letters to Sanjay Singh, confirming the illicit relationship between the two.

The courts have released her, Sanjay Singh and Akhilesh Singh and, therefore, in the eyes of the law, they are not guilty of the murder of Syed Modi. The same court, however, held that the four who were present at the scene of the crime on July 28, 1989 —Amar Bahadur Singh, Bhagwat Singh@Pappu, Balia Singh and Jitendra Singh@Tinku—the hired killers in the employ of Akhilesh Singh, a friend of Sanjay Singh are the murderers of Syed Modi. The material collected against the four satisfied the court, but the material collected against the remaining three was not considered good enough to even make them face trial. Personally, I consider the investigation conducted in this case to be of the highest order, though the court held otherwise and released the three whom the CBI claimed had masterminded the murder through the four hired killers.

How does the investigator look upon all this after matters have been laid to rest? When there is evidence, the statute requires the entire material available be compressed in a chargesheet and that chargesheet be filed in court and, leave it to the court to decide who should face trial. The courts have held, that the evidence against Sanjay Singh, Ameeta Modi and, later, even Akhilesh Singh was not good enough to drag them through a trial and that is final. We thought otherwise and many who read her letters to Sanjay Singh and her meticulously written diaries, as well as the welling from the heart of two others Syed and Garima, may also share our perception.

A question often asked is why Ameeta Modi did not seek a divorce from Syed Modi, considering her infatuation for Sanjay Singh, and her own strained relationship with Syed Modi. To seek a divorce, one has to be legally wedded and there are valid grounds to hold the view. Ameeta and Syed were not legally man and wife, and their so-called marriage was not solemnized under any legally or socially accepted norm. The date of marriage is reported as 14-5-84 in an affidavit sworn by the couple and it is shown as taking place under The Special Marriage Act at the residence of Sanjay Singh and the witnesses were Sanjay Singh and his PRO Alam. No one was present from Syed's family and there was no other outsider either. The marriage officer ADM City was not in Lucknow on 14-5-84 either. Sanjay Singh who was a State Cabinet Minister was a active participant in the drama of the hush-hush marriage and he got a document from a magistrate who was not the notified marriage officer of the state that "this marriage is not registered but it subsists" whatever that may mean. The case of the prosecution was that she chose to be a widow and not a divorcee. This evidence could have been tested, if there was a trial, and as there was none, it remains a unsubstantiated theory of those who investigated the murder.

(3)

मेरे प्रिय,

अमेठी मुझे भेजने के बाद दो दिन तक आप लखनऊ मे ही रुके रहे। कहिए तो सच है न। यदि आप चाहे तो किसी व्यक्ति से कहल दूं। आप की मर्जी क्या है? स्पष्ट कहिए। मुझसे बारम्बार झूठ बोलना धोखा देना। उसमे प्रेम की जड़ उखड़ना है। यदि आप मुझ से कहीं अच्छा साथ चाहते है तो आपको इतना बहाना बनाने की जरूरत नहीं है। मैं अपने बच्चो समेत आप का रास्ता साफ कर दूंगी। बच्चो को ले कर कहीं डूब मरेंगी।

महाराजा ने भी इसी बात कि पुष्टि की है कि आप ने जनाब मोदी को

(19)

प्र. ने जन्मदिन के उपलक्ष में अमेठी बुलाया है। तो जायें सब कोई। मैं आपके सामने न पडूँगी। जहाँ सम्मान न हो वहाँ बारम्बार मुँह दिखाने से क्या है।

कहते हैं कि विश्वास करो मेरा। विश्वास शब्द का उपहास करने को जी करता है। घाव पर घाव। अहा! खूब मिले पति से। कैसी मूर्ख हूँ मैं भी? अब अन्त आ गया है। मैं हृदय से पुकारती हूँ माँ मुझे अब छुटकारा दिलाओ इस असह्य वेदना से। मुझे शीघ्र मृत्यु दो ताकि विश्वासघात से बच सकूँ। देख लेना, माँ ~~मेरी मेरी~~ अपनी माँ, जरूर सुनेगी,

पीछा छूटा पति नाम के भयंकर [illegible] से

हा। हा। हा। हा। हा। हा।

प्रियंका (8) (1)

यह letter मेरे दिल कि आवाज है।

यह तुमोर लिए नही लिख रहा हूँ मै अपने दिल कि आवाज निकाल रहा हूँ। मै आज रो रहा हूँ। लेकिन किसी को अपनी आवाज नही सुना सकता। क्यों कि इस दुनियां मे मेरी आवाज सुनने वाला कोई नही है। एक तुम थी जो सुनती थी लेकिन अब तुम किसी कोऔर आवाज सुनती हो। तुम्हे अब हमारा फोन का भी इन्तजार भी नही रहा। क्योंकी तुमे बहुत बडे लोग फोन करेते है। तुमे प्यार करेने वाले बहुत लोग हो बहुत भरोसा था तुमोर ऊपर। आदमी क्या सोचता है क्या हो जाता है। तुम ऐसी लडकी नही थी। शायद मेरा नसिब ही खराब है। यह लिखते वक्त मै रो रहा हूँ। लेकिन मेरी आवाज सुनने वाला अब मेरा नही रहा। मुझे तुमसे जो प्यार मिल था उसी के सहारे थोडे दिन और जी लूगां। मै किसी को और चाह नही सकता यह हमारी कमजोरी है यह ही हमारी सबसे बडी कमजोरी है। यही हमारी जिन्दगी की सबसे बडी भूल है की

(2) 17/8/88

हमने तुमको प्यार किया। और चाहा और
विश्वास किया। यहा पर जब एक दुसरे को
देखता है तो क्या होता है यह मै नही लिख
सकता। अगर मै चाहुँ तो यहा पर लड़की मिल
सकती है। पर क्या जिन्दगी मे लड़की ही
सब कुछ है। हमारे ख्याल से नही जो
लोग अपने बीबी से प्यार नही कर सकते
उस आदमी से कोई कितने दिन का उमिद लगा
सकता है जब आदमी अपनी बीबी का नही
हो सकता तो क्या दुसरे का हो सकता।
हर आदमी के जीवन मे तुफान आता है उस
तुफान मे जो लोग नसिब वाले होते है बच
जाते है हम तो नसिब वाले है ही नही।
तुम्हारे वजह से हमारा नसिब बदल गया था
और अब तुम्हारे ही वजह से हमारा नसिब
बदल जाये गा ऊपर वाला भी जितना देता
है हिसाब रखता है। लिखते मै रो रहा
हुँ मेरा प्यार टुट रहा है तुमको तो बहुत
लोग प्यार करने वाले है क्या कि तुम तो
ही प्यारी। मुझे लगता है अब जिन्दगी
मेरा साथ नही देगा अगर मै अब नही

रहा तो कोई बात नहीं। अब मैं तुमसे
शिकायत नहीं करूंगा थोड़े से ज़िन्दगी में
तुमने हमको प्यार बहुत दिया। इतना काफी
है उस बदनसीब के लिए। अगर तुमको कभी
मेरी जरूरत पड़ जाये तो याद करना हम मर
कर भी तुम्हारे रहेंगे। अब जैसा चल रहा
है अब और दिन नहीं जी सकता। हमारे
रूम में तुम्हारी फोटो है। जो देखता है वह
तुमको देखना चाहता है। तुम हो ही इतनी
प्यारी कि सब लोग तुम्हारी फोटो मांगते हैं
मेरी ज़िन्दगी इतनी ठीक से चल रही थी
शायद ऊपर वाले को मन्जूर नहीं थी।
मैं तुम्हारे साथ हर तरफ से खुश था मेरा
उठना बैठना पीना खाना सब कुछ तुम्ही थी।
मैं इतना तुम्हारे साथ खो गया था कि मुझे
पता भी नहीं चला कि ज़िन्दगी में क्या
मोड़ आने वाला है। हर कोने को मैं अपना
कोना समझता था लेकिन मैं भूल गया कि
अब वह बात नहीं रही। ज़िन्दगी में अब
एक नैया मोड़ ले आया। मैं एक किनारे पर
रह गया। उसमें मैं तुम्हारी गलती नहीं

मानता। क्यो कि तुमको ऐसा ही सिखाया
गया है। मै अपने को बहुत ही बदलना
चाहता था लेकिन नही कर पाया।
अपने ही प्यार को लुटते देखता रहा।
मै यह गम और नही सह सकता। मै तुमसे
अलग तो नही नही हो पाऊँगा लेकिन यह
दुनिया जरूर छोड़ दुंगा। मै और कुछ नही
मांगूगा मै अन्दर से खत्म हो रहा हूँ तुम
नही समझ सकती हमारे ऊपर कैसा लग रहा
है। क्यो कि जिस गम मे मै जल रहा हूँ वह
तुमने नही देखा। ऊपर वाले से यही कहूंगा
कि तुमको वह कभी न दिखाये। तुमको
प्यार करने वाले हमसे ज्यादा प्यार करते
है। जो कि अपनी बाबी से भी नही करते।
इस छोटी सी उम्र मे इतना बड़ा सदमा सह पावूँ
गा कि नही। जिन्दगी एक धूप छांव है कभी
धूप कभी छांव लोग कहते है कि तुम्हारी
बीबी तुमसे कितना प्यार करती है। और
मै जो हूँ। कि तुमको गलत ही समझता हूँ।
शायद एक वक्त आयेगा कि तुमको
हमारे ऊपर प्यार आये। लेकिन बहुत देर

हो गयी होगी। शायद मैं इस दुनिया में
नही होगे। तुमने कभी समझेन कि कोशिश
नही कि। हम तुम्हारी हर बात मानेत थे
सिर्फ मुझे यही हमेशा अच्छा नहीं लगा।
जब लोग दुसरे की बीवी के ऊपर हसेत थे
मैं भी हसता था। लेकिन आज जब मैं
मेरे ऊपर आया तो पता लगा कि कैसा लगता
है किसी के ऊपर हसना मेरी खामोशी मेरा अन्दर
से खून पी रही है। मैं हस रहा हूँ सिर्फ
दिखाने के लिए। ऐसा कभी नही हुआ कि
जिस दिन मैं ठीक से सो सकू। तुम चाहती
तो मुझे संभाल सकती थी। लेकिन तुम ऐसा
नही करती। अब मैं तुमको सिर्फ देखना
चाहता हूँ। मुझे पता कि तुम्हारा सिलसिला
चालू रहेगा अब मेरी एक ही तमन्ना है
कि तुमको एक बार ठीक से देख लूँ
मुझे बहुत सारे दिन याद है तुम्हारे प्यार के
उस प्यार के बाद और कुछ नही चाहिए
मुझे। तुम मेरी जिन्दगी मे सब कुछ थी।
तुमने मुझे इतना प्यार दिया था कि मैं और

सब भूल गया था। मेरी मौत मेरा
प्यार ले के जाये गी। इस Letter के बाद
मैं तुमको एक Letter और लिखूं गा लेकिन
जाने के बाद ही दोनो Letter हम तुमको
दे कर जाये गें। अगर तुमको लड़का
हो तो उसे बड़ा खिलाड़ी बनाना। यह मेरी
तुमसे आखरी बिनती है। मैंने तुमसे
ही प्यार किया। अपने जिन्दगी में तुम्हारा
ही आदर्श माना। तुम जिन्दगी में जुदा बनो
ही हमारी चाह है। उसके बाद मैं एक
और Letter लिखने वाला हूँ वह मेरा आखरी
Letter होगा। सिर्फ तुम्हारा

SONA

(20) Lucknow.
13th Aug. '85

My dearest

Thought I must pen you a few lines because I think this is probably going to be the only sort of communication left between the two of us.

I was rather let down since meeting you yesterday. You said things which hurt and did not say certain things which also hurt. I had expected a much warmer union, moreso because this was quite a painful separation. No doubt we have been separated a couple of times before, and twice for over a month, when I was abroad playing but this separation was the worst of them all, because for the first time in two years, we had become very close. Yes, close we always were but both of us had not openly confessed it to each other. This time there was a totally different dimension to this closeness of ours. It's true, very true, I love you, but there are many, many restrictions in this blind love of mine. I can never forget the fact, however hard I try, that we are both married to two different individuals and our first duties are towards them. It's all easy to say, but I know, we can't leave them, however we might want to be and

(can't leave them, however we might want to be and)

(19)

guess we will have to find a via media to this
today, you happened to say in the car 'But how long
will you make a man wait?' Does this mean that you
not going to be able to wait? Does it mean that I what take
you for what you say, cause you've often said 'For you,
I can wait a life time'? Does it mean you say something
when you are emotional and don't mean it later
when you get more down to earth? Does it mean that
I cannot depend on you when I need you most? Why
have these doubts started coming again? You had given me
a certain amount of confidence, but you are taking it back
Please tell me, can you wait even if it means a year or
more? Let me also prepare myself because if I have to be
shattered the sooner the better. I am seeing dreams!

Today I am really confused, lost, lonely. At one side I am
losing my husband's love, faith, trust infact everything, and
now I feel at the other end I am losing you too I am
already facing the awful sarcasm, criticism of this awful
world for being so close to you but the most unfortunate
thing is that I am not even assured of your love. In any
case, I am not writing this to ask for your support or

confidence but I am merely writing to you to assure you of my love. Don't ever doubt that I am becoming weak or I am scared or might not be able to face the situation. I promise you I will never let you down. No doubt I may not be able to be by you when you need me or should I say when you are next free but try I always will. After all you too cannot assure me of your time if I am next free. Can you? I am sure you are not liking my writing to you like this but why not? If we love each other I am sure we have the liberty to atleast be frank.

Anyway I would certainly like to talk to you very seriously if you can spare a couple of hours for me. Let's hope it's possible sometime before this misunderstanding between the two of us reaches a stage where there can be no understanding at all.

I hope I can rely on you for the best out of this slight misunderstanding.

With all my love + kisses

Affectionately

Always yours + only yours

[illegible]

Chapter-8

Rajiv Gandhi and CBI
Uncovering the Cover-Up

Rajiv Gandhi was still the Prime Minister but VP Singh was already charting out his destiny, independent of his former mentor. Arun Shourie, of *The Indian Express,* had earned a name for his fiery journalism. Bhure Lal, a VP Singh favourite, later to control CBI through the PMO, had just been removed as the Director of Enforcement Directorate, and was moving in the Finance Ministry looking after the Mints in 1988.

It was around this time that *The Indian Express* carried a letter, issued by the Deputy Director of the Enforcement Directorate, Calcutta, addressed to his Director at Delhi. It was written when Bhure Lal was still the Director. This letter described a search operation in Calcutta of a firm with which Mr Kamal Nath, a Congress MP from Chindwara, and his father were connected. It alleged violations of the Foreign Exchange Act by the company, and described recovery of evidence. It damningly added, that midway through action, the operation was called off, on the orders of some big wig in the Finance Ministry. The Prime Minister already dismayed by Mr VP Singh's posture was—as related by Mr Katre, CBI Director, to me—furious.

He believed that the letter was a forgery and suggested that, Mr Bhure Lal and Mr Arun Shourie had created it to embarrass him. He wanted them to be nailed. Katre ordered me to search them both and, if any material was found, to arrest them. Bhure Lal and Arun Shourie were at that time, icons. Their integrity was beyond doubt, I felt. I knew Bhure Lal personally and respected him. Arun Shourie, I did not know at all but his journalism had earned my respect. I reminded Mr Katre of their reputation and suggested, that a search on any one on such flimsy material would be incorrect. Certainly, the grounds were flimsy. I recorded my views and assured him that if investigations revealed that the letter was a forgery, Mr Arun Shourie, who had used it, would be criminally liable. The important thing was to find out if it was a forgery.

True on that date, under the same dispatch number, another letter on the same facts was available in Calcutta and Delhi Office of the Directorate. I wanted more material to hold the letter published in *The Indian Express* to be a forgery. Mr Katre considered my points, probably spoke to the Prime Minister and allowed me time. I was a DIG but, reporting to the Director directly at that time. I dispatched Inspector A.K. Ohri to Calcutta with instructions and soon after followed myself. Ohri had by then picked up all the shorthand notebooks used by the Deputy Director, Enforcement Calcutta, which were lying in the record room awaiting weeding out and destruction. A short hand stenographer had commenced transcribing them one by one. Within a week, the letter Arun Shourie had published, was found. It had been actually dictated and sent to Delhi. Since the search had been stopped, apparently on certain instructions, that letter too was destroyed and another letter —suggesting that the search yielded nothing on the same date— had replaced it. That letter was not dictated but, typed straight on the typewriter in Delhi. The earlier letter was to be destroyed but, one copy remained which Arun Shourie procured for his paper. He also produced it in a Parliamentary Committee to prove his point, that he had committed no forgery. At this point, I was shifted to another posting so the rest is not known to me.

Arun Shourie, the journalist, had uncovered what became a scoop. Bhure Lal and he are friends. At a marriage, which I attended, they came together. It is anybody's guess, how copies of a letter, that someone powerful had got replaced, were not all destroyed. Nevertheless, here was a case of political interference exposed. Rajiv Gandhi had no idea that his Cabinet colleague had interfered to stop the search, and get the Congress MP and his father off the hook. Had he known, surely he would not have called in the CBI. What was established by the investigation was that the letter Mr Arun Shourie had published in *The Indian Express*, was not a forgery. Admittedly, other questions now cropped up but, I did not even attempt to answer them as 1) I was not a part of CBI's anti-corruption wing and 2) My brief was limited to investigating the alleged forgery and find out the persons responsible for the forgery. Now, that the forgery was no longer an issue, I decided that I had no further role to play. The point that Arun Shourie had made, however, was that corruption at the highest level had led to the heat being taken off Kamal Nath and his father's alleged FERA violation. In fact, Bhure Lal himself was away from Delhi when his No. 2 had received instructions reportedly from Arun Nehru, to stop the investigations in the Kamal Nath case. Faced with a *fait accompli*, Bhure Lal had acquiesed to the cover up. Arun Shourie had helped him to liberate himself. There was, therefore, definitely a need for a CBI investigation into the cover-up but, this did not happen.

The sad part is that both Bhure Lal and I, had allowed ourselves to be a part of a cover up, which if fully investigated would have exposed the level of interference by Rajiv Gandhi's cabinet in investigations. The strangest part here is that the cover-up was ordered and completed, when Mr VP Singh was Finance Minister and Bhure Lal was the Director, Enforcement, both fiercely proud of their probity. If Bhure Lal had made available, the copy of the letter to Arun Shourie, he had taken the grave risk of implicating himself as he was the Enforcement Director at the time of the cover up. Probably he felt that he deserved this ordeal by fire for allowing the cover up – rather the ordeal than allowing the cover-up to remain unexposed. The CBI had let him down, and had let itself down by not investigating the corruption by public servants, through its anti-corruption division, after the CBI's own special crime division had succeeded in establishing that Arun Shourie had exposed a foul cover up in *The Indian Express*. Mr Katre was the head of both divisions and, he and succeeding directors must take the blame for not investigating the cover-up.

Chapter-9

The Krishnamurthy Saga

Mr V Krishnamurthy was Member, Planning Commission, in 1992, when an inquiry was ordered against him. He was alleged to have asked the Big Bull, Harshad Mehta, for Rs 25 lakhs. This was apparently for his son's company and a cheque from the personal account of Mr Harshad Mehta, for that amount was issued by Mohan Khandelwal, the Power-of-Attorney holder, for Harshad Mehta in Delhi. This amount went to the company as requested for by Mr Krishnamurthy. I was joint director, heading the anti-corruption division of the CBI, and was asked by Mr SK Dutta, Director, CBI, to enquire into this episode through one of the units under me. When the enquiry was started, Krishnamurthy was not asked to relinquish office. His status was that of a Minister of State and, therefore, I am right in assuming that the Prime Minister had cleared the investigation against him.

The permission to investigate Mr Krishnamurthy was a surprise, as everyone knew the power he wielded. His habit of calling rich businessmen, to pay up ostensibly for the purpose of business, and then, conveniently forgetting to repay the instalments, was not a very well kept secret. His victims included RP Goenka, CK Birla and Vijay Mallya. Mr Narasimha Rao who, according to Mr

Krishnamurthy himself, took instructions from him, when Rajiv Gandhi was Prime Minister, had ordered this enquiry out of pettiness. It is possibly true as Mr Rao, a "first rate Prime Minister and a third rate man" to quote Veer Sanghvi, could have stooped to that level. I realized the extent of Mr Krishnamurthy's powerful network, as soon as the enquiry started. I was subjected to such enormous peer pressure, that I decided to use a sledge hammer to investigate him.

After four days of a full-throttled secret enquiry, I was satisfied that the charges against him required a deeper probe. I ordered a search at his residence, all his offices in various parts of the country, took him and his elder son into custody, arranged for arrest warrants against his younger son who lived in the United States. He and his elder son were taken on police remand and thoroughly interrogated, during the remand period. He was confronted with Harshad Mehta who had also been taken into custody in another case under investigation, with a different unit under me at the same time. After the police remand was over, they were not released but sent into judicial custody. Of course, each action against him had the approval of the court under whose jurisdiction the investigation was being conducted. There was no pressure during the period of his arrest, his interrogation or his dispatch to jail.

When the investigation reached the stage where it was possible to find assets in Swiss banks, problems were faced by investigating officers. The first step was to stall the investigations in Hongkong and Japan. Investigations in Switzerland to reach their Swiss bank accounts were still possible but, that too was frustrated. It is interesting to recount my conversation with Mr Nishikant Sinha, Joint Secretary in the Prime Minister's Office. We had already approached the competent court to grant us permission to move the competent Swiss Court and obtain details of all bank accounts that Krishnamurthy and his sons operated in those banks. Under the procedural law, before issuing the letter rogatory, the court had to have an assurance from the government that the information received would be used only for the case under investigation and, if a similar request was made by the Swiss authorities, it would be heard and dealt with under the laws of the country. Therefore, we had moved the government for the assurance and the Prime Minister's Office was at that time considering the issuing of this assurance to the competent court. Mr Sinha, on receiving the request, called me up. His call was not only very warm, he also gave me an assurance that the PMO was ready to issue the assurance required by the court.

A week later, he called up again and this time he was a bit worried as the secretary to the Prime Minister, Mr AN Verma, had appeared unwilling and had asked for some clarifications, which he was seeking from me on the phone to expedite matters. In the meanwhile, the court was continuously giving us dates to appear with the assurance, so that it could issue the letter rogatory. On each occasion, we were forced to inform the court that the assurance of the government was awaited. When his third telephone call came, Mr Sinha was an angry man, and he asked me quite angrily, as to why the CBI had moved the court without seeking the government's permission to seek letter rogatory in case of Krishnamurthy's accounts in Swiss banks. My answer that we came to the government on the court's direction and, we had followed the same procedure that was followed in the Bofors case, where the government had taken exactly one and a half days to issue the assurance to the court. I also said that the law does not call for a prior approval. "We will change the law", he said. I expostulated that this is a procedural law, and a recent entry in the criminal procedure court in this country which is aimed to detect corruption and crime abroad. My contention that apart from Bofors, it had been similarly used, when gold mohurs from the Nizam's treasury in Hyderabad were surreptitiously moved to certain vaults in Switzerland, seemed to have no effect.

I added, that if the Government of India, was of the considered opinion that we should not investigate the Swiss accounts of Krishnamurthy and his sons, it should go on record, and we will inform the court that the assurance is not forthcoming. The letter rogatory would be denied to us. Already, the government had denied us permission to investigate Krishnamurthy's Sumitomo links in Japan. This was not palatable. Soon afterwards, I was shifted to the crime division of the CBI. Apparently, in the Krishnamurthy case, the idea was only to expose him and not any others, who might have shared in the crimes committed by him since, they enjoyed the goodwill of the present dispensation. The sledgehammer technique that I adopted, was to escape the odium of being labelled the cat's paw. At the risk of speculating, I could say that it "frightened" others. Both the investigations—taking the Rs 25 lakh bribe from Harshad Mehta, and stashing away ill gotten money in Swiss banks—were dropped. The former by the court after eight years spent in just having arguments to assess if the material before the court warranted Krishnamurthy's and his two sons' trial. The latter was dropped by the government, as it considered the material collected as insufficient to arraign him court. No investigations had been permitted in Japan, and Switzerland reference was delayed by years, and whether enquiries were at all carried out in Australia, Singapore and Germany is not known to me. Incidentally, the boast of the PMO bureaucrat about changing the law was not an idle one either and, as of now no prayer for issue of letter rogatory to a court can be sent without a clearance from the Government of India. Since India's Criminal Procedure Code could not be amended, recourse has been taken to a issue of a directive to that effect by the Ministry of Personnel , CBI's controlling Ministry and this Ministry is under the Cabinet Minister who is usually also the Prime Minister of India. A sort of a permanent interference in all investigations that require evidence from abroad.

Long before VKrishnamurthy became our Czar of the Public Sector, he was a General Manager of the Bharat Heavy Electricals in Trichy. He fell foul of the CBI but his Minister of Heavy Industries in 1977 pooh poohed CBI's adverse report and, he survived to reach the esoteric heights that he did. The same minister is in deep shit, as Tehelka tapes forced him to resign as India's Defence Minister.

Chapter-10

Truth of Hawala Scam

The Hawala case is a story of calculated interference. Consider the facts: The Hawala diaries were chanced upon during a search and raid operation by the CBI, under Deputy Inspector General, CBI, Mr OP Sharma, on May 3, 1991. Mr DP Singh, DSP, in the CBI's terrorist cell recovered the diaries from the house of one Jainender Jain in Saket. Jainender was an employee of Surender Jain, and the case under investigation was under the Terrorist and Disruptive Act. On June 16, the CBI's OP Sharma was trapped by the CBI receiving Rs 10 lakhs, allegedly the last instalment of bribe money for not arresting Surender Jain under TADA, which brooks to bail.

The Hawala diaries, thereafter went underground, to resurface in March 1993, when Mr SK Dutta, the CBI Director, directed that Joint Director (Anti-Corruption) - that is myself - to investigate the case. The instructions came with a note of caution that the investigations should not antagonize Surendra Jain and his associates, as they are the main prosecution witnesses against O. P. Sharma. Investigations were commenced under case number RC 5/S/91/SIV-V/ACU-VI/AC-II JD/NE. The diaries became public property when on August 24, 1993, the newspaper, *Jansatta*, carried the story under the banner "Karoro Ke Ghapla Purr Kundli Maree

Baithee Hai, CBI". On September 2, 1993, Mr Ram Jethmalani addressed a Press conference where he detailed the contours of the case and alleged that the CBI was covering up the diaries. The facts of the case were that investigations had started, cautious and careful, in March 1993. The DIG in charge was Mr Amod Kanth. He was hardly happy that this cauldron had been handed over to him.

Footnote: OP Sharma had made the cardinal mistake of agreeing to hush up a crime. The diaries were not being investigated, he claimed, on orders from the top. Yet, he started playing footsie with one LK Kaul and kept in touch with Surendra Jain through him. If the diaries were closed and sealed from May 4, 1991 - as he had disclosed to Sanjay Kapoor in his book on Hawala, *Bad Money, Bad Politics* – he had really no business to be investigating the diaries as late as June 15, 1992, when he got trapped, receiving Rs 10 lakhs from LK Kaul acting as emissary of Surendra Jain.

My instructions on the file of the case will bear out the extent of guidance and persuasion that was required to get him and his team to move forward. Mr Jayeed Chaudhary, was then, the Director of Enforcement. When I asked him to associate himself with this investigation, he turned on me and wondered what faith he could have in an organization, which sat on the diaries from May 1991 and, whose own DIG was trapped receiving Rs 10 lakhs. In short, he shamed me.

The disclosures in the Hawala diaries were catastrophic, indeed. The writer of the diary and, on his disclosure, other Jains should have been arrested on May 3 itself. In custody they would have explained the abbreviations in the entries: RG, LKA, JHK, VK, etc. and in custody they should have been made to identify in person each of them. The diaries were written upto April 1991 and hence, custodial interrogation would have certainly spilled the beans. Instead, OP Sharma, allegedly took a bribe and then CBI Director, Mr Vijay Karan, froze any investigation on the diaries.

There may be some reason, weak though, not to investigate the Jains after June 16, 1991 pursuant to OP Sharma being caught in the act. Why no investigation took place between May 3, 1991 and June 15, 1991 – almost a month and a half - when there was enough time to rip the case wide open is anyone's guess. An informed guess would be that the CBI was interfered with or that it allowed itself to be interfered with, giving OP Sharma an opportunity to be corrupt. Once the chance to pounce on the case was lost, further investigation became a belated effort. Also, missed was an opportunity to locate people abroad who were using the Jains hawala channels and get them to confess, and name the politicians and public servants who fitted the abbreviations. With this loss, the only option was to use the diary against the writer and slap tax and other penal offences against him. I would have done that. However, the Supreme Court took over, urging the CBI to get the big wigs.

In the Indian system of jurisprudence, evidence is one that is incontrovertible. Even if there is an iota of doubt, the accused gets the benefit of it. However grave, suspicion is never proof. In the Hawala case, what was incontrovertible was the existence of the Hawala diary. These diaries were regularly maintained. They had both credit and debit entries and the accounting was explained at the end of each day. The amounts received in foreign exchange were converted into rupees in accordance with the day's sterling exchange rate. The initials were allegedly acronyms of some politicians and public servants. There was grave suspicion but not proof enough to establish the point in a trial. This was always in doubt till somebody actually testified to these facts as a witness. The maintenance of the diary, however, straightaway invited investigations under the Income-Tax Act and FERA offences against the Jain brothers and their employees. Notwithstanding this simple argument, the CBI selectively chose to prosecute certain politicians on charges that they had helped Jain in his business for pecuniary considerations. This was apparently done on the Supreme Court's directions, deliberately closing eyes to the evidentiary value of the results of the investigations. The result is that all the charges have been dropped, and the Hawala diaries belong to a chapter that has been closed.

To go back into time to understand the process of investigation-interference and end result: a long progress report on the investigation had been received by me and on September 21, 1993, I had issued detailed instructions regarding further investigations. I had never been convinced, that payments reflected in the Hawala diaries were bribes, paid by Surendra Jain and others to Ministers and public servants to obtain facilities. Some payments may have been of such a nature, and I doubt that, but the payments amounting to over Rs 64 crores in foreign exchange, was in my view, payment received by both politicians and public servants from channels abroad, for services rendered to parties abroad or for other considerations or their own foreign exchange kept abroad clandestinely and, Surendra Jain only acted as the conduit making payment at the market exchange rate. That is why, I recommended an investigation abroad and this was carried out both in the United States of America and in the UK by DIG, Mr Amod Kanth. Though this evidence was not then available, later, by a strange quirk of circumstances, I did learn, from almost the horses mouth, that a part of the payments reflected in the Hawala diaries was definitely money collected in foreign exchange for individuals, and parties, and sent through Surendra Jain, who not only gave the best exchange rate but, also kept the information to himself.

It so happened that in June 1996, when I was facing a severe attack on my integrity over the urea scam, from the *Financial Express* and its editor, Mr Prabhu Chawla, I was introduced to Mr Arun Jaitley, by Mr S Swaminathan, then of *Business India*. I wanted an informal legal opinion to proceed against the *Financial Express* in the Press Council. Mr Jaitley was kind enough to give me a whole afternoon whereafter, I took Mr Chawla to the Press Council and got him censured, with the *Financial Express* withdrawing the story with an apology. Subsequently, Mr Jaitley took me through the chargesheet filed against the then BJP President, Mr LK Advani and all the papers in support of the chargesheet, which he as the defence lawyer was then carefully examining. It was shocking to see the paucity of evidence, and I was non-plussed, as to how on the material available the chargesheet against Mr Advani had been filed in court as the first chargesheet in the Hawala case.

Mr Advani as "LKA" has been recorded in the Hawala diary for the first time when he was not a member of the Parliament, and as such, not a public servant. Mr Jaitley said, that the entry recorded against these intitials had actually been received by Mr Advani and was reflected in the BJP account books. For this entry, he could not be prosecuted as he was not a public servant. As such, the basis of his prosecution was not the entry in the Hawala diary, but an entry in a loose sheet, which was separately found during search. There was nothing else beyond this loose sheet of paper, to support the prosecution's case. The case was bound to be thrown out, and in fact should not have been prosecuted, as the number 1 case in the Hawala diary matter. Here was startling evidence to prove that the Hawala diaries were authentic and Mr LK Advani, who received money from abroad for the BJP, admittedly through a conduit, and not through the RBI channel, would have been a very important witness to establish the authenticity of the Hawala diaries and, satisfy the court that these diaries were regular books of accounts maintained in the course of business.

Instead, with this chargesheet against Mr LK Advani on virtually no evidence on record of the case, not only was the chargesheet against him thrown out of the High Court, the entire Hawala diary became inadmissible, as evidence before the trial court. The end result was that, other individuals against whom there was much more than just diary entry e.g. close friendship with the Jains, favours from ministries of which they were heads, evidence on that line also got away scot free on the grounds, that the hawala diary had already been determined to be inadmissible evidence, and that the trial court could not rely upon it.

Had some other politicians, say Mr Arif Khan or Mr Vidya Charan Shukla, or public servants like VK (V. Krishnamurthy) chargesheeted first, there was some chance that the diary would survive. There was some proof that they extended favours to Surendra Jain as a *quid pro quo* THAT IS FOR BEING THE CONDUIT FOR TRANSFER OF THEIR SECRETED FUNDS STASHED ABROAD. Mr Advani, on the other hand, had extended no favour to the Jains; he was not a Minister —and clearly in no position to extend a favour - and was in fact free from the taint of corruption. His sin, if at all, was to receive money collected for the BJP - at that time a party without power - abroad through channels not approved by the RBI. In the instance chargesheeted, there was nothing more than a loose sheet, the flimsiest piece of material. Yet it was the first Hawala case pushed in court. Worse, the Hawala diaries were always available against Surender Jain and his family members. Even that opportunity was lost by the prosecution while it courted disaster by going against Mr Advani first. One may justifiably ask what guided the CBI Director, Mr Vijay Rama Rao, who was hardly a babe in the woods of investigation. Whatever may have been the logic or the absence of it, the Hawala disaster will forever remain a black spot in all annals of investigation. On a personal level, I cannot resist mentioning that the Director first got rid of me, and then of Mr Amod Kanth. The Hawala diaries were destroyed by professionals at the behest of politicians and the Supreme Court was the unknowing cats paw, as it played in the area of criminal investigation which is not its normal cup of tea.

The Supreme Court's role in egging the CBI to get the 'big fish' - read politicians - was only partly responsible for the final wrap up that is the fate of the Hawala diaries. It gave the CBI and its Director the occasion to claim, that politicians were prosecuted at the behest of the Supreme Court. The truth is that, the investigating agency is the only judge of facts when it launches the prosecution. In the absence of conclusive proof against the politicians, there was no need to heap ridicule on the agency by chargesheeting those against whom there was only suspicion. As the Indian courts say, suspicion, however, grave, cannot be the basis of conviction. This is what emboldens one to emphasise that the Hawala diaries were literally destroyed under instructions from the then CBI Director. Earlier, the diaries had been buried by Mr Vijay Karan, after June 16, 1991, under instructions from Mr Chandra Shekhar and then Mr Narasimha Rao. Mr SK Dutta revived it in March 1993 and Mr Vijay Rama Rao did the final honours with the destruction. The lesson and a hard one at that is that the Lakshmanrekha is evidence and proof must sustain the chargesheet. Otherwise it will fail, burying even that part of the chargesheet that was well documented. In the case of the Hawala diaries, the diaries were also evidence against the writer and, could not also be converted into evidence against the politicians and public servants for want of cogent proof. The only course, howsoever unpopular and disgusting it may have seemed, available to the CBI was to save the evidence of the diaries against those who wrote it. Professionals have no business to stray from their path when gathering evidence to cater to and satisfy the popular mood. The result of such transgressions : is that the diaries have now sunk without trace, leaving the guilty unscathed for reasons that are shameful and sordid. Income tax and inforcement authorities continue their efforts to make some headway but with the diaries dead, declared so by the courts, they may achieve very little despite all their motions. The diaries were genuine entries recorded from day to day but, both CBI and Supreme Court made so heavy weather of establishing this truth, that in the process the diaries were destroyed as documents proving commission of serious fiscal crime by great many household names. One group of people who did not figure even once in these diaries were our politicians from the Leftist parties, which again is a point to prove these diaries were genuine as, however, black they may be painted, never has the Left in India been charged with stashing funds in the immoral West. The Hawala Diaries are dead and buried.

Copies of Relevant Pages of Hawala Diaries

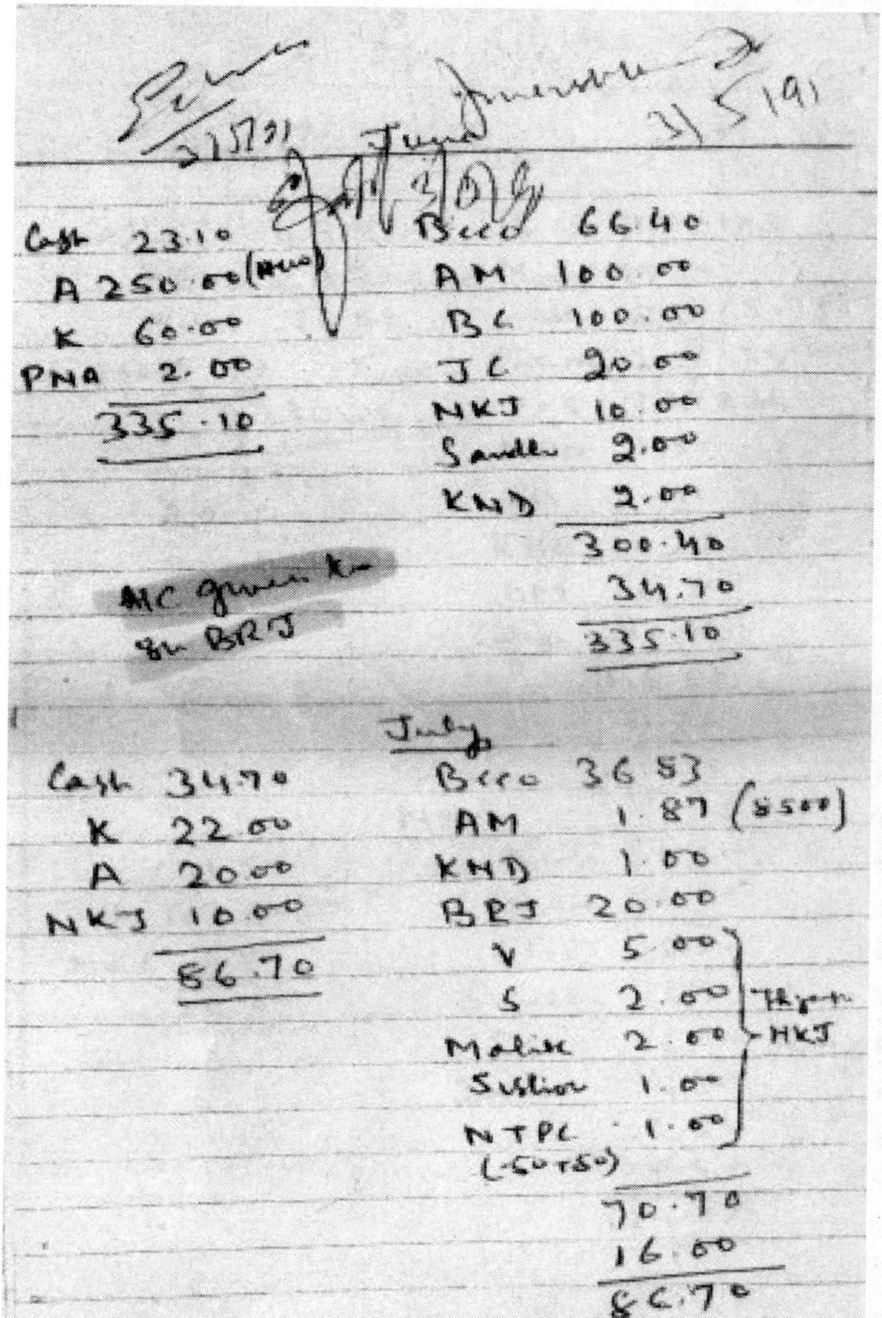

21/5/91

21/5/91

Cash	23.10	Bcco	66.40
A	250.00 (...)	AM	100.00
K	60.00	BC	100.00
PNA	2.00	JC	20.00
	335.10	NKJ	10.00
		Sandu	2.00
		KND	2.00
			300.40
			34.70
			335.10

MC given to
BRJ

July

Cash	34.70	Bcco	36.53
K	22.00	AM	1.87 (8500)
A	20.00	KND	1.00
NKJ	10.00	BRJ	20.00
	86.70	V	5.00
		S	2.00
		Malik	2.00
		Sushion	1.00
		NTPC (-50+50)	1.00
			70.70
			16.00
			86.70

Through NKJ (V, S, Malik, Sushion, NTPC)

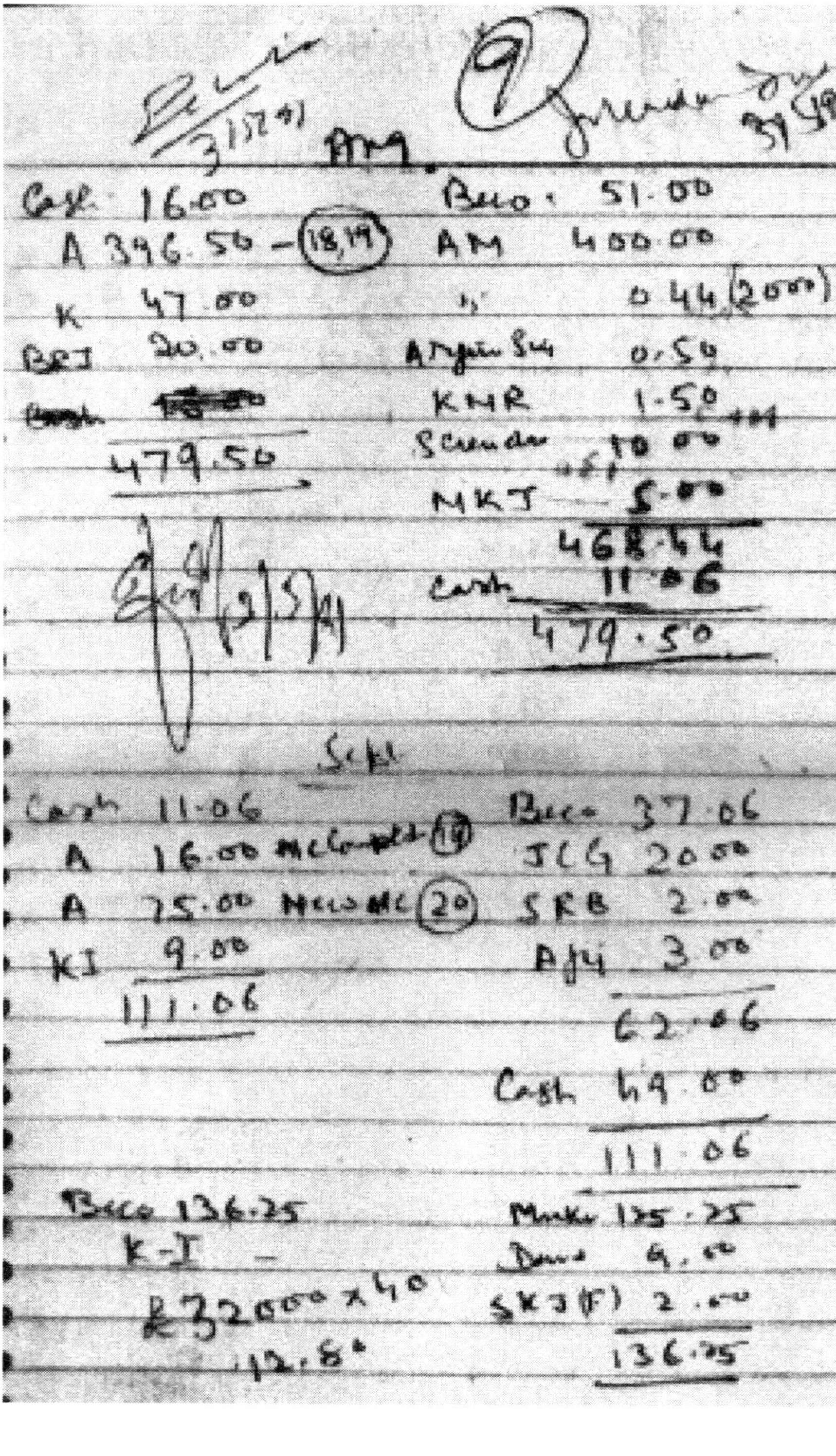

Cash 16.00 Beco 51.00
A 396.50 – (18,19) AM 400.00
K 47.00 " 0.44 (2000)
BPI 20.00 0.50
KMR 1.50
479.50 Scindia 10.00
MKJ 5.00
468.44
Cash 11.06
479.50

Cash 11.06 Beco 37.06
A 16.00 (19) JCG 20.00
A 75.00 (20) SKB 2.00
KJ 9.00 3.00
111.06 62.06
Cash 49.00
111.06

Beco 136.25 135.25
K-J –
32000 x 40 SKJ (F) 2.00
12.80 136.25

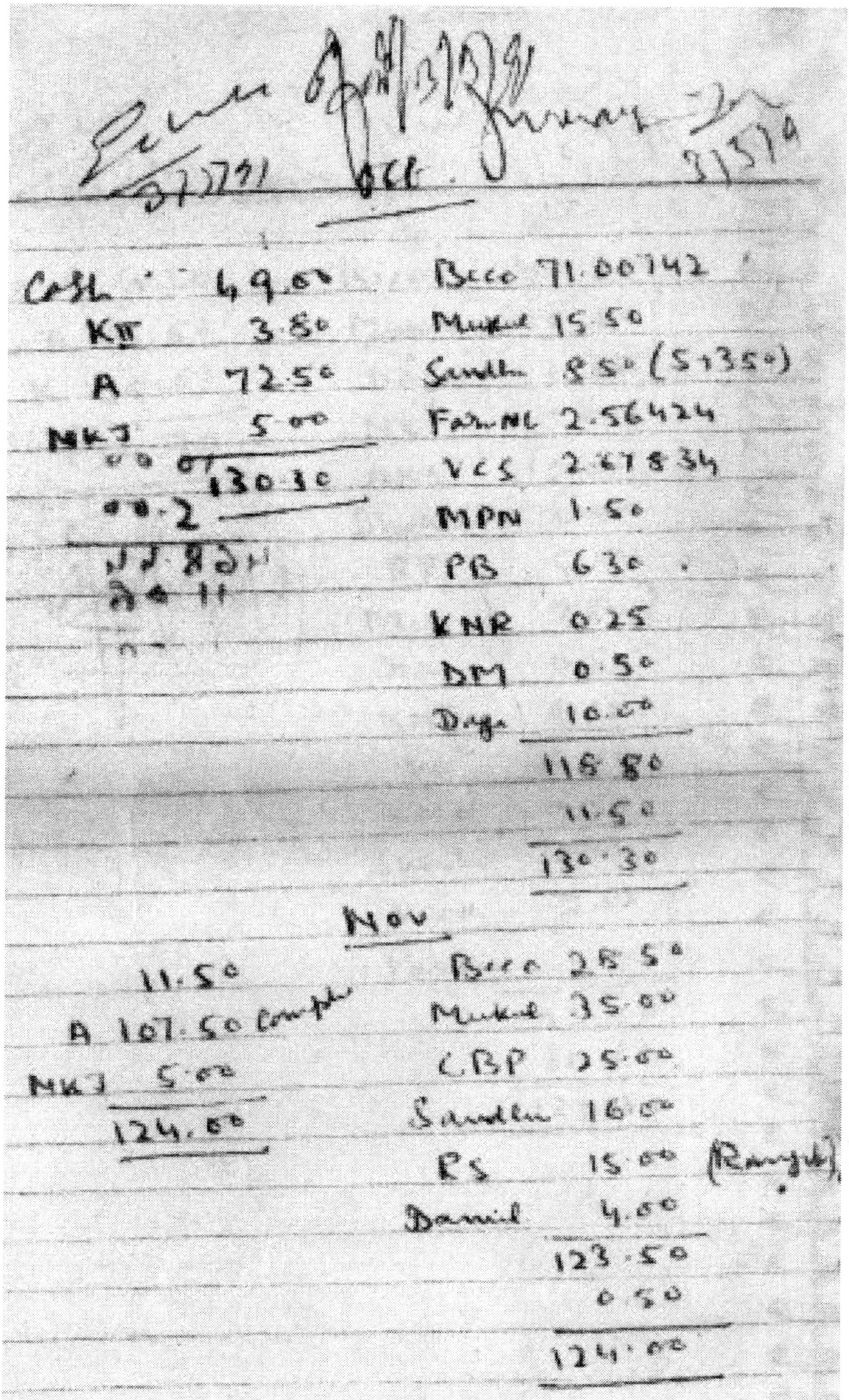

Cash 49.00
KII 3.80
A 72.50
MKJ 5.00
130.30

Bcco 71.00742
Mukul 15.50
Sandhu 8.50 (5+3.50)
Farm NL 2.56424
VCS 2.67834
MPN 1.50
PB 6.30
KNR 0.25
DM 0.50
Dogra 10.00
115.80
11.50
130.30

Nov

11.50
A 107.50 complete
MKJ 5.00
124.00

Bcco 28.50
Mukul 35.00
CBP 25.00
Sandhu 16.00
RS 15.00 (Ranjit)
Daniel 4.00
123.50
0.50
124.00

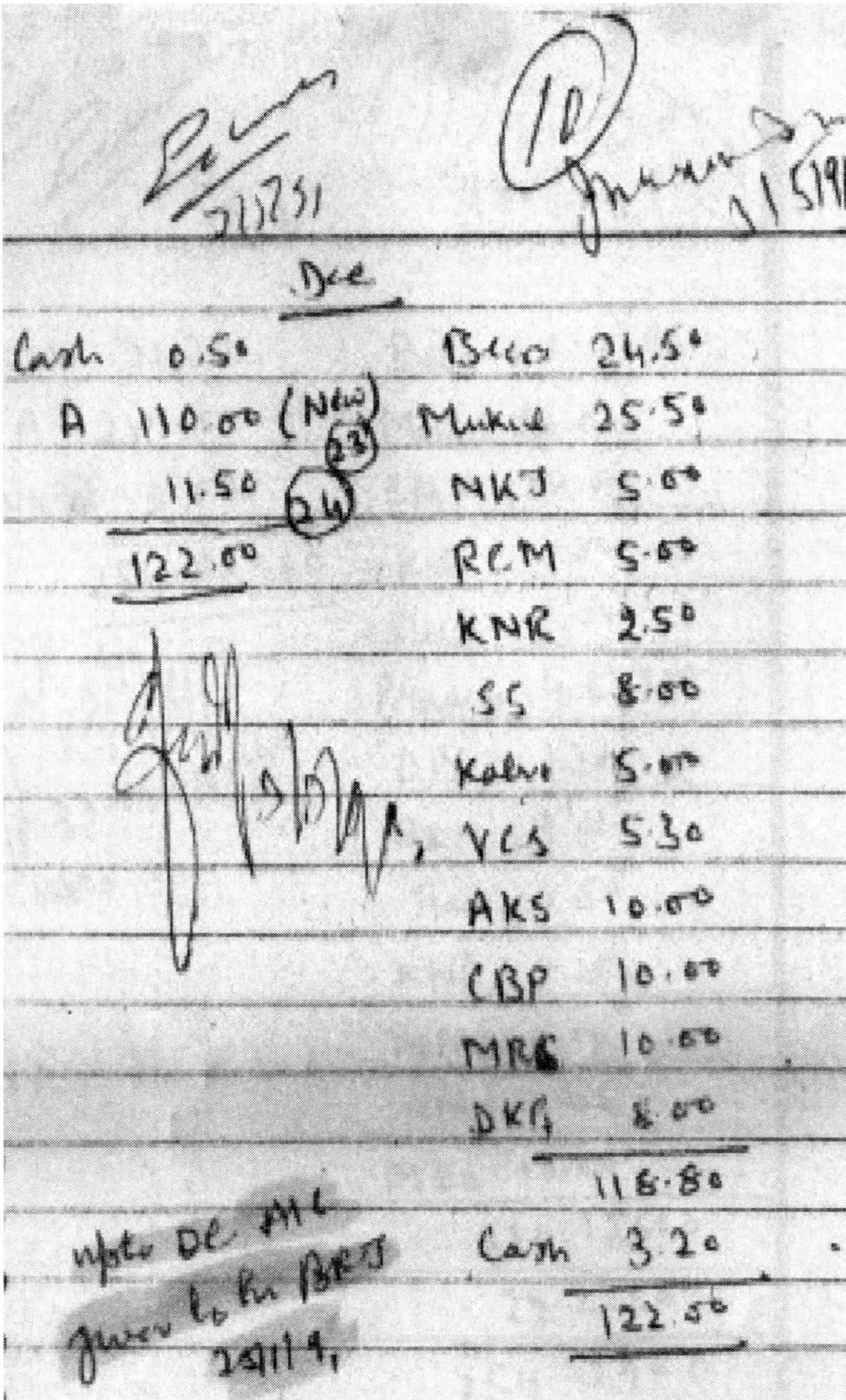

Due

Cash	0.50	BCCO	24.50
A	110.00 (New)	Mukul	25.50
	11.50	NKJ	5.00
	122.00	RCM	5.00
		KNR	2.50
		SS	8.00
		Kalvi	5.00
		VCS	5.30
		AKS	10.00
		CBP	10.00
		MRG	10.00
		DKG	8.00
			118.80
		Cash	3.20
			122.50

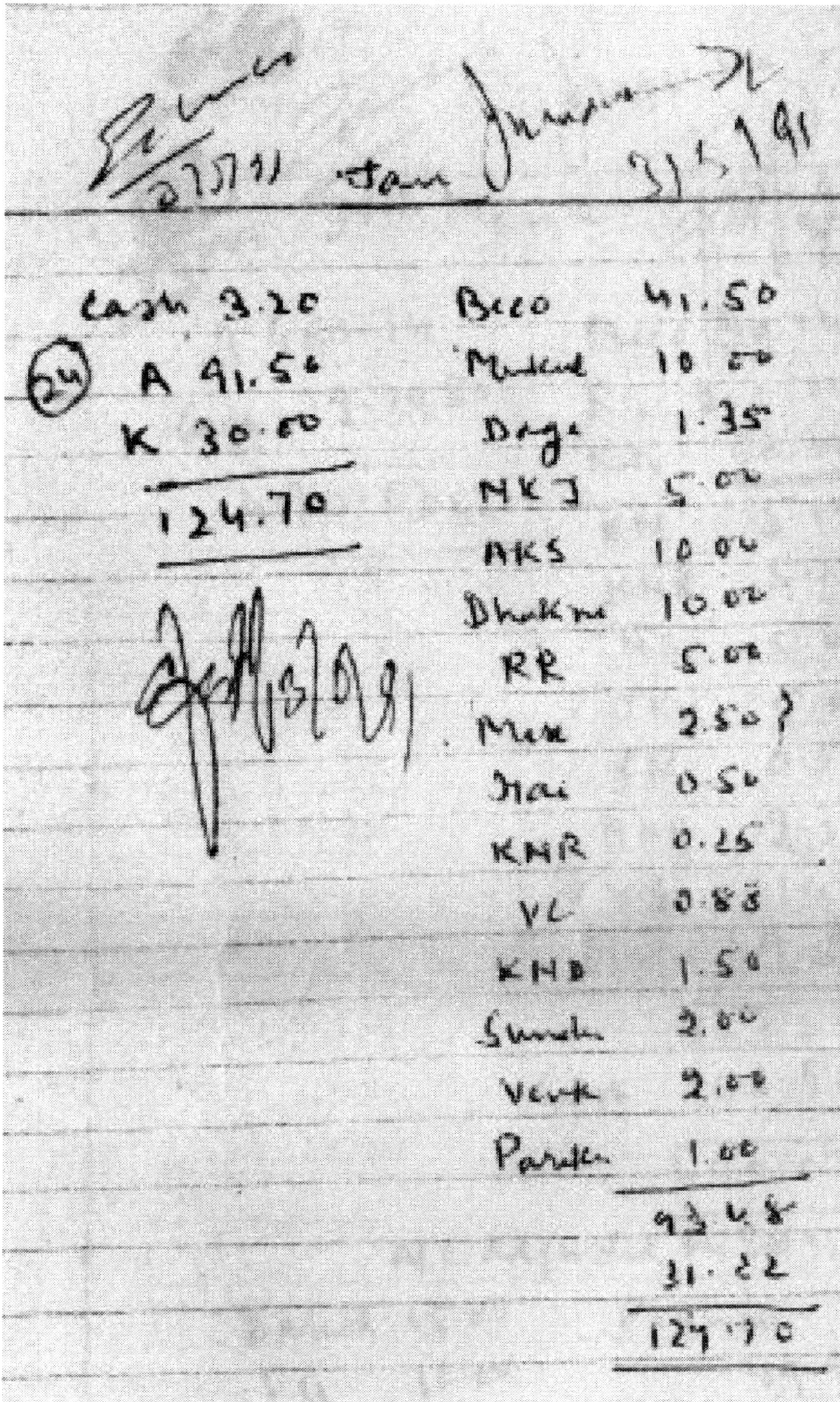

27/5/91 31/5/91

Cash	3.20	Bcco	41.50
(24) A	91.50	Mukul	10.00
K	30.00	Daga	1.35
	124.70	NKJ	5.00
		AKS	10.00
		Dhakm	10.00
		RR	5.00
		Mee	2.50
		Mai	0.50
		KNR	0.25
		VC	0.88
		KMB	1.50
		Suresh	2.00
		Vevk	2.00
		Parikh	1.00
			93.48
			31.22
			124.70

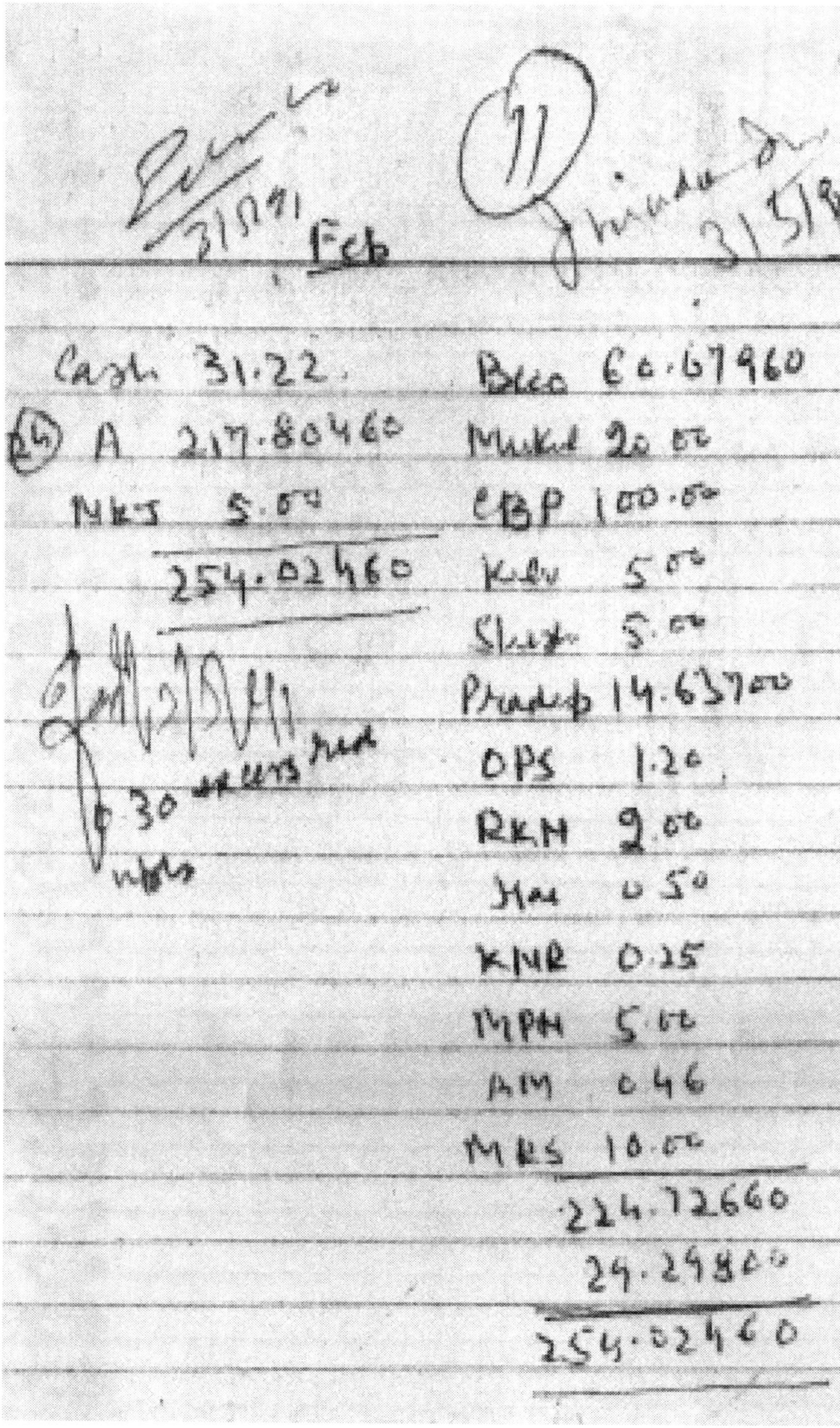

Feb

Cash 31.22

A 217.80460

NKJ 5.00

254.02460

30 ... ... nots

Bkco	60.67960
Mukul	20.00
CBP	100.00
Kulv	5.00
Sheeja	5.00
Pradip	14.63700
OPS	1.20
RKH	2.00
Har	0.50
KNR	0.25
MPH	5.00
AM	0.46
MRS	10.00
	224.72660
	29.29800
	254.02460

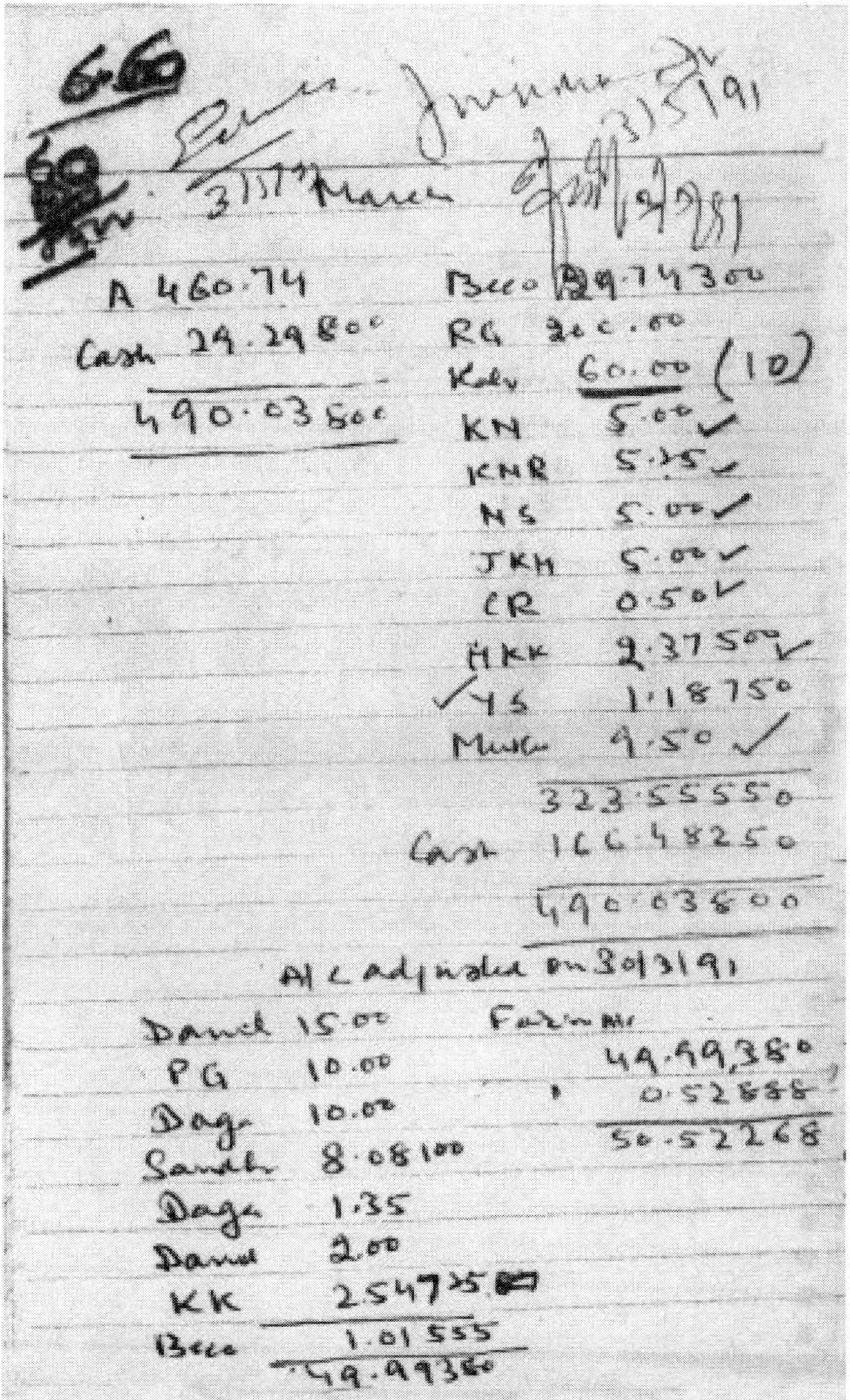

3/5/91

31st March

A	460.74	Bcco	29.74300
Cash	29.29800	RG	200.00
	490.03800	Kalv	60.00 (10)
		KN	5.00 ✓
		KMR	5.25 ✓
		NS	5.00 ✓
		JKH	5.00 ✓
		CR	0.50 ✓
		HKK	2.37500 ✓
		✓YS	1.18750
		Murli	9.50 ✓
			323.55550
		Cash	166.48250
			490.03800

A/c adjusted on 30/3/91

David	15.00	Farm	
PG	10.00		49.99,380
Daga	10.00		0.52888
Sandh	8.08100		50.52268
Daga	1.35		
David	2.00		
KK	2.54725		
Bcco	1.01555		
	49.99380		

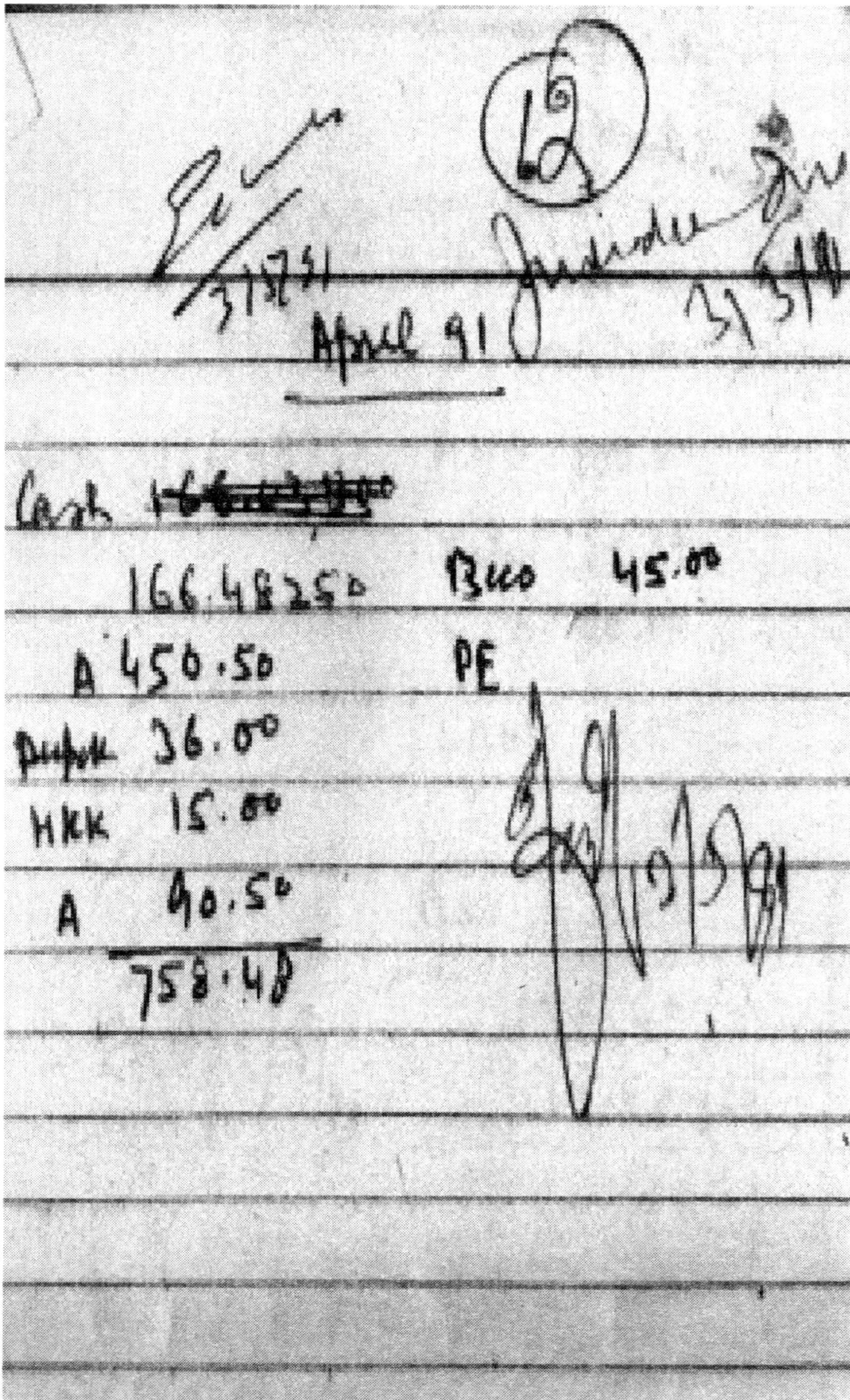

62

3/5/91 3/5/91

April 91

Cash

166.48250 Buco 45.00

A 450.50 PE

[illegible] 36.00

HKK 15.00

A 90.50

758.48

3/5/91

3/5/91   3/5/91

A/C for March

A	460.74	Bcco	29.74300
Cash	29.29800	RG	200.00
	490.03800	Kalvi	60.00
		KN	5.00
		KMR	5.25
		NS	5.00
		JKH	5.00
		CB	0.50
		HKK	9.37500
		YS	1.18750
		Mukul	9.50
			323.55550
		Cash	166.48250
			490.03800

3/12/91

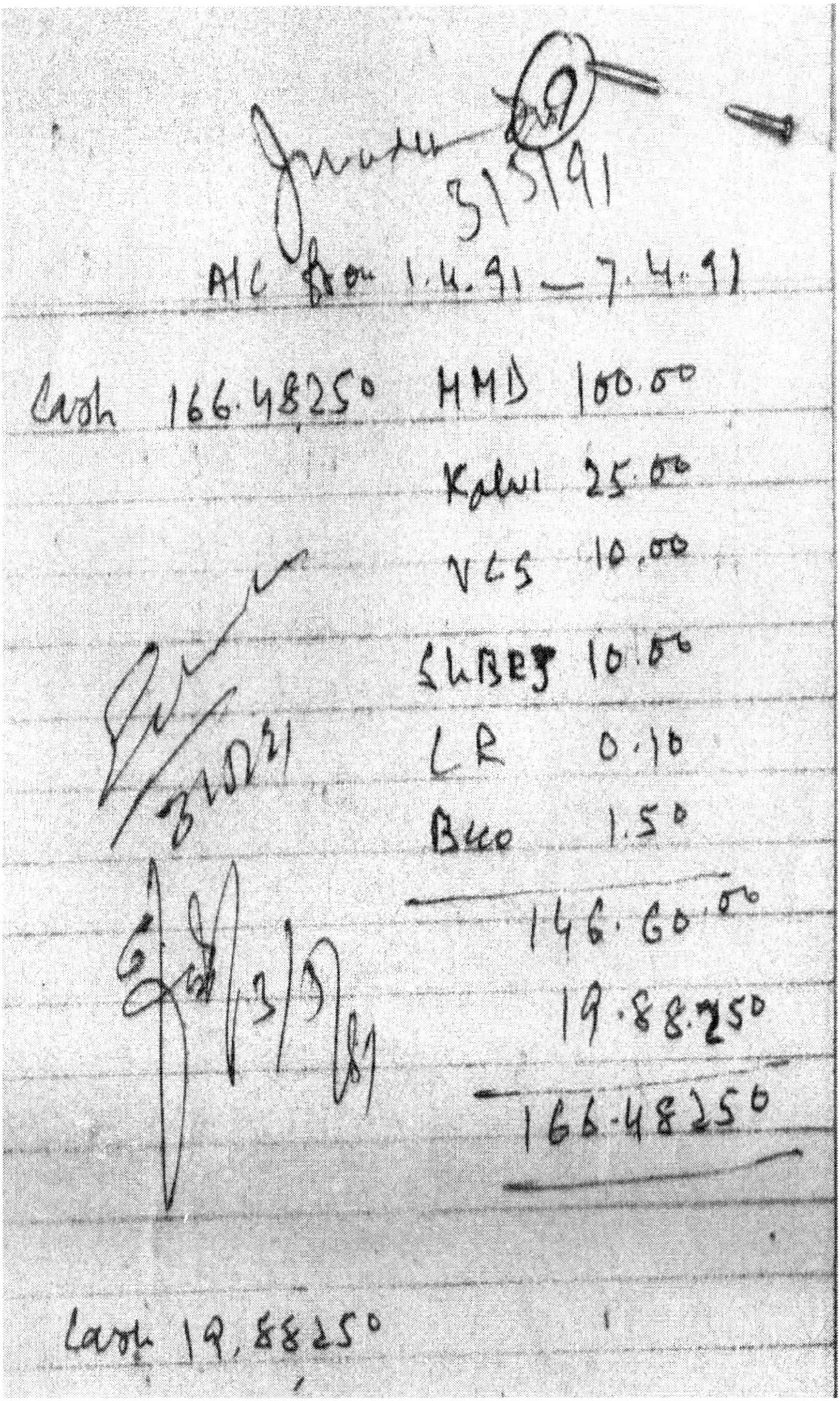

3/5/91

A/C from 1.4.91 — 7.4.91

Cash	166.48250	HMD	100.00
		Kalwi	25.00
		VCS	10.00
		SUBEJ	10.00
		LR	0.10
		Bkco	1.50
			146.60.00
			19.88.250
			166.48250

Cash 19,88250

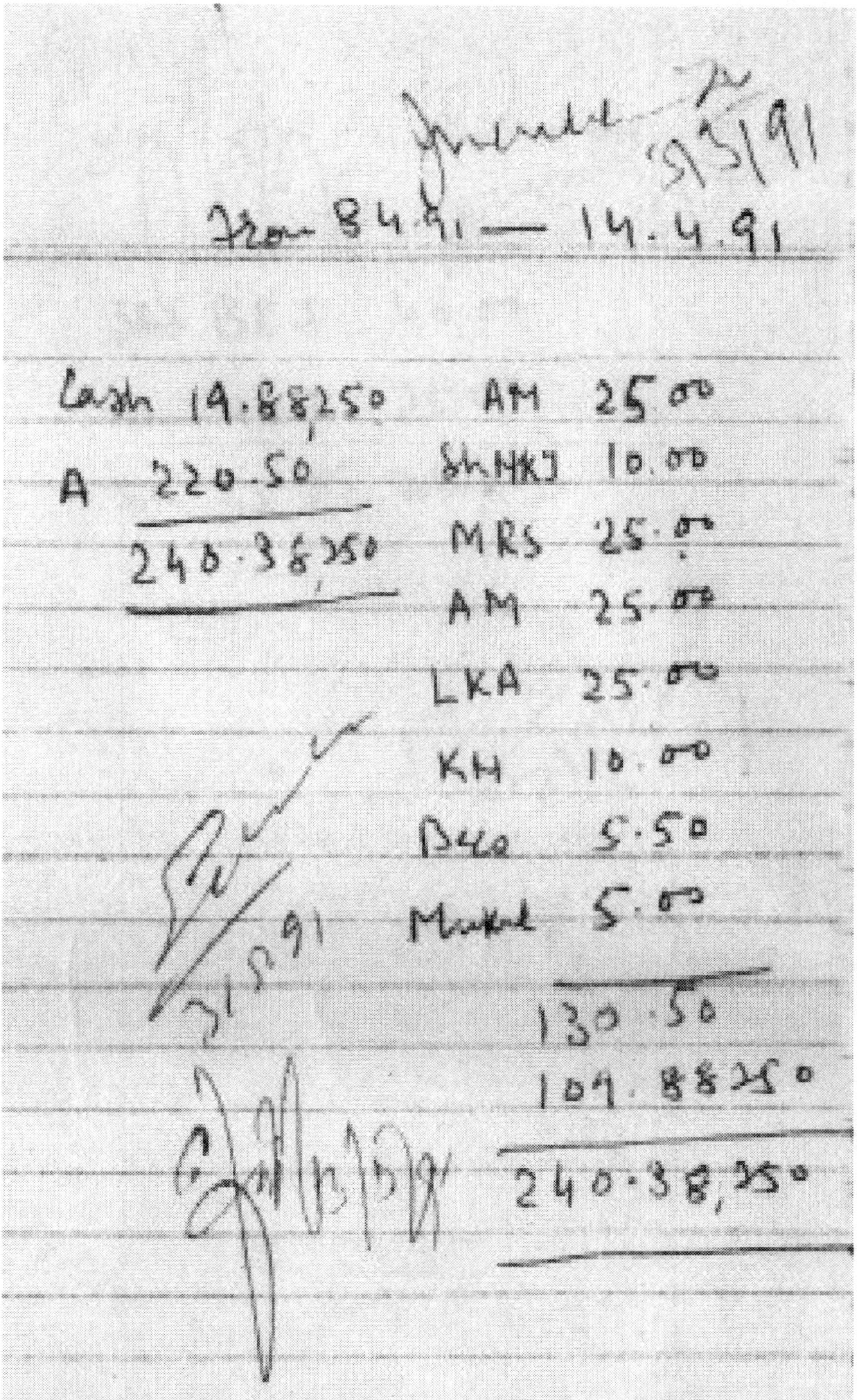

From 8.4.91 — 14.4.91

Cash 19.88,250
A 220.50
240.38,250

AM 25.00
Sh HKJ 10.00
MRS 25.00
AM 25.00
LKA 25.00
KH 10.00
D40 5.50
Mukul 5.00

130.50
109.88,250
240.38,250

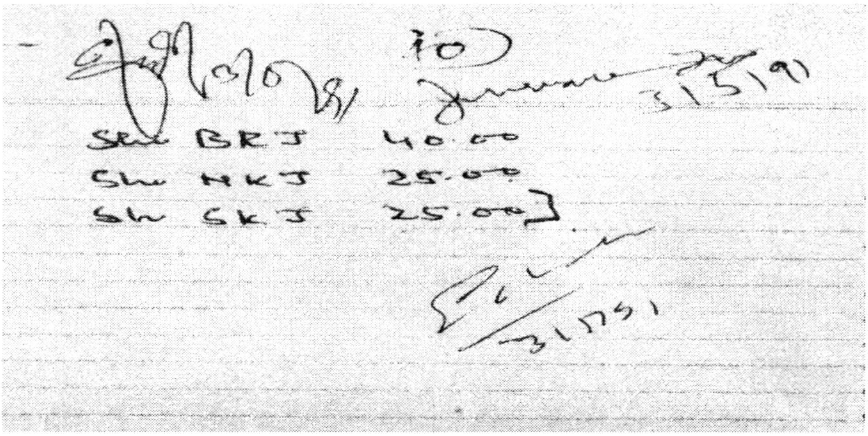

(10)

31/5/91

Shri BRJ 40.00

Shri HKJ 25.00

Shri SKJ 25.00

31/5/91

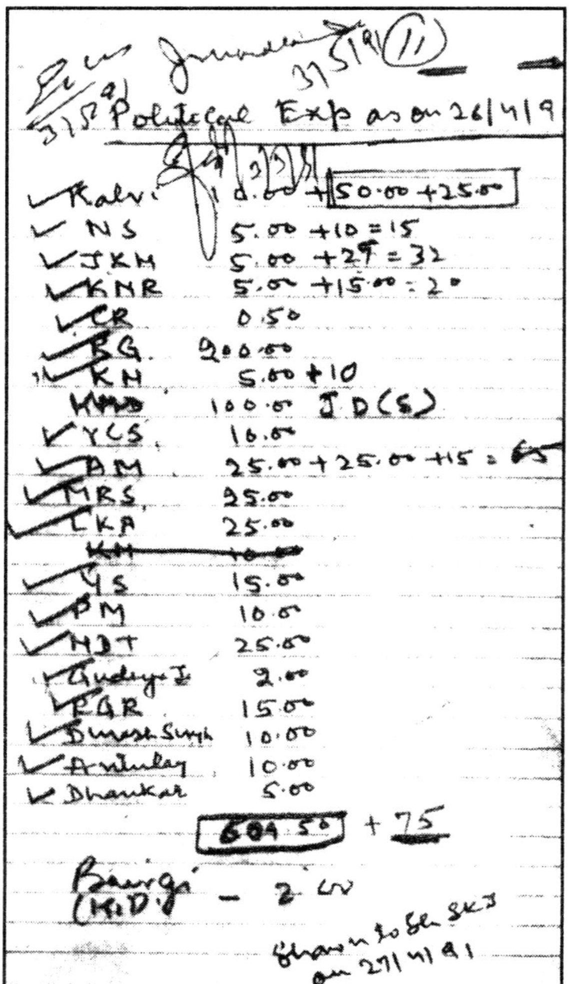

(11)

31/5/91

31/5/91

Political Exp as on 26/4/91

31/5/91

Kalvi 10.00 + 50.00 + 25.00

NS 5.00 + 10 = 15

JKM 5.00 + 27 = 32

KNR 5.00 + 15.00 = 20

CR 0.50

BG 200.00

KH 5.00 + 10

HMD 100.00 JD(S)

YCS 10.00

AM 25.00 + 25.00 + 15 = 65

MRS 25.00

LKA 25.00

~~KH 10.00~~

YS 15.00

PM 10.00

HDT 25.00

Gudiya J 2.00

RGR 15.00

Suresh Singh 10.00

Antulay 10.00

Dhankar 5.00

604.50 + 75

Bangi (H.D.) – 2 cr

Shown to Sh SKJ on 27/4/91

Chapter-11

The PM's Forger

Forty seven years down the memory lane, in 2014, it is the memory of the drive through the downpour that survives more than anything else. On that wet night, however, nabbing the master forger, whose claims to fame included passing off the forged signature of the Prime Minister as genuine, was no mean achievement. Not so much for myself, then a Deputy Superintendent of Police, but for the ingenuous driver, who beat the driving rain—all along the 400 kilometer Dhanbad-Banaras route in the dead of night—to ensure that we reached the temple city before the suspected associates of our accused got a whiff of what was chasing them and covered their tracks.

Ram Surat Rai was a dismissed public works inspector of the Indian Railways. There was nothing wrong with his selection, selected for the job to begin with but something was drastically wrong with the papers, that served as a basis for his selection. They were forged! Even as the Railways dispensed with his services though, Rai had realised that he was on to a good thing. The Railways may have had no use for his talents but he, himself, did. Forgery was then to be the career of this otherwise normal man - who chose the life of a politician - who married and had a happy family with a child. The quintessential rustic politician, whose brother was a muffussil pleader, Rai a smooth conversationalist, claimed the first benefit of his position: he travelled on a forged railway pass for himself and his family. Indeed, it was this pass that had taken him to the Bokaro Steel City with his family, where he met his nemesis.

Rai was a man with a sense of triumph. He had earlier sent a letter written and signed by the Prime Minister, Mrs Indira Gandhi, to the authorities at the Bokaro Steel Plant recommending that the position of a teacher at their school be given to his spouse. Instructions from the Prime Minister are not something that the Steel Plant could ignore and Rai's wife was interviewed. It so happened that the Secretary of the Steel Plant was visiting New Delhi, and called on the PMO to assure them that the PM's instructions were being carried out, when the cat came out of the bag. What instructions? The Prime Minister had sent nothing of the kind. Enter the CBI. Someone was forging the Prime Minister's signature, and this was a matter of great consternation. The case came to me, and found me in Bokaro, where I got the Steel Plant to send a telegram to his wife saying: "Selected. Please come for final interview," confident that the lady would be accompanied by her errrant husband.

Enter the triumphant Rai, little knowing that it was all a trap laid in a mock interview. Rai was invited to the official interview and admitted to having got the Prime Minister to recommend his wife for the position in the presence of the interview board. This admission was necessary for purposes of providing compelling evidence.

What followed was an arrest, and Rai was promptly lodged in the Dhanbad gaol while his wife—who may or may not have been an accomplice—was escorted back to Banaras by train. Meanwhile, we rushed to his Banaras home by car before anyone back there got wind of things. The rain, harsh and incessant, did its best to play spoilt sport. The slush on the Grand Trunk made matters a nightmare for the Bokaro Steel driver, Panditji, in more ways than one. However, Panditji and his station wagon, were quite a match for the downpour as he swerved, ducked, drove the van through paddy fields, used the vehicle at will—cursing all the while—managing to reach us to Banaras before the wife could alert anyone or indeed tamper with the evidence at home. The evidence existed in heaps, literally. A collection of official stamps, letterheads of ministers, Prime Ministers, Members of Parliament, a selection of perfect second class railway passes to be used at will and a world of forged letters from every possible Minister—from KC Pant to Dr Karan Singh—telling the world that they knew Rai and that he should be helped.

Two cases were filed, at the Lucknow magistrate's court and at the Patna magistrate's court for the Dhanbad incident. Rai was convicted in both. In the best tradition of collecting evidence, I had marched off to the Prime Minister to obtain her specimen signature - in itself an act of some bravado for a junior officer in those times. Mrs Gandhi readily obliged; her private secretary confirmed that the signature had been taken in his presence and the file with the forged and genuine sent off for expert opinion. The expert confirmed that the signature on Rai's letter was forged—"prepared by tracing process"—and since the forged document was used by Rai, it was circumstantially held, that he was the one who had forged it.

A simple story. Yet, a story that may have turned out quite differently, had the simple trick to trap Rai, not been practised. This is what ingenuity is all about. Equally worthy was Panditji's role, because had he not got us to Banaras on time, Rai's accomplices may have got rid of the tell tale signs!

Meanwhile, the signature of Mrs Indira Gandhi, taken for the purposes of nabbing the simple forger from Banaras, remains in the CBI museum, often flashed on television whenever the museum is covered by the electronic media.

Notes

Chapter-12

Inside Job

In 1968, the State Trading Corporation was still a young organisation. Balancing accounts was very important. Maheshwari, the banking officer, broke out in cold sweat on a December morning while going through the bank statements. The State Bank of India had debited the Corporation Rs 10,989 in May 1968, against a cheque issued for Rs 10, in favour of Messrs Laxmi Corner, 4311 Bhairon Street, Nai Sarak, Delhi. Again in November 1968, the SBI had debited the Corporation Rs 38,300 against a cheque of Rs 38, issued in favour of Messrs Nath & Company, 4439, Bhairon Street, Nai Sarak, Delhi. Maheshwari was worried: Rs 50,000 had vanished and the STC did not have a clue about who was responsible.

The Central Bureau of Investigation was asked to investigate by Mr Prakash Tandon, then Chairman STC. The investigation, handed over to me, took me to Bhairon Street as the two banks - the Oriental Bank of Commerce, Chawri Bazar and the Allahabad Bank, Hauz Qazi, where the amounts had been credited - could offer no clue as to the identity of the account holders. They were introduced to the bank by the *paan walla* in the same building, who had introduced thousands of account holders. The focus then had to be on Bhairon Street—an ancient Delhi lane with houses clustered on both sides, most of them ramshackled and filthy.

Luck generally plays a part in intelligent investigations. One was sure that this was an insider job. The criminal had to our good luck left a tell tale sign in the first address - Laxmi Corner, 4311, Bhairon Street, was a valid address. Nath & Company's was not. The intelligence and luck factor had to be complimented with persistence and it was necessary to establish whether or not any STC employee lived in that community of people - some 40 families - living in the same house. The survey of residents had to be discreet and the first survey by an assistant sub inspector was infructuous. Like a doctor, confident of his diagnosis, who is reluctant to accept contra report without a double check, I ordered another survey, this time by a more lowly-placed, but highly intelligent head constable, Narendra Singh Chawla. Chawla struck pay dirt. Ramesh Chandra Sharma was an employee of the STC's public relations department till December 1968. At the time of the survey he had been shifted to the imported car cell. He had married a year ago. The two inflated cheques were payments made to parties through the public relations office. Sharma was clearly our man but he was not in Delhi. Sharma had gone to Alwar to his in-laws with his wife, where he was picked up within a day in the presence of his wife and brother-in-law. A little questioning was all that was required to get a confession out of him and Sharma alone was arrested and brought to Delhi.

The room he shared with his extended family was searched in his presence. Among the material picked up were letters from his wife suggesting that he should not waste his newfound earnings and a diary that showed an entry on May 9, 1968: "cheque was issued in favour of Messrs Laxmi Corner, Delhi, in the above date." It was now a matter of gathering conclusive evidence that would stand up in a court of law. Identification by persons and identification by writing were the two areas of collection of evidence open to me. No officer of staff of either the Oriental Bank of Commerce or the Allahabad Bank agreed to identify Ramesh Chandra Sharma, as the operator of the accounts in their banks on the grounds that the bank had so many account holders. This ruled out identifying the suspect in a line-up.

Identification by handwriting was the only option then. The banks where the account holders, M/s Laxmi Corner and M/s Nath & Company had accounts, were made to produce every piece of paper connected with the two accounts and seized. All this, while Sharma was in police custody, and asked to write on sheets of paper on blank bank documents, on blank cheques in the presence of witnesses. He was asked to write while sitting, standing and lying. Chance had disclosed that he was ambidextrous and, therefore, he was asked to write with both his hands. As a staff of the imported car cell he had filled in requisitions for booking of cars, which were seized from the STC. As we were later to realise, the turning point of the case was the thoroughness with which Sharma's handwriting had been obtained.

His immediate boss, Manjuran, who had identified his writings on various documents turned hostile when the matter went to trial court, where he said that he could not recognise Sharma's handwriting. Manjuran's wife working for the ONGC, had, in the meantime, got on the wrong side of the CBI, in another matter being investigated by me. The saving grace was that the corroborative expert opinion that remained valid on the basis of other handwriting evidence, though a large mass of exhibits was considered invalid by the trial court on account of Manjuran's *volte face*. The trial court - thanks to Manjuran - threw out both cases against Sharma because Manjuran's was direct evidence. It refused to take cognizance of the STC accounts officer's evidence. He had testified that while he had not seen Ramesh Sharma writing, he could still identify these requisitions to be written by him as he had against these requisitions made payment to Sharma for use of taxis, cars and other chores that he ran for the imported car cell. This was another stroke of luck because as a typist, Sharma left no samples of his handwriting at the PRO's office.

We had to go to the High Court to seek relief from the trial court. The High Court rejected the trial court's finding that the official documents were seized from the STC, as Sharma's writings were invalid, as they had been identified by an accounts officer, who had seen Sharma's writing during the course of his official work. It, therefore, upheld the expert opinion. As the expert opinion was corroborated on the basis of information contained in his wife's letters to Sharma, where she had responded to his communications about his coming into a lot of money. Matters would have been strengthened had I got hold of Sharma's letters to his wife - which I did not take away from the tearful young bride, when I had an opportunity to do so at Alwar at the time of his arrest.

They were folded and tied by a blue thread in her tin box. I saw them, opened them but returned them without reading. This was poor investigation, and I could have rightly been punished for allowing emotions to get the better of investigative training. The High Court said: "The observation made by the learned additional sessions judge that his (expert) evidence was not sufficient to prove that official documents (exhibit BU 14/J-116) were in the handwriting of the respondent is on the face of it erroneous, to say the least. Criminal trial is not simply a game of wits, and rules of assessment of evidence are not artificial. While crime is a reality, the criminal trial itself is not something divorced from realism. In this case, admitted writings (requisition slips) were proved partly from official records dealt with by the accounts officer."

Sharma was convicted in both the casees by the High Court in its judgement of October 12, 1979 - 11 years after the crime. In his confession, Sharma had told me that he got the idea of the crime from the casual manner in which payments were approved in the PRO's cell. He had got two seals made in the names of M/s Laxmi Corner and M/s Nath and Company. He first submitted, under Laxmi Corner's stamp, a claim of Rs 10 for having supplied gift wrappings. The bill was passed without any problem. He then proceeded to use a blade and simulated the handwriting of the writer of the cheques that now read Rs 10,000. The expert had corroborated which part of the handwriting was forged. Having succeeded the first time, Sharma went for a bigger kill the next time under Nath & Company. This time the amount was increased from Rs 38 to Rs 38,000. In the first case, he was sentenced to rigorous imprisonment for one and a half years and a fine of Rs 2,000. In the second case, he was sentenced to a rigorous imprisonment for two years and a fine of Rs 10,000.

STC too learnt its lessons. The CBI's advise to it was to have perforated cheques that could not be forged by other Ramesh Chandra Sharmas.

Chapter-13

Supreme Court Recognises An Expert after Denying him Recognition for 30 Years

Krishan Sikand was thirty-nine with one unfortunate marriage behind him. But in October 1982, he was in love. Rani was a war widow who had married again but the marriage had turned sour. Two souls with unhappy marriages behind them, had found happiness and looked forward to a life together. But fate willed it otherwise when in the afternoon of 2nd October, 1982, a booby trap sprung in a parcel blasted him to pieces.

A service hand grenade of Pakistan Ordnance Factory fitted with an igniter/detonator manufactured by Ammunition Factory, Kirkee, Pune, in 1964 exploded in his face. This happened as he untied a parcel addressed to him as Shri Krishan Sikand, 98, Sunder Nagar, Delhi, from Delhi Metals, 290, Hauz Quazi. Delhi-700 006. The address was fictitious. The hand grenade had been put inside a badminton shuttlecock (tube wheeler) box used to pack plastic badminton shuttlecocks. M/s. Artex Industries, Bombay, used these boxes. This particular box in common with other similar boxes had a white plastic lid each at both ends of the box. The box used had been cut to a size, which made it, possible to place the hand grenade inside it in a manner where the lever of the hand grenade placed and expertly packed in this case with the help of twisted copper wire found at the scene of the crime, is released as soon as the pressure of the packing material is eased. This is what happened when Krishan opened the parcel. Death was instantaneous and horrible. The entire body was disfigured and burnt. The haemorrhage and shock bled the vital organs with heart and lungs stopping, kidneys bleeding and the brain dying.

Who did it? The finger of suspicion pointed at Rani's estranged husband Lt. Col. SJ Choudhari @ Jeeti, a dashing armoured corp. officer decorated for gallantry in action. He had married Rani, then a war widow in 1976, after his first marriage had ended in a divorce. When Krishan and Rani met in 1979 around Diwali she had left Jeeti and was in the midst of a bitterly contested divorce proceedings in Delhi. Jeeti contested the divorce at every step, even to the extent of seeking a review petition in the Supreme Court. He denied Rani the custody of their only child Sonal and Rani capitulated to escape what she felt was a marriage that had failed with no chance of ever reviving. Not only did he fight the divorce through every court hearing, he sought to make her withdraw the case through the intervention of friends, failing that issued threats verbally and in writing to kill her and her lover, and repeatedly followed Rani and Krishan when they were together, making life quite unpleasant for them. Together with the weapon used and the diabolical manner it was planted, his complicity in the crime was certain. Evidence was needed to send him to trial particularly so, as he was a serving Army officer with a distinguished past, a top golfer and the only son of a former police chief of Delhi. He had enough goodwill to interfere in our investigation. In fact, for slightly more than six months from 2-10-1982 to 19-3-1983 when CBI took over the case from Delhi Police, the original investigation agency, was effectively stymied. In view of the above facts and circumstances if our work was not good enough in the field of collection of evidence, our investigation could come unstuck.

Without a single eyewitness, the circumstantial evidence collected during investigation against him, became the key, the only key, in fact, to indict him. The said compact and closely knitted evidence disclosed the only and only one hypothesis and that was the involvement of Jeeti Choudhari in the murder of Krishan Sikand on 2-10-1982. The evidence of a vital expert, the typewriter expert in this case, was denied to the prosecution by the Trial Court first and thereafter, by the High Court on account of an old ruling of the Supreme Court (Hanumant Nergundkar v. State of M.P. -AIR 1952 SC 343) vide which the typewriting expert's opinion was not found admissible u/s 45 of the Indian Evidence Act. Even the Division Bench of the Supreme Court was unable to remedy the lacunae. It was a bench of five judges of the Apex Court that finally allowed the evidence of this vital expert.

The legal battle was hard fought and long. It was during trial, on 27-3-1987 that the Addl. Sessions Judge, New Delhi, S.C. Jain disallowed the expert to tender evidence. The revision petition filed by CBI challenging his orders in Delhi High Court was rejected by Justice MK Chawla on 20-5-1987. Their Lordships of the Hon'ble Supreme Court by an order dictated by Justice (as he then was) JS Verma and concurred by four of his colleagues GN Ray, NP Singh, Faizan Uddin and GT Nanawati on 13th February, 1996 allowed the expert to tender in evidence his opinion as a typewriting expert under Section 45 of the Indian Evidence Act, 1871. This is the story of this effort, how it was conceptualized, labored upon, put in court, where it was lost successively, and finally won.

The blast in the first floor bedroom of Krishan Sikand on the afternoon of 2nd October, 1982 had brought in the Delhi Police to investigate the case. Six months later, the unsolved crime was on the lap of the CBI on the orders of the Government of India. Within CBI, the investigation was assigned to a unit headed by me, the then Superintendent of Police. This unit was located in Lok Nayak Bhawan, very close to Khan Market, New Delhi. I assigned the investigation to MP Singh, then a Deputy Superintendent of Police who had AK Ohri, then an Inspector for Assistance. Another senior Deputy Superintendent of Police BR Puri was roped in to provide expertise. I devoted most of his time to actively participate in the field investigation. Whenever it could not be done, I was able to get a feedback on the day-to-day basis.

After taking over the case from Delhi Police, Singh and I visited 98, Sunder Nagar, to inspect the scene of crime, a hallowed system that heralds the shree ganesh of all investigations. But that was not to be, as with concurrence of the police and the court, that place (Krishan's bedroom) had been restored. This was a setback. Three of us Singh, Puri and myself held a council-of-war to consider alternatives. The result was that we called on Dr. GR Prasad, the then Head of Ballistic Division, General Forensic

Science Laboratory, CGO Complex, Lodhi Road, New Delhi. The entire debris, including the remnants of the parcel and its contents had been packed in different parcels by the Delhi Police, sealed and shipped to him for a forensic opinion. He had opened the parcels on 12th October, 1982 to examine the contents. Prasad in his preliminary delving into the debris, had unearthed enough bits and pieces of the parcel to partially piece together the outer covering, to reconstruct partially the typewritten name and address of the addressee, Krishan Sikand as well as the address of the sender. A detailed discussion with Dr. Prasad encouraged us to have a close look of the entire debris kept in the CFSL for expert examination. The two of us spent over nine hours, spread over two days, scrutinizing each and every piece of the debris. The hand grenade, too, was partially reconstructed as was the tubular box for shuttlecocks which held the deadly explosive. The copper wire that controlled the grenade lever, set to trigger the grenade on, as soon as the pressure eased, and the pieces of thread used to tie the parcel, etc., provided real good leads to pursue the investigation further. This helped us to overcome, to a certain extent, the disadvantage of not being able to sniff around the scene of crime in this case.

When we took stock of what we had seen and what could throw light on a crime that had so far defied solution, we came to the conclusion that the case could be cracked. The reconstructed parcel, the hand grenade pieces, the length of the copper wire, the pieces of thread were keys that could fit the lock of the door behind which the skulking killer had remained in hiding so far. The entire team of Investigating Officers started to work to that end. With bits and pieces slowly coming together, the decision was taken to throw the book at Jeeti Choudhari, who had emerged as the suspect number one. A number of CBI officers under the command and control of Singh searched the house of Jeeti Choudhari at Friends Colony, his suite in Pragati Vihar Hostel, his office near Vayu Bhawan, New Delhi and his Standard Herald Car and recovered significant materials as legal exhibits. When examined by the experts, the pieces of thread recovered from his office drawer, a wire cutter recovered from his car tightened the screws against Jeeti Choudhari. The only material exhibit which remained to be linked to him was the parcel cover of the booby trap which bore the typewritten address of the deceased and that of the fictitious sender, postal stamps and the tape. If it could also be linked to him, the evidence would amount to something that he would find difficult to wish away. The team, therefore, needed to closely and continuously question their primary suspect which appeared to be the only option left at that moment. Finally, the die was cast and we decided to take Choudhari in for interrogation. He was called to the Lok Nayak Bhawan office for interrogation on 1-8-1983. After some hours of questioning, finding him obdurate, stonewalling all efforts of the team to pry defiant and even arrogant, he was arrested by Singh. The next day on 2-8-1983 he was produced in the Court of the Metropolitan Magistrate, KC Lohia and police custody for more questioning was sought. He was remanded to police custody till 6-8-1983.

Custodial interrogation is a science and needs meticulous preparation. This team had done that. Singh acted the toughie, Puri with his Punjabi connections, same mother tongue, etc., the softie brimming over with sympathy and I in spite of the same background, and age rude and hell-bent to fix him by hook or by crook. In the background, was Ohri again a Punjabi who showed that he wanted to be kind and considerate, but was scared of Singh and frightened by even my shadow. These actors continued interrogation of Jeeti Choudhari relentlessly for two days and three nights after remand. On 5th August, 1983, the iron will of Jeeti Choudhari ultimately collapsed. Sustained questioning by the team in the atmosphere that had been created by the different actors in the team saw him succumb. The team needed the typewriter, and to that end the grilling was directed. Finally, in the afternoon of 5th August, he made a statement, which was recorded in the presence of witnesses at 6 p.m. He was willing to disclose the place where he had got the addresses of Krishan and Delhi Metals typed. It was a commercial typing college at Lajpat Nagar market centre in South Delhi. Jeeti Choudhari, in custody, took the team to Lajpat Nagar and pointed to the place where he had gone to get the addresses typed. The place he identified was the Janta Commercial College, L-43, Lajpat Nagar-II. A pointing out memo was prepared at 7 p.m. on 5th August itself, within an hour of his confession. This college had 13 typewriters. Specimen typescript of all the said thirteen typewriters were taken that very evening in the presence of witnesses. Already, the typewriters were in use for ten months after the day Choudhari had paid a visit and, therefore, it was necessary to obtain admitted contemporaneous typed scripts also from these typewriters, if they were available. They were. It was a college to teach typing to the learners. Different learners had typed different sheets on all the said typewriters which were checked by the trainer of the college and kept with him date-wise. These typed sheets which were about

740 in all were taken charge off from the said commercial college. The arrest and scientific interrogation of the accused thus, paid off.

The next step was to seek the expert opinion on the abovesaid typed materials. It was exceedingly important to prepare the reference so comprehensively, that the expert could give an opinion on the questioned documents. But, the law as it stood pronounced by the Supreme Court of India way back in 1952, in *Hanumant Nergundkar v. State of Madhya Pradesh* had held, that an opinion on typewritten material could not be called an Expert Opinion under Section 45 of the Indian Evidence Act, 1872. This opinion was long debated by among ourselves, and also with others knowledgeable. Was it possible to overcome this opinion? But more to the point was the need to go on with the investigation. The team had to find the typewriter first and, thereafter, the person who had typed the same. The said person may become the star witness in the case. The team understood within themselves, that even if the expert gave opinion on the typewriters, it would be an opinion that would not be acceptable either to the Trial Court or to the High Court. Even a Division Bench of the Supreme Court would not be able to have it accepted as evidence. Only a five-member Bench of the Supreme Court could affect that miracle. We were preparing to achieve a miracle in legal terms. The reference to the expert, his opinion if it supported the prosecution case, would be exhibited in all the courts of Appeal, including the Supreme Court, without being once mentioned in the order yet, its base would be the supporting Supreme Court judgment. Singh prepared the reference to the expert who in this case was SK Gupta, Assistant Chemical Examiner, the Head of the Document Division in the Central, Forensic Science Laboratory, CGO Complex, Lodhi Road, New Delhi. In Singh's own words how he went about his task was 'Herculean.' The reference went to Gupta from Singh on 6-8-1983 and it was supplemented on 10-8-1983.

Then, it was Gupta's turn to burn the midnight oil. If he confirmed that the typewriter in the Janta Commercial College had actually typed the name of Krishan Sikand, etc., on the envelope, then the pointing out by Choudhari on 5th August would become evidence, that would link Choudhari with the murder. Gupta's detailed opinion dated 26thSeptember, 1983 is worth its weight in gold, in the annals of expert opinion detecting crime. To our team, it was reward for the dogged determination in zeroing on the murderer the "expert" way, despite knowing that the path was blocked. Gupta connected the questioned typed addresses on the booby trap parcel to 90 typed sheets of the corresponding period, and one sheet of the specimen typed script taken from one of the thirteen typewriters found kept in the Janta Commercial College, Lajpat Nagar, on 5-8-1983. The typewriter which was in the special knowledge of Jeeti Choudhari was thus identified by the expert.

The murder was thus out. I, wrote, summing up the result of investigation. "The entire evidence is circumstantial. But this evidence is an inextricable net comprising evidence of motive, of threat, of dexterity, of involvement, of conduct and it's tightly laced with the evidence of experts_ _ _ _." Surajit Choudhari @ Jeeti thus became a number in the Court of Addl. Sessions Judge S.C. Jain, 56/83 facing charges u/s 302 IPC (murder) and 3 & 4 of the Explosive Substances Act. This was in November 1983.

The turn of the expert SK Gupta to give evidence came. Bawa Gurbachan Singh, the defence counsel, opposed his appearance. The issue was argued at length. SC Jain by an order dated 27-3-1987 disallowed Gupta's evidence. He faced with the opinion of the Supreme Court in *Hanumant Nergundkar and another v. State of Madhya Pradesh* (AIR 1952 SC page 343) had little choice to decide otherwise. He wrote in the penultimate para of his judgment. "Hon'ble Judges of the Supreme Court meant that such evidence cannot be brought on record and be evaluated by the court. It is well settled if their Lordships of the Supreme Court clearly intended to declare the law on a particular point then even though the observation be *'obiter dictum'*, they are nevertheless binding upon the High Court and subordinate courts." The Delhi High Court (Hon'ble Justice M.K. Chawla) dismissed the criminal revision filed against this order on 20-5-1987 with the observation. "No interference in the impugned order is called for. The petition is dismissed." Both these orders were expected.

Normally, when two successive courts dismiss the case, the Government rejects a further attempt in the higher court but here, the Government of India concurred with the CBI, and the issue of opinion on typed document being an expert opinion or not was taken to the Supreme Court. PK Choubey, Advocate, assisted by CS Sharma, Senior Public Prosecutor and Singh set themselves and launched their preparation for the last judgment. They were thorough, laborious and meticulous in their research. Their object was to convince the Supreme Court of India, that the 1952 *obiter* dictum is required to be looked into and overruled. In their study they piled up enormous data. All of that then had to be chronologically and logically built up as an argument and put down on paper which, in the language of the court, is called, the paper book.

The reference that was made, was on a question of law and the short point was whether the opinion of the typewriting expert is admissible under Section 45 of the Indian Evidence Act, 1872. This became vital, as this prosecution was very acutely dependent upon this expert to prove the charge of 302 Indian Penal Code (murder) against Jeeti Choudhari. Therefore, though the reference was on a pure question of law since, it was raised during the trial of this murder case, it also became a question of fact, though this remained in 'purdah'. Annexure 'G' of the paper book was SK Gupta's report on his examination, reasoning and opinion on the questioned typed documents. The Supreme Court's pronouncement made no reference to this annexure, but during arguments it was examined and debated by the parties with the Bench, raising pertinent points on the validity of this opinion. Shri Choubey provided logical and to the point answers, to all the queries of their Lordships. This opinion from the Document Division of the Central Forensic Science Laboratory under SK Gupta's hand remained the determinant factor which governed the Apex Court's favourable response and yet not, even its shadow is allowed to colour the verdict. The highest court restrained itself. Its views on the opinion would have impinged upon the freedom of the subordinate court trying Choudhari for murder and this is impermissible. The Supreme Court held, that "the examination of typewriting, and identification of the typewriter, on which the questioned document was typed, is based on a scientific study of certain significant features of the typewriter, peculiar to a particular typewriter, and its individualities, which can be studied by an expert having professional skill in the subject and, therefore, his opinion on that point relates to an aspect in the field of science, which falls within the ambit of Section 45 of the Indian Evidence Act."

The effort, the hard work that went in the investigation to seek an opinion on typed documents, knowing that such an opinion is no evidence, was in the hope, that the highest court of the land could, on the basis of the opinion and other material, revise a law which had stood firm for more than thirty years (on the date of the murder). This hope came alive. Such is the splendour of dogged determination facing odds and hurdles that appear, at first sight, is insurmountable.

Jeeti Choudhari was given a life sentence by the trial court .

Chapter-14

With Lt Governor (LG) Delhi (April 2007 to July 2013)

Prosecution in the state of Delhi is almost an impossible job without certain reforms. A proactive and legally refurbished judiciary, close administrative monitoring of prosecution and absence of political interference are needed to better prosecution. It has not been possible to usher in such reforms in last so many decades.

I joined as a part of LG Delhi's Administration on July 24, 2007. The Home Department, Delhi which includes Delhi Police, Delhi Prisons, Delhi Fire Services and Prosecution reported to LG Tejendra Khanna through me. The Prosecution Department reported to the Law Minister and only those matter where acquittal in trial was proposed to be appealed was submitted to LG for his orders. LG did not get to see the work of the prosecutor on a day to day basis. Yet poor results in court reflected on the LG as Delhi Police reported to him and investigation was done by Delhi Police.

Police is, judged, broadly by its record in preventing crime, record in detecting crime and its record in the area of prosecution of accused arrested after detection of crime. Its the third area, the percentage of conviction it achieves in the cases it sends up for trial Delhi Police has fared poorly. The percentage of conviction is about 30%. The percentage of detection is 80%. So 80% detection ends in only 30% conviction. Either investigation is poor or prosecution is shoddy.

In most developed countries the decision to send for trial rests on the Director of Prosecution. They are known by different nomenclature in different countries. It's the District Attorney (DA) in America. We have a provision u/s 25A CrPC to appoint a Director of Prosecution who will have similar powers. LG Delhi considered this provision carefully. It was discussed first in a meeting of the LG with the Commissioner of Police and all senior officers of Delhi Police specially called for the purpose. Home Secretary, Delhi ,was present and so was the Chief of Prosecution Delhi at the bidding of the LG. The issue was poor prosecution and the blame game between Delhi Police and the Prosecution Branch of Delhi Government. The latter was of the view that Delhi Police officers did not render sufficient assistance to the prosecutors during trial. The Delhi Police , on the other hand, complained that prosecutors of Delhi Government did not prepare well for the court trial. The net result is that an almost 80% rate of detection of crime is reduced to less than 30% conviction by courts.

The LG was informed during the discussion that the remedy might lie in invoking the provisions of Section 25A CrPC. This provided for a Director of Prosecution in a State. In Delhi it would mean this legal deity, an appointee of the Delhi High Court and reporting to the High Court through the LG would independently review the evidence before the case was put in court. It will be his decision to send the case for trial. If he found the evidence weak, based on statements of unreliable witnesses or tutored ones or otherwise fabricated evidence, he could refuse to send up the case for trial. The power to decide if a charge sheet is to be filed presently lies with the investigating officer. Countries like Singapore and Malaysia who practice similar criminal jurisprudence as we do, have already immensely benefitted by acting similarly. The Director Prosecution there checks the evidence word for word, witness by witness and ensures that the evidence collected does stick. Conversely, he also determines that it does not stink. The numerous court judgments are proof that both happens, enough to raise hackles. Such instances do not come to light till the trial concludes, years later. The Chief Minister Delhi and the Government of Delhi turned down the suggestion of the LG. I believe that Sheila

Dikshit's Government did not want to loose the advantage of its hold on the Prosecution.

It is unfortunate that LG Delhi was not allowed by Sheila Dikshit's Government to bring in this reform in Prosecution, between 2007 and 2013 in the area of detection and prevention LG Delhi did make an impact. In 2007 there were only 700 Police Beats in Delhi. By 2013 the number were increased to 2100. In some areas of criminal activity, crime in Delhi has been substantially reduced/controlled. Many terrorist crimes have been prevented in the last four years. Similarly fatality in motor vehicle accidents have been brought down in appreciable terms. Street crimes including looting of cash from people, withdrawing funds from banks, snatching from ladies out in the market place, rape of call centre girls returning from duty in the early hours of the morning, crimes against people from the north east, stalking of university female students, slaughter of cows by Mewati gangs etc., have come down, shady tenants are almost a thing of the past and crime by servants, have to some extent been controlled. The functioning of several tiers of grievances cells at all responsible ranks of the Delhi Police hierarchy has improved police response at the ground level to complaints against inaction. Creation of a Police Complaint Authority, the first in India has been a step in the same direction. Corporate Social Responsibility (CSR) has joined hands with Delhi Police's PARIVARTAN and YUVA to lessen the proclivity of crime in the J J clusters. These are areas of impressive performance by Delhi Police in the sphere of prevention of heinous crime. Yes, in many areas of poor detection persist. Rape figures are escalating, murders still take place even where they are preventable, dowry deaths are continuing, domestic violence, wife beaten by husband violated, abused by her in- laws, children sexually abused still happen in disconcerting numbers. Old dependent parents are often uncared and abused. There are many streets which at night are not safe for women. Senior citizens are still unsafe. And then, there is corruption that singes many ranks in Delhi Police. The LG Delhi can never rest on his oars and his efforts to keep Delhi Police performing have to be unceasing.

Delhi Police record of detection of certain types of crimes is impressive. Between 2007 to 2013, virtually, no sensational crime have remained undetected . L G efforts to tackle poor performance in court, however, was a non-starter.

What is true of Delhi may well be true for all States. The Indian Criminal Justice System needs this one reform. Section 25A of the

Code of Criminal Procedure (CrPC) 1973 provides for a Director of Prosecution. He must now come to occupy his rightful place in the Indian Judicial system in the same manner as he/she has taken his/her place in many erstwhile Commonwealth countries following the tradition of Great Britain since 1880.

Corruption in Delhi was/is, as else where, rampant in the services. The watch dog was the Anti- Corruption Branch(ACB). It was headed by an Additional Commissioner on attachment from Delhi Police. All officers and men in the ACB were attached to this Branch from Delhi Police. It reported to the Vigilance Department of Delhi Government. Vigilance was the responsibility of the State and in officialise it was a Transferred Subject. All Departments that comprised Transferred Subject were excluded from LG's direct superintendence and files from the State Government were submitted for LG's perusal and approval as a Constitutional Head of State. There was an Additional Secretary ranked officer in the LG's Secretariat who saw and submitted to the LG all files received from all the Transferred Departments. However, in the Distribution of Work assigned to me all matters relating to the Anti Corruption Branch were included.

When the incumbent Additional Commissioner (Anti-Corruption) reverted to Delhi Police soon after the new LG took over a new Additional Commissioner of Police had to be selected. Among the panel of names forwarded by the Commissioner of Police was Dilip Kumar. The choice was left to LG and it was Dilip Kumar who became the new Additional Commissioner Delhi ACB in September 2007. He had spent seven years in the CBI Bangalore Branch and enjoyed a fine reputation. Within months of joining he arrested the Member, Engineering Jal Board, in a corruption case. This very much upset PK Tripathi Pr Secretary to the Chief Minister and a former Chief Executive Officer of the Delhi Jal Board. He called me up and I know how angry he was that Delhi Jal Board(DJB) which was headed by the Chief Minister (CM) should have its Member arrested without the CM being informed about it. He always spoke the Chief Minister's mind and from that day on Dilip Kumar found himself on the wrong side of Delhi Government. He, however, continued to be fully backed by LG Delhi. Dilip Kumar went about his work with dogged determination. He investigated officers of Social Welfare, Transport, Delhi Jal Board, Municipal Corporation Department Delhi, New Delhi Municipal Corporation, Delhi Police. He proved his cases and obtained sanction for their prosecution. He trained the lay complainant to record demands of bribe on camera and used that evidence to fortify his charges against them in court. He worked hard on restructuring the department to get over the incorrigible cases of huge vacancy in the ACB in all ranks. He scouted for better office space as their present accommodation was cramped and unsightly. Many of the corrupt in ACB received marching orders. He got laptops for his officers. He got over transport problems by getting approval for hiring vehicles. He regularly took on the officers of the Vigilance Directorate to expedite orders on his numerous well documented proposals. The ACB officers began to look at with some respect. But none of his proposals of restructuring the ACB succeeded. They were blocked at various levels. Long term proposals did not go through but short term ones which were irritants succeeded, But he was a marked man. His penchant for laying traps for the corrupt by private complaints had upset many. His action against Social Welfare Secretary made many more enemies. He persisted with his efforts to book the corrupt and had LG's backing, but not the CM's. His promotion by the MHA to the rank of Joint Commissioner of Police provided her with an opportunity to recommend to the LG that his services on promotion were not required by ACB. When it was pointed out that the MHA order specifically stated that all those who were promoted were to assume their new ranks in their present post it did not cut any ice. When LG was not inclined to accept this argument as another officer in Delhi Government in Home Guards had, in identical circumstances, become a Joint Commisioner of Police and was allowed to assume his new rank in his old post LG was informed that he too would be sent back to Delhi Police. The underline message was that this decision was not on caprice but on policy that higher ranked officers should not hold on to post which are meant for their juniors. Dilip Kumar was relieved. Thereafter the other officer to whom the guillotine was also to fall managed a stay and continued in Delhi Government. The policy so proudly touted on the file to facilitate Dilip Kumar's exit went into a limbo .

Anti-Corruption measures taken by Dilip Kumar received a set back after his exit. While individual acts of corruption, on specific complaints only, were acted upon joint corrupt practices in departments like the Social Welfare Department, Jal Board, Municipal Corporation of Delhi detected by the Anti- Corruption Department under him no longer came to light. The corrupt practices in the Transport Department detected in the selection, appointment and monitoring of the private firm appointed to report on pollution of commercial transport was ruthlessly suppressed by the Government of Sheila Dikshit. The Comptroller and Auditor General of India has alleged a scam in the expenditure of Rs 2000 crores shown as spent on non-existing civic infrastructure to forty lakh residents of unauthorised colonies in her tenure. This is an allegation of huge siphoning of public money. There are similar allegation in the working of Delhi Jal Board. ACB Delhi has been kept stunted by successive Governments of Delhi. LG Delhi Tejendra Khanna took decisive steps to give it teeth. Sheila Dikshit as Chief Minister Delhi effectively spiked these steps.

My efforts in converting ACB Delhi into an organisation with teeth annoyed powers that be. Rohini Singh of the *Economic Times* rang me up in August 2013 that P S Mehrauli is investigating me in FIR No 420 dt 23/06/2013 on the complaint of M A Usmani, officer Wakf Board. Usmani, on behalf of the Board on receipt of a communication from one Bahadur Abbas Naqvi, alleging sale of Wakf land in 2009 in a fraudulent sale supported by forged and fabricated documents, accused me to be a party, along with others, to this crime. Bahadur Abbas Naqvi and his legal adviser Mohammed Pracha had held several conferences with me during my tenure in the Rajniwas Secretariat. Mohammed Pracha was also part of Sheila Dikshit's legal support appearing on her behalf in courts. Naqvi was an office bearer of Anjuman-Hyadri and along with Mohammed Pracha was channelizing efforts to take possession of land measuring 8 acres of land in tony Jorbagh and 2 acres of land in Mehrauli in South Delhi. The approximate value of both these land parcels is Rs 3000 crores. These claims were doubtful and though Ahmed Patel sent many messages to the Lt Governor Tejendra Khanna and also spoke to him in their support it was repeatedly blocked. My role was limited to prevent violence and book those who indulged in violence. Naqvi was booked for violence. I blocked all efforts to drop charges against him and his supporters who had attacked a police officer and injured him in the eye. The cases were not dropped despite pressure from Ahmed Patel and Shinde as well, at some stage. Usmani's complaint forwarding Naqvi's allegations conveyed Sheila Dikshit Government's approval. Mohammed Pracha was her legal adviser. The allegations relate to 2009 and were trumped up as charges in June 2013. My tenure in Rajniwas ended on 9th June 2013.

Dilip Kumar went back to Delhi Police and worked first in Police Headquarters Vigilance Department and later in Land and Building. In the year 2011, if I remember correctly the MCD needed a Director of Vigilance and LG selected him to clean up the Augean stables. This time the MCD Councillors of the majority party were very reluctant. He did not become the Director of Vigilance MCD Delhi. Since MCD reported to the MHA, his appointment required the approval of the Central Vigilance Commission (CVC). Dilip Kumar found out that the MCD Councillors who were in the majority managed to convince one Vigilance Commissioner who came from Karnataka, incidentally under Bharatiya Janata Party (BJP) rule, that Dilip Kumar was a wrong choice. My tenure also came under a cloud around the same time. The Home Minister of India, Mr. Chidambram twice told the LG that he should not have me as consultant any further. The L G did not pay any attention to calls for my removal by the Home Minister of India, I write this on the authority of what L G Tejendra Khanna himself told me. My appointment was co-terminus with that of the incumbent LG. The new LG took over on 9th July, 2013 forenoon and I decided that I ceased to be a part of LG Delhi's team at the same time. I had informed the LG on or around the 7th July about this decision. I did not meet the new LG .

Tejendra Khanna is a brilliant man with a photographic memory. He retains with dates and time all that he hears and reads and that too without an effort. I think he can read a page in a minute and then recite the main points without referring to it at all. Monitoring the work of Delhi Police was very important to him. Regular fortnightly meetings with the top brass of Delhi Police and looking into grievances of the citizens of Delhi against Delhi Police personnel were the main planks to advise, direct, control and discipline Delhi Police. Within a few months he overhauled the pattern of the fortnightly meetings. He demanded a summary in a few pages, a note from his office, which I started preparing, about what was right and wrong in the workings in the fortnight which would be reviewed in the Police Districts, Ranges, Headquarter Divisions like Crime, Anti-Terrorist work, Economic Offences, Intelligence, Vigilance Operations, Court Trials a day before the fortnightly meeting. The meetings lasted nearly two hours and each head made a presentation and responded to specific queries from him. Whenever he concluded that a particular performance needed to improve, he issued what he described as "Bullet Point" These were recorded and put up to him and after he approved they were issued as decisions recorded for implementation. In order to show all this to posterity I made an exercise to compile the bullet points, the major ones under separate heads. Between 30.04.08

and 30.05.13, bullet points were issued in various areas of work of Delhi Police. These are a dozen areas that comprise Law and Order, Security of Women, Security of Senior Citizen and Children, Traffic, Terrorism, Community Policing, Prevention of Encroachment of Public Land, Publicity, Prosecution, Police Administration, Use of Technology and Training. These bullet points were monitored and every three months Joint Commissioner Headquarters informed the LG the progress made in implementing the directives issued. There was never anything routine in the follow-up. Terrorist acts likely and its consequences was one topic that was reviewed every fortnight without fail. Disciplinary action should be immediate and not kept hanging like a Damocles sword was a regular refrain in these meetings. Back log of disciplinary cases was cleared at his insistence.

The other area was grievance monitoring. While written complaints during his tenure ran into thousands and were monitored by the grievance cell of the LG, great importance was given to those who personally registered every morning from 11am to 2pm and demanded to be heard. I was under instructions to hear them personally and put up some of them to the LG for his consideration. During this tenure I heard four thousand three hundred and eighty five complainants. Each one was heard the day the complainant registered himself/herself. His grief was reduced into writing and sent to the Commissioner of Police with a copy personally handed over to the complainant and copy sent to him by the office through post. In urgent cases I would speak to either to the Deputy Commissioner of Police/Joint Commissioner of the Range/if necessary the Station House Officer too and ensure relief to the complainant. The LG would be briefed in my periodical meetings. Information from study of these grievances often became the source of bullet points. The Special Commissioner Vigilance, unfailingly, presented a graphic picture how the grievances had been acted upon. Specific action taken against delinquent police men who, deliberately caused the grievance, was also reported by him.

Before signing off a matter relating to the Commonwealth Village and the murky blame games played must be narrated. The facts are within my domain knowledge .Tejendra Khanna had completed three years as Lt Governor Delhi when the Games ended. The normal tenure is 3 years. Many were wanting him out. They include Sheila Dikshit and P Chidambram among the politicians and the Punjab cadre IAS colleague of the Lt Governor in the PMO, TKA Nair, Principal Secretary to the PM, was their points man. He selected VK Shunglu a former CAG and an ex IAS, to enquire and report on the allegation of financial irregularities in the Commonwealth Games. He chose to indict Tejendra Khanna. He accused him of forcing his "subordinates" to "endorse" his decision in "the matter of fixation of price per sq.ft. for purchase of flats in the Games Village from the Developer's share at Rs 11,000 without taking up the matter with Delhi Development Authority." VK Shunglu never sought clarification from Tejendra Khanna either directly or indirectly on any issue that finds mention in his report.

All his charges were unfounded and LG rebuttal in his nine page report to the President in March 2011 amply demonstrated that the Shunglu report was an attempt to malign him. He failed. Tejendra Khanna had two tenures as LG Delhi and together constituted the longest tenure ever of any LG. His second tenure alone was for six years and three months. It must be admitted, however, that two officers, one Additional Secretary to LG dealing with all DDA matters in LG's Secretariat and Finance Member DDA were called upon to explain their misconduct by the LG when consequent to Shunglu Report against him, LG found both along with others unknown suppressed a document from him while giving VK Shunglu the impression that the price was fixed on consideration of that very document. This was a communication from the Developer addressed to the LG seeking a particular price. Enquiries conducted by me on written orders conveyed on behalf of the LG by the Principal Secretary to the LG established that Additional Secretary to LG who received this communication addressed to the LG as it fell within his charter of duties, hid it from the LG and additionally quite improperly handed over the original to the Finance Member DDA and that too without keeping any record in his office. By their action and Finance Member's false information to VK Shunglu, both aided and abetted the Shunglu Committee in coming to the erroneous conclusion resulting in the indictment of the LG. They were serving the interest of those who wanted the LG ousted. Both of them were suborned by those who wanted the LG Delhi ousted for corruption after the Games concluded in 2010. This was politics dirty and touching nadir .

LG 's nine page report to the President for March 2011 was not seen by the Prime Minister. TKA Nair had ensured it. In June 2011 the LG learnt of this from Prime Minister. I ensured, with my contacts in the SPG to send a copy to the Prime Minister at his residence. The Annexure will fill the gaps in this episode.

सत्यमेव जयते

प्रधान मंत्री

Prime Minister

New Delhi
6 June, 2011

Dear Shri Khanna,

I have received your letter of 1 June, 2011 forwarding a copy of your report for the month of March 2011, sent to the President.

With warm regards,

Yours sincerely,

(Manmohan Singh)

Shri Tejendra Khanna
Lieutenant Governor of Delhi
Raj Niwas
Delhi - 110054

उपराज्यपाल
दिल्ली
Lieutenant Governor
Delhi

सत्यमेव जयते

दिल्ली-११००५४
RAJ NIWAS
DELHI-110054

Confidential

01 June, 2011

Subject: Copy of Monthly Report for March 2011 sent in April, 2011 to Respected Rashtrapati Ji, Vice-President, Prime Minister and Union Home Minister.

Respected Sir,

When I had met you briefly last evening at the Reception hosted by our President in honour of Mrs.Angela Merkel, Chancellor of Germany, after conferment on her of the Jawahar Lal Nehru Award for International Understanding-2009, I had mentioned that in my Monthly Report for March, 2011 sent to the country's highest dignitaries, I had brought out the correct factual position vis-à-vis certain erroneous observations of the Shunglu Committee concerning the role of L.G., Delhi. These concerned the purchase of flats by DDA from the Developer of the Commonwealth Games Village, in the context of the severe financial stringency and serious consequential delays being experienced in the execution of the Games Village project since 3 November, 2008, following Delhi High Court orders.

Since you kindly mentioned that you had yet not seen the above Monthly Report, I am sending a spare copy directly to you at your residential address, for favour of kind perusal of the relevant portions in the very opening paragraphs, concerning my stand on the observations of the Shunglu Committee. You will kindly appreciate that whatever steps were taken by me in this matter were completely transparent and in the national interest.

With Kindest Regards,

Yours sincerely,

TKhanna

(Tejendra Khanna)

Encl: As above.

Dr. Manmohan Singh,
Hon'ble Prime Minister of India,
South Block,
New Delhi.

CONFIDENTIAL

Office of the Lieutenant Governor: Delhi

REPORT FOR MARCH 2011

1. Shunglu Committee Report

In my monthly report for March 2009, while apprising progress/ preparation for the Commonwealth Games, I had brought to the notice of Hon'ble President of India that a scheme was being worked out at the request of the Emaar-MGF group, who had been developing the Commonwealth Games Village and experiencing financial stringency due to a sharp fall in booking of flats by private investors, to buy a certain number of flats from Emaar-MGF group, out of their share, and thus improve their liquidity.

1.2 The Second Report of the High Level Committee (HLC), constituted by the Government to look into issues relating to the organizing and conduct of Commonwealth Games-Delhi 2010 headed by Shri V.K. Shunglu, was submitted in March, 2011 and was immediately in news regarding its findings directed at the office of Lieutenant Governor, Delhi. **It may be mentioned that the Committee had at no stage cross-checked facts from the office of LG, Delhi and evidently based its findings without caring to gather and judiciously evaluate the full facts, with a seemingly predisposed intention to tarnish the image of the incumbent Lt. Governor, Delhi.** Shunglu Committee has clearly not understood the position of LG, Delhi as the ex-officio Chairman of DDA, who chairs the meeting of the Authority. The Chief Executive of DDA is the Vice-Chairman (VC), who is assisted by a number of senior officers and several thousand staff members on a day-to-day basis. While detailed comments on Shunglu Committee Report are being submitted by DDA to

Contd...2

Ministry of Urban Development, for proper appreciation of the context in which a decision was taken for DDA to purchase a certain number of flats from the share of the Project Developer in April-May 2009, the following facts need to be borne in mind:

1.3 On November, 3, 2008, while hearing a Writ Petition lodged by certain Environmentalists regarding location of the Commonwealth Games Village along the Yamuna River Bed, a Double Bench of the Delhi High Court observed that all investments made on the project etc. would be at the risk of the builder/investor.

1.4 The above order led to a sharp fall in the booking of flats by private investors and resulted in serious cash-flow problems for the Developer, Emaar-MGF. The Project Developer had been writing to various authorities in DDA and Ministry of Urban Development, GOI since November, 2008 for financial assistance due to adverse effect of ongoing litigations on booking of flats and credit squeeze due to economic meltdown. None of these letters was addressed to LG, Delhi.

1.5 The Project Developer also informed the Monitoring Committee, set up to monitor the Commonwealth Games Village Project and comprising of an independent member, Shri B. Mazumdar, Director General (Retd.), CPWD and one member each from DDA and the Project Developer, at its meeting held on 11th December, 2008 that the litigation about the Village site was severely hampering the progress of the work. The funding from the bank and customer was in jeopardy. The result is that the progress of the work had slowed down. The Project Developer requested the Monitoring Committee to intervene in the matter. Subsequent monthly requests of the Monitoring Committee also stressed the need for reversing the serious slow-down in pace of work of the Village.

1.6 On 30.12.2008, Chief Minister of Delhi, Smt. Sheila Dikshit called on L.G. at Raj Niwas and urged him to work out some financial bridging arrangements to tide over the serious financial stringency being experienced by the Project Developer which had led to major slow down in work at the Games Village site.

1.7 At a meeting of senior officers of DDA at Raj Niwas on 17.2.2009, after discussing various options such as grant of loan to the Developer and cancellation of contract on account of non-performance etc., it was felt that purchase of flats by DDA may be the best option in the given circumstances. That afternoon, at a meeting of Committee of Secretaries called by the Cabinet Secretary to review the progress of Commonwealth Games projects, the then VC-DDA, Shri Ashok Kumar Nigam, mentioned that DDA was contemplating purchase of some flats from the Developer's share to overcome the serious financial stringency being experienced by them. However, he wrongly mentioned that Lt. Governor, Delhi had already given approval to DDA for making purchase of flats out of its own funds. The original minutes of the meeting held at Raj Niwas on 17.2.2009 forenoon, approved by the then Principal Secretary to LG, Shri R. Chandramohan, and issued on 24.2.2011, only recorded that note had been taken of the slowdown of work in the Commonwealth Games Village due to financial stringency being experienced by the Project Developer.

1.8 After issue of the approved minutes on 24.2.2009, the then VC-DDA, Shri Ashok Nigam requested through a fax message dated 25.2.2009 to Shri A.K.Acharya, Additional Secretary to LG, an amendment therein to the effect that LG had "decided" that purchase of flats would the best option. Shri A.K. Acharya amended the minutes of meeting of senior officers of DDA held on 17.2.2009 under the Chairmanship of LG, Delhi at his own level without obtaining approval of Principal Secretary to LG, who had approved the original minutes of the said meeting issued on 24.2.2009, or my approval and issued the amended minutes on 26.2.2009. No copy of the amended minutes was marked to my Private Secretary or Principal Secretary to LG.

1.9 In fact, no such categorical decision to purchase the flats had been taken at the said meeting held on 17.2.2009. It was only the consensus view in the meeting of the senior officers that purchase of some flats may be the only workable option in the given circumstances. In the Cabinet Secretary's COS meeting on 17.2.2009 afternoon, it was decided that an "out of box" solution involving purchase of flats by DDA from the Developer after proper valuation etc. may be taken forward to resolve the unusual financial crisis faced by the Project Developer which had led to serious slow down in this project of critical importance for staging of CWG-2010.

1.10 Following the above decision taken at the Cabinet Secretary's meeting, on 12.3.2009, the LG ordered constitution of a four-agency Valuation Group consisting of representatives of National Building Construction Corporation (NBCC), Housing Urban Development Corporation (HUDCO), CPWD and DDA. Several meetings of the Valuation Committee were held under the chairmanship of the Executive Director, HUDCO, Shri R.K. Safaya at the HUDCO office. No details of these meetings were ever brought to LG's attention nor were so required to be done under the normal working procedure of DDA. After receipt of the Valuation Committee's report, the Finance member, Shri Nand Lal and VC DDA, Shri A.K. Nigam suggested that a Negotiating Committee headed by Finance Member, DDA including Chief Accounts Officer of the DDA and Principal Commissioner (Commonwealth Games) may be set up to negotiate the matter further with the Project Developer. This proposal was approved by the LG on 13.4.2009. The details of the negotiations held were again never brought to the notice of the LG nor were they required to be brought up to him.

1.11 At a meeting on 23.4.2009 by Vice-Chairman DDA, Shri Ashok Nigam in the presence of Finance Member, other Members of the Negotiating Committee, DDA's Financial Consultants and the Project Developer, Emaar-MGF, a purchase price of Rs.11,056/- per sq.ft. was worked out by adding cost of finance, overheads and 15% Developer's margin as per CPWD's norms, to the original price band proposed by the Valuation Committee. The Developers signified the acceptance of a purchase price of Rs.11,000/- per sq.ft. It was also noted by senior officers of DDA, including Vice-Chairman and Finance Member, DDA that prevailing booking rates for flats before the onset of the crisis ranged between Rs.13,000-13,500 per sq.ft.

1.12 **It is only at this stage that LG was informed that an agreed purchase price of the flats had been worked out which was well below the market rate.** LG then decided to call a meeting at Raj Niwas on the afternoon of 24th April, 2009 to consider the purchase price rate being recommended and requested Secretary, Ministry of Urban Development, Shri M Ramachandran and Jt.Secretary, MOUD, Shri M.M. Kutty also to join the meeting as the Ministry had been closely monitoring the crisis at the Games Village.

1.13 The Shunglu Committee in its report has referred to a letter dated 22.4.2009 sent to LG by the Project Developer which also cites an earlier letter of 21.4.2009 stating that they had been offered a price of Rs.10,100 per sq.ft. by the Negotiating Committee which was not acceptable. However, a price of Rs.11,000 per sq.ft. which would cover their overheads, cost of capital and margin would be acceptable. The Developer pointed out that prevailing market price of the flats ranged between Rs.13,000 to Rs. 13,500 per sq.ft.

1.14 **It is very significant to note that neither of the two letters allegedly sent on 21 April, 2009 and 22 April, 2009 by the Developer to the Lt.Governor were ever received in the LG's Secretariat, as per LG Secretariat's Dak Registry.** Inexplicably, the original letter of Emaar-MGF dated 22 April, 2009 addressed to L.G. but marked "For kind attention of Shri A.K. Acharya, Additional Secretary, Raj Niwas" was lodged with DDA and was incorporated in DDA's Negotiation Committee records without any endorsement or order, whatsoever, from either LG's office or the LG himself. Many months later, on 22.8.2009, a photocopy of Emaar-MGF's letter of 22nd April, 2009 was marked down to his staff by Shri A.K. Acharya but was never shown/ put up to LG. This letter was wrongly relied upon by Shunglu Committee to insinuate that it was LG's intervention which had resulted in a price of Rs.11,000/- per sq. ft. being approved for purchase of flats from the Developer and that LG had got his decision in this matter ratified by some "subordinates" including Secretary, MOUD, Government of India. The fact is that this letter was never received or seen by LG at any stage.

1.15 **As already clarified earlier, LG played no role whatsoever in the actual valuation or price determination of the flats and his role in the entire process was limited only to the following four steps:**

(i) **At the senior DDA officers' meeting on 17.2.2009, chaired by LG, it was felt that purchase of flats of DDA may be the best option to save the CWG Village project in the given circumstances. However, the actual decision to pursue the purchase option was taken in the COS meeting of 17.2.2009 afternoon presided over by the Cabinet Secretary, after the briefing given by VC-DDA.**

(ii) **On 12.3.2009, LG approved the appointment of a four-agency Valuation Committee comprising NBCC, HUDCO, CPWD and DDA.**

(iii) After receipt of the Valuation Report by VC DDA, at FM/VC's recommendation, on 13.4.2009, LG approved the setting up of a Negotiating Committee to negotiate the purchase of the flats by DDA. This Committee was headed by Finance Member, DDA, Shri Nand Lal, and included some senior officers of DDA.

(iv) LG called a High Power Committee meeting at Raj Niwas on 24.4.2009 afternoon consisting of Secretary, Ministry of Urban Development, Government of India, Vice Chairman, DDA, Engineer Member, DDA, Finance Member, DDA, Jt. Secretary (Delhi Division), MOUD to consider the purchase price of Rs.11,000/- which had been worked out by the Negotiating Committee after a final round of discussion with the Developer under the chairmanship of the then VC-DDA, Shri Ashok Kumar Nigam on 23.4.2009. A copy of the Minutes of the High Level Committee meeting is enclosed for ready reference as Annexure III.

1.16 It may be mentioned that the price of ₹ 11,000 per sq. ft., agreed to between the Negotiating Committee and the Project Developer, was well below the then prevailing market price of the flats. At the current reported price of ₹ 18,500 to ₹ 19,000 per sq. ft., DDA stands to gain more than ₹ 450 crore, which will yield over 70% gross profit on its investment on the flats bought by it. Besides, this timely action achieved the invaluable objective of getting the best ever Commonwealth Games Village ready for the Mega event.

1.17 The decision taken by the High Power Committee in this regard was ratified by the Authority at its meeting held on 03.06.2009 on the basis of a formal Agenda item. Convening of Authority meeting for prior approval of purchase of flats out of the Developer's share was not required as per rules of conduct of business of DDA and would have delayed the project further.

Lieutenant Governor of Delhi : Report for March 2011

1.18 It is also not true that the LG got the matter of fixation of prices per sq. ft. endorsed by his subordinates. As the matter was both very sensitive and important in nature, the Secretary, Ministry of Urban Development, Govt. of India who was keenly aware of the severe financial situation and the delay dogging the Games Village Project since end of 2008, was kept informed in the whole decision making. Several communications had been sent directly by the Developer to the Ministry. Secretary, MOUD was also aware of the discussion in the meeting of CoS under the Cabinet Secretary held on 17.02.2009 regarding resolving the problem at the earliest. He had not attended the meeting called by me on 24.04.2009 as a subordinate Officer.

1.19 **It will thus be seen that the unfounded criticisms and allegations of the Shunglu Committee, vis-à-vis the role of LG are totally mis-conceived, misplaced and reflect malicious intent. A copy of the letter which had been sent on 6 May, 2009 by Shri M. Ramachandran to the Cabinet Secretary endorsing a copy to Shri T.K.A. Nair, Principal Secretary to Prime Minister and to Smt. Sindhushree Khullar, Secretary (Sports) on the subject is enclosed (Annexure IV). The concluding part of this letter was, "It is expected that the above decision will enable DDA to take further necessary action to complete the Games Village Project in time for the Commonwealth Games."**

1.20 Following findings of the Shunglu Committee pertaining to the office of LG, Delhi have to be weighed in the background of the preceding paragraphs, as shown in the following Table:

Lieutenant Governor of Delhi: Report for March 2011

(True Copy)

S.N.	Finding of Shunglu Committee	Para No. of this Report containing my comments
1.	That the Developer approached LG vide letter dated 22nd April 2009 suggesting an acceptable rate of Rs 11,000 per sq. ft. while rejecting the rate of Rs 10, 000 per sq. ft. offered by the Negotiation Committee.	**1.13 & 1.14**
2.	That the LG held a meeting on 24th April 2009 under his Chairmanship and decided the purchase price of flats under the Bailout Package to the Developer.	1.7 to 1.12 & 1.15
3.	That the amount of Rs 11.000 per sq. ft. fixed by the Evaluation Committee and approved by the Group of Officers under Chairmanship of LG is unjustified.	1.16
4.	That the meeting convened by the LG on 24th April 2009 had no authority to take such a decision and the matter should have been taken to the Delhi Development Authority, which is the body, empowered to take such decision.	1.17
5.	That the LG did not take up the matter of fixation of price per sq. ft. to the Delhi Development Authority and got the same endorsed by his subordinates.	1.18

Chapter-15

Autonomy to the Central Bureau of Investigation (CBI)

Successive governments, whatever their politics, have remained obdurate in the face of demands of the major opposition parties that the Central Bureau of Investigation (CBI) should be autonomous. Many ordinary people believe that the autonomy to the CBI is in order. They are in error, the CBI cannot be autonomous. It cannot have the powers of the C&AG or the Election Commission of India. It cannot have any constitutional status. It will be what it is, a police organization subordinate to the civil authority and through it to the Government of the day. Sometimes the Supreme Court or the High Court may, in a particular investigation or enquiry, require the CBI to report stages of investigation only to it and the CBI will dutifully file the reports in a sealed cover to the court in question. Such instances will be few and far between. In every case after the final sealed cover report is filed and some times before, the superior civil authority of the CBI, Ministry of Personnel, Pensions and Grievances, will be in the know of all the investigations done and through it to the Government. Court supervision has never stopped the Government being privy to what is exactly CBI's finding or from receiving instructions from the Government or proceeding with the enquiry/investigation bearing in mind about those instructions.

The demand of autonomy for the CBI cannot be conceded for the simple reason that it's a non starter. The organization is by law required to discharge its responsibilities as specified in the laws passed by the Parliament or the State Legislature and assented to by the President or the Governor as the case may be. The flexibility available to the CBI officers while working under these specified law is, therefore, limited. CBI becomes extortionate and criminal when the moral fibre of the investigator and his superior breaks free of the constraint imposed by the laws and rules that control all investigations under the Code of Criminal Procedure (CrPC). The Code decides the flexibility available to the CBI officer. The corrupt behaviour of a CBI officer is subject to laws of the land. A corrupt behaviour is open to investigation under the Prevention of Corruption Act. It is also controlled by the Conduct Rules of the Government and any violation of the rules must lead to administrative action like warning, censure, reduction in rank and even dismissal. In other words, there is in-built autonomy to CBI officers in the discharge of their investigation responsibilities. As long they act within the law and are not tempted by any type of illicit gain, each CBI officer has complete autonomy in investigation and prosecution.

When the demand for autonomy of the CBI is raised in various forums, it is to ensure that the CBI officers are not subjected to any influence or pressure from the Government at any stage of their work either during investigation or during prosecution. This freedom to act independent of extraneous influence, to refuse to carry out incorrect or illegal directions of superior officers is available to all CBI officers. If some CBI officers are perceived to act as 'caged parrot', the fault lies with them individually. The fault is in the training, it is in the lust for post retirement benefits which the government can bestow, it is greed for lucre, it is for recognition, not regular, from Government. They are corrupt officers and are not satisfied with the recognition by way of a meritorious service medal or the higher distinguished service medal. They lust for a post retirement five-year or a ten year government sinecure which has power, authority and glamour and for assets disproportionate to their known sources of income. Ever since 1963 when CBI was created, largesse has been distributed by the government to selected superior officers of the CBI. It is this temptation that persuades even the best officers to expect to be benefited by extension of service, re-employment, gubernatorial postings and more. They then work as caged parrots and their subordinates then have to toe the line. This behaviour worsens when the CBI officer is also corrupt. Fortunately, a majority of CBI officers are not so tempted.

As yet CBI officers can always act strictly in accordance with law. To allow this to happen no temptation should be dangled before serving CBI officers or officers who have served CBI. Laws prohibit accepting financial benefits from private persons both during service and after retirement. Laws should also prevent any largesse from Government. No CBI officer should be eligible for any post retirement jobs where the President is the appointing authority. Also every CBI officer, irrespective of his rank, should be assessed for his integrity periodically and also without warning. This assessment should be meaningful. This exercise should include his/her dependent and/or those who have been dependent on him/her. CBI officers deal with the future of the service life of public and government servant both highly placed and otherwise. They must prove as long as it is required of them that they have it in them those virtues that qualify them to do what they are assigned to do. If they, at the end of their service life, emerge worthy of trust let them be rewarded. For instance, allow them to draw as pension their last pay and allowances for five years more. Let them also enjoy the facility of retaining government accommodation or in lieu receive house rent for five years. These are illustrations only.

It is only when the CBI officers function uninfluenced by the temptations of sinecures and gubernatorial posts the ignominious appellations like caged parrots, Congress Bureau of Investigation, Corrupt Bureau of Investigation etc. for CBI could end. Demand of autonomy to CBI to ensure investigation free from influence, is just a red herring when the Director CBI is compromised.

DIRECTIONS TO DELHI POLICE 2008-2013
BULLET POINTS

Improving Security of Women Bullet Points For Delhi Police 2008-2013

I Maintenance of Law & Order

II Improving Security of Women

III Security of Senior Citizen and Children

IV Decisions for Improvement in Traffic

V Prevention of Terrorism

VI Community Policing, YUVA & PARIVARTAN Schemes

VII Prevention of Encroachment of Land and not allowing Civil Dispute on property to be converted into criminal cases

VIII Publicity

IX Prosecution Improvement

X Police Administration

XI Introducing Technology, Infrastructural Development and Preparing studies of important cases to achieve better policing

XII Improving Training

Maintenance of Law & Order

19.06.2008

1. Certain relatively mild 'drugs' should be considered for deletion from the NDPS Act. Users thereof could also be placed in a distinct category with a more lenient punishment. *(Action: Pr. Secretary (Home)*

01.07.2008

2. A report may be sent on the pendency of cases filed before SDMs involving illegal groundwater extraction to the Divisional Commissioner with a copy to Pr. Secretary to LG. *(Action: Spl. CP/Vigilance.)*

3. An advisory may be sent to all the car manufactures for installinganti-theft gadgets before selling their cars. An advertisement may also be given in the newspaper to educate members of public on car security measures. *(Action: Jt. CP/Crime)*

04.09.2008

4. An adveltisement advising people not to carry huge amounts of cash on their person without proper security may be released.

18.09.2008

5. To seek wide participation of public through greater alertness and provision of inputs regarding suspicious factors for improving the security environment. *(Action: Spl. CP/Intelligence)*

22.01.2009

6. Entry of illicit arms from neighbouring states should be curbed by suitable screening at the entry points. *(Action : Jt. CPs/Ranges)*

16.04.2009

7. Nobody should be permitted to block fire/emergency exits in high rise buildings. *(Action: Joint CP of all ranges)*

18.05.2009

8. Database of jhuggi dwellers should be collected by Delhi Police as a step towards a secure Delhi.

25.05.2009

9. CP will take steps on grounds of security to identify residents living in jhugi jhopri where there is information that illegal immigrants from across the border are staying with false identity papers.

10. Incidents of clandestine cow slaughters are being repeatedly taking place. This situation has seeds of disruption of communal harmony. A drive with a special force should be initiated to investigate all such cases and bring the Culprits to book as soon as possible.

11. CP should initiate a proposal to reduce the age of juvenile criminals to be tried by Juvenile Court from the present age stipulation. There are instances of serious crimes being perpetrated by such persons who are showing signs of adulthood though they continue to be technically known as juvenile as per statute.

12. Crime of snatching on the road has gone up by 25%. CP has taken note of the serious repercussion of such crimes and will make a concerted effort to reduce their spate in NCT Delhi.

28.05.2009

13. List of Bad Characters should be made and their be kept under constant surveillance. *(Action: Jt. CP/Ranges)*

14. Surprise and unobtrusive inspections should be carried out to check the alertness of private security agency staff deployed at malls, cinema houses, hotels etc. *(Action: Jt. CP/Ranges)*

15. The police should focus on action against the "big fish". Police action should not be taken only to build up statistics. *(Action: Jt. CPs/Ranges)*

16. Beat Constables should keep a close eye on active criminals in their respective beats. *(Action: Jt. CPs/Ranges)*

17. During night patrolling, PCR Vans should check suspicious vehicles moving around residential colonies. *(Action: Spi. CP/Int. & Ops.)*

18. Appropriate briefing should be given to PCRs so that they are on watch even while stationary. *(Action: Spl. CP/Int. & Ops.)*

01.06.2009

19. Identification of suspect elements living in Jhuggi/Jhopri should be continued at good speed so that there is a database of suspect criminals/terrorists in Delhi living in Jhuggi/Jhopri.

03.08.09

20. LG directed the CP to ensure compliance of the Cabinet decision that stated monuments under the ASI should be protected from visitors who go there to perfom religious rites. Only in the case of those protected monuments were already orders exist permitting religious rites, such rites will be permitted by Delhi Police as laid down in the notifi cation. A copy of the notification has been made available to the CPO.

17.06.2009

21. Instructions were issued that checking at Barricade set up by the police should ensure that anyone without proper identity and a suspect is properly identified and his biometric data prepared. The number of such detections should be reported to the LG in the reports sent to LG.

13.07.2009

22. On security the extent of lawlessness created by huge spurt in crime in residential colonies, presence of criminal elements freely moving in the residential colonies and parks and their criminal activities in areas of snatching, motor vehicles thefts, drug peddling, molestation of women was discussed and the need for more policing as proposed by the CP was urgently felt. Municipal Magistrate would also need to be proactive along with the police in the field.

23.07.2009

23. Instructions may be issued to the effect that DDA must obtain the recommendations of Special Branch of Delhi Police before proposing/making any allotment to religious organizations. Special Branch will take into account, inter alia, the population composition of the locality.
(Action: Principal Secretary (Home)

24. The attempts at revival of old mosques as places of worship on a regular basis should be carefully gone into by Union Home Ministry to evolve a clear policy and line of action. *(Action: All concerned)*

25. Proper checks on people coming to buy chemicals which can be used for explosives should be undertaken. *(Action: All concerned)*

26. It is observed that there is increase in crime in areas having inhabitants of lower socio-economic and educational status. It was felt that deployment of more police force in such areas is likely to have greater deterrence. Accordingly, the proposals of Delhi Police for opening 29 more police stations may be sent to MHA.
(Action: Joint CP (Crime)

06.08.2009

27. The data base of Guest House owners should be shared by Add!.CP/Lic with Jt. CP/Special Cel!. *(Action: Addl. CP/LIC)*

28. Follow up action on the lessons learnt from mock drills need to be taken scrupulously. The matter of delayed response time during mockdrills at Lajpat Nagar and Nehru Place may be taken up with Fire Department. There should be zero tolerance for any deficiency noticed during mock drills so as to ensure full preparedness. *(Action: Jt. CPs/Ranges)*

29. Further, to control the increase of robbery/snatching, etc. barriers can be set up near the banks and verification of Motor Cyclists need to be expedited. A pilot plan to place spotters near banks, etc can also be considered to check the anti-social elements who keep an eye on people visiting banks for ulterior motives. *(Action: Jt. CPs/Ranges)*

20.08.2009

30. Bank Branches where usually large cash transactions take place should be identified and kept under surveillance. *(Action: Jt. CP/Crime)*

31. Proper surveillance near liquor shops and vends should be maintained to prevent eve teasing, drinking outside the permitted "ahata" premises.
(Action: Jt. CPs/Ranges)

32. Number of buses checked on the move and the number of criminals arrested with knives should be intimated. Habitual knifers should be externed. *(Action: Jt. CPs/Ranges)*

22.09.2009

33. On the Issue of taxi drivers and TSR drivers Since more than registered drivers are illegally driving such vehicles, it is necessary for reasons of security to ensure that bio-metric data of authorized taxi drivers and TSR drivers is collected and recorded. All authorized drivers be issued public service badges. The delay in issue of such badges specially in respect of the Airport both domestic and International should not be allowed to continue. LG has instructed the Chief Secretary to hold a meeting with the Transport Commissioner and the Special Commissioner (Int.) so that a time frame for the completion of this important work in respect of cab drivers in the Airport is determined and the work compl eted within that time frame.

19.10.2009.

34. Bio-metric identity of taxi drivers and auto-rickshaw is necessary in the interest of security. LG was apprised by the CS of the Transport Department effort in this area. The CS was directed to hold regular meetings with the Transport Commissioner towards implementing the exercise of completing Bio-metric identity of taxi and autorikshaw drivers within a specific time table. CP who was present was directed to ensure that Special Commissioner (Int.)/Jt. Commissioner (Operations) was present at these meetings.

26.10.2009

35. LG has directed that whenever Residents Welfare Associations (RWAs) report to the SHOs of the concerned Police Station that there is congregation of "worshipers" in old AST protected or listed disused former religious structures like former old disused mosques grave etc., then SHOs of concerned Police Station must immediately step in to prevent misuse of such ASI protected property within residential colonies. CP has been communicated as instructed.

09.11.2009

36. Instances of Bikers attacking teachers and students as they wait forthe morning bus to take them to school were noted by the CP for corrective action.

08.12.2009.

37. In areas around International and Domestic Airport, Delhi continous security monitoring of residents living close to the airport be carried out to prevent any breach of security when planes land or take off from these Airports at Delhi.

04.01.2010

38. Public representatives, Hon'ble MPs, MLA and Municipal Councillors have repeatedly been writing to the Hon 'ble LG on the subject of non-registration of cases in their constituency. These largely relate to incidents of robbery, snatching, molestation of women and car thefts. The CP explained that unless there is verification of the incidents reported, cases are not registered. In many cases, it has been found on verification that in an incident which is not a cognizable offence, it is manipulated so that it is converted into an incident of snatching, robbery, molestation of women etc. Regarding car thefts, he admitted that an FIR is registered only after attempt to recover the car fails and therefore there is some delay in registration of car thefts. This is done with the consent of the complainant who also does not want the stolen car to become a stolen property once it recovered after registration of a case.

15.02.2010

39. LG reiterated that CP's proposal regarding extension of powers to Issue notification u/s 144 CrPC to ACP should be immediately reconsidered and the file recalled from Home Dept. for consideration and LG's orders.

40. The issue of a committee as directed by the Hon'ble Delhi High Court to consider guidelines for what has come to be known as Trial by Media was discussed with the CP and LG passed orders regarding the constitution of such a committee.

41. It was agreed that among the core function of Delhi Police, the role of watch and ward has no place. Wherever such duties are required, the owners of the premises should make arrangements. This matter arose as the CP was asked by the Union Home Ministry to secure venues for Commonwealth Games as soon as they were ready. The LG assured the CP that he would take up the matter with the Group of Ministers (GoM) to ensure that these orders are reviewed. *(CP has confirmed that orders have been withdrawn)*

25.02.2010

42. Arms License may be issued to five star hotels which meet all licensing requirements for enhancing their internal security preparedness. *(Action: Addl. CP/Licensing)*

43. Mewat area lacks educational facilities. A note on lack of educational facility in Mewat area should be sent to the CS with a copy to the LG. Efforts should also be made to get central police forces station their Battalions in the vicinity of Mewat villages to prevent a drift into lawless behavior. *(Action: Spl. CP/Int.)*

44. NCC cadets may be included in the 'Eyes & Ears ' Scheme. *(Action: Jt. CP/PHQ)*

02.03.10

45. Areas in Delhi where large groups of foreigners who have a muslim background live should be surveyed, put on surveillance on a regular basis and on occasions when festivals take place, special care be taken to watch suspected elements from amongst them.

46. In structures which are considered vulnerable if personnel are out sourced to work in these places such out sourced private persons should be screened for security before being allowed access. They should be allowed to work as out sourced personnel only when they are so screened to ensure that these institutions are secured from disruptive elements.

08.03.2010

47. LG directed that police should register more cases against those who are violating laws on Preventing of Cruelty to Animals in GNCT.

11.03.2010

48. Private security guards posted at vulnerable places should be screened by Police for suitability and written advisories in their behalf issued to management of these vulnerable places. *(Action: Joint CPs/Ranges)*

49. A biometric data-base of youngsters from outer areas of Delhi with propensity to commit crimes may be developed on a time-bound basis. *(Action: Jt. CPs/Ranges)*

01.04.2010

50. Surprise checking by putting barricades at strategic locations may be carried out. (Action: Jt. CP/Ranges)

51. The blockage of carriageways by spillover of worshippers at places of worship is to be controlled/minimized in consultation with heads of such places of worship. Availability of land for construction of places of worship may be identified in consultation with DDA so that worshippers can avail of the facility of prayers/worship close to their place of residence. *(Action: Jt.CPs/Ranges)*

52. Strict action may be taken against criminal elements coming from neighouring states who indulge in cow slaughtering. *(Action: Jt. CPs/Ranges)*

53. Crime analysis may be divided into two parts, offences against property & offences affecting the human body. *(Action: Jt. CP/Crime)*

15.04.2010

54. Delhi Police should obtain collapsible barricades and deploy them without prior notice in areas of Delhi for checking at random vehicles/motor cycles pedestrians. The feedback of these surprise checking carried out with the help of collapsible barricades should be obtained and necessary action to ensure security and safety of Delhi be undertaken. Feedback on surprise checking done at pickets and other points may be given at the next law and order meeting. *(Action: Jt. CP/Ranges)*

55. At selected sites where random checking of vehicles and motorcycle riders is done, some spotters accompanied by at least two Constables with weapons should be present. *(Action: Joint CsP/Ranges)*

56. In the reporting of kidnapping and abduction cases, gender break up of victims should also be given. *(Action: Jt. CP/Crimes)*

19.04.2010

57. The LG directed that all Asstt. Commissioners of Police posted in the districts should themselves periodically conduct checking on the roads by setting up mobile check posts and submit written reports as a result of the checks carried out by them to their immediate supenor. CP will monitor and apprise LG of the results periodically.

26.04.2010

58. CP will issue advisory to shops within the jurisdiction of Delhi Police selling high valued items to take steps to secure these establishments by employing security guards and taking all other requirements both technological and physical to prevent unsolicited access to these establishments.

59. Market's Associations shall also be issued advisory to employ adequate security guards and install security cameras to keep surveillance over markets when they are closed for business.

60. The issue of raising armed battalions by Delhi Police for meeting requirements of strategic nature ensuring security of vital installations in Delhi was considered and CP has been directed to adequately deploy members of the Delhi Armed Police for security duties. LG agreed this will be possible after the recruits selected will complete training of one year which will commence from I st June 2010 and thereafter complete three months of field training. This will be possible from October 2011.

03.05.2010

61. Mobile check posts should be frequently placed in all areas where criminal elements are known to be on the move and all cases of successful detection of criminals should be recognized and suitably rewarded by the CP.

03.05.2010

62. Watch and intercept suspected disruptive elements who may be planning to create mischief in areas of Delhi where there is continuous and constant footfall.

63. Mobile check posts should be frequently placed in all areas where criminal elements are known to be on the move and all cases of successful detection of criminals should be recognized and suitably rewarded by the CP.

06.05.2010

64. Interrogation of apprehended juvenile bad characters reveals that socio-economic reasons where the main factor of their taking to crime. Delhi Police may consider setting up a vocational centre where counseling may take place to prevent youngsters from stepping into crime. *(Action: It. CP/Ranges)*

65. Consumption of liquor in front of licensed vends should be stopped. *(Action: Jt. CP/Ranges)*

10.05.2010

67. A Standing Operating Procedure (SOP) should be drawn up by the Pr. Secretary (Home) to determine how Delhi Police will seek the assistance of the armed forces U/S 130 of the Cr.PC. Once the procedure is drawn up in black and white, LG will determine the civil authority who will exercise the powers U/S 130 Cr.PC to requisition the armed forces to assist the Delhi Police when the situation so warrants.

17.05.2010

68. In view of escalation of crime by bikers, verification of motor-cycle users has to be resumed in right earnest. CP confirmed that he has issued orders to that effect.

10.06.2010

69. Warning signs may be put up outside liquor vends notifying that drinking in the vicinity of a vend is an offence. CCTV cameras be also got installed covering the opening area outside such vends. *(Action: Jt. CP/Ranges)*

24.06.2010

70. The problem arising out of issue of arms licenses in Doda District (J & K) to non-residents has a bearing on Law & order in Delhi. Chief Secretary, Delhi was requested by the LG to write to Chief ecretary (J & K) on this issue. MHA should be kept informed. Jt. CP, Special Cell will send details to the Chief Secretary, Delhi to enable him to write to Chief Secretary (J & K). *(Action: Jt. CP, Special Cell)*

71. Drinking in the area just outside liquor shops is becoming a serious problem reflecting Law & Order. CP will write to Chief Secretary, Delhi about the necessary steps that should be taken to incorporate regulation in excise laws to curb this menace, including fixing of CCTV Cameras. *(Action: CP, Delhi & CS Delhi)*

72. PCR Vehicles and officers should confront potential trouble makers in their area of duty. Jt. CP PCR was directed to adequately brief and debrief PCR staff to ensure they are proactive. *(Action: Jt. CP PCR)*

73. SHOs of Police Stations should carry out verification of antecedents of propelty dealers to prevent property frauds. *(Action: Jt. CP/Ranges)*

19.07.2010

74. LG issued directions to the CP to ensure that both the LG's office and the Chief Secretary's office has direct/hot line connections from the Command and Control Room of the Delhi Police.

75. PCR vehicles are reportedly not visible, specially at night. The CP explained the shortage in the number of PCRs which is responsible for this blemish in a rapidly expanding capital. When the number of PCRs is raised to 1000 as has been proposed the position will improve but only slightl y. Delhi needs at least 3000 PCRs if all areas are covered and they are visible 24 x 7 according to the CP.

76. LG also directed that PCR staff should be pro-active in matters of crime control.

26.07.2010

77. CP agreed that Delhi Transport Corporation (DTC) bus drivers and cleaners should also be galvanised to act as Eyes and Ears of Delhi Police.

78. LG reiterated the need to exercise diligent precautions on the roads of Delhi and on the borders of Delhi to spot potential disruptionists.

20.09.2010

79. The CS offered 43 CCTV Cameras to Delhi Police for installation and use.

27.09.2010

80. On the Issue of prisoners escorted in trains, the escorting party entitled to higher class of travel are compelled to travel in the lower class authorized to the prisoners. The prisoner's class of travel should be upgraded so that the escort party can travel in the class they are entitled.

11.10.2010

81. Pr. Secretary (Home) was directed to ensure that next excise policy implements administrative orders issued regarding prohibition of drinking near liquor vends in Delhi.

21.10.2010

82. Surprise checking of persons with motorcycles who are just hanging out should be carried out in order to prevent crimes on the road.
(Action; Jt. CP/Ranges)

04.11.2010

83. Beat patrolling may be intensified in crime infested areas in the outskirts of Delhi. *(Action: Jt. CPs/Ranges)*

15.11.2010

84. All Police Stations are required to be fitted with CCTV cameras and it has to be ensured that these CCTV cameras keep a week's record of their footage.

18.11.2010

85. The police stations which have registered a large number of robberies/ snatching should be strengthened by way of deployment of more PCRs, intensive preventive action, etc. *(Action : Jt. CPs/Ranges)*

86. Loudspeakers should not be allowed to operate after 10 p.m.
(Action: Jt. CP/Ranges)

22.11.2010

87. PCR Vans were directed to keep a Log Book to register complaints of individuals who suffer a crime within the vicinity of the PCR Van and come and report the

same to the person incharge of the PCR Van. LG also emphasized the urgency to keep the proposal for ensuring that the mega city of Delhi is secure by creating a fire ball round it is on the fast track in the MI-IA.

29.11.2010

88. LG directed that cab drivers of BPO should be issued instructions to ensure the safety and security of the passengers they carry from call centres to their residences at night. Dehi Police should devise ways and means to check whether these instructions are being implemented and those who are negligent should be criminally prosecuted.

89. Existence of unsafe buildings in Delhi reveals that there is general non compliance of people to laws and instructions issued regarding construction of safe buildings. That generally there is non-compliance to laws has to be curbed by Delhi Police by taking action against those who break the law.

90. Licenses of those who use two wheelers should be checked to ascertain their criminal background.

02.12.2010

91. A polite letter should be written by the area SHO to religious institutions concerned in case it comes to notice that its public address system is being used at a raised volume particularly after 10 PM and during early morning hours. *(Action: Jt. CPs/Ranges)*

21.12.2010

92. In view of stolen vehicles being used in Crime, LG directed that notification u/s 144 Cr.PC be issued to mandate that the sellers of the vehicles and its buyers should be identified by pasting their attested photographs on the sale documents that are filed with the Transport Authorities. The notification should stipulate the period during which all documentation should be completed.

93. Wherever CCTV cameras are installed and will be installed in future they should have a recording provision of 30 days. CP may ensure that this directive is implemented through necessary notifications/directives etc.

23.12.2010

94. As a crime prevention measure, in order to reduce/prevent crime, it is necessary that healthy sports activities are organized for the youth who are idle and at a loose end. Delhi Police Officers should look for public land, especially in areas of Police Stations where crimes take place by youths, and recommend construction of sports grounds on the patterns of SOCCO-5. DDA will then be advised to take follow up action. *(Action: Spl. CP Crime/VC DDA)*

95. It should be examined whether police could formulate some arrangements of title verification of properties till a Titling law on the basis of Torrens system is enacted. *(Action: Spl. CP/Crimes)*

96. Whenever Beat constables come across a car with tinted glasses, they should locate the owner of the car. If the owner lives within the Beat, he should ask him to remove the tinted film from the car failing which he should be prepared to face prosecution by Traffic Police. *(Action: Jt.CP Ranges)*

97. Whenever Delhi Police participates in removing vendors from public land

at the instance of a land owning agency, it should be ensured, to the extent possible, that some alternative place for vendors is assigned by the land owning agency.

(Action: Jt.CP Ranges/Commissioner MCD/VC DDA/Divisional Commissioner)

98. Instances of snatching are on the rise in some Police Stations, at a particular time of day or night. Such Police Stations should be identified and mentioned in the Law and Order presentations with full details. These areas should be better policed at those hours when snatchings occurred. *(Action: Jt. CP Ranges/Spl. CP/Crime)*

99. The fact of arrest of robbers in nearly one-third of cases of road robberies may be publicized seeking further public co-operation in such cases.

(Action: Jt. CP Ranges/Spl.CP Crime)

100. There are many areas where illegal parking is taking place at the instance of the mafia and muscle men. Such areas are not authorized by the land owning agencies. The parking sites proposed by MCD may be jointly inspected with them and decision of Delhi Police regarding grant of NOC to these sites expedited. *(Action: Spl. CP Admn)*

27.12.2010

101. Arrest and apprehension of Biker gangs in Delhi needs to be continued in an organized manner.

06.01.2011

102. In view of stolen vehicles being used in crime, orders should be issued under appropriate provision of law making it mandatory for agents selling such veh icles to provide photographic details of both buyers and sellers to Delhi Police within one week of the transaction. The order should also stipulate the period by which all documentation of selling/buying is to be completed.

(Action: Spl. CP/Crime)

103. A significant number of crimes of murder take places on account of enmity between parties. A conscious effort should be made by Range and District Officers to prevent murders on account of known cases of enmity between persons/groups by taking preventive measures well in time.

(Action: Jt. CP/Ranges)

17.01.2011

104. At least 100 PCR cars will be deployed with Sub-Inspectors at the wheel along with one Head Constable with instructions to be multi tasked to prevent crimes on roads and also to check traffic violations.

03.02.2011

105. A list of compames which are providing transport services to employees of BPOslMultinational companies should be made. The proprietor/managers of these companies may be called to brief them about the security measures they are required to adopt. *(Action: Spl. CP/Crime)*

106. Crime Branch may collect the figures of persons arrested andrecoveries made during surprise check ing carried out by putting up barricades.

(Action: SpI.CP/Crime)

107. Action against touts be taken under the newly enacted Anti-touting Act.

(Action: Jt. CPs/Ranges)

108. It should be confirmed if all the liquor vends have installed CCTV Cameras as directed. *(Action: Jt. CPs/Ranges)*

109. Need to notify early that vehicles should give way to ambulances and police vehicles proceeding on emergent law & order and relief duties by keeping the extreme right lane free for them. *(Action: Spl. CP/Traffic)*

21.02.2011

110. In view of the fact that Delhi Police is tackling juvenile crime which commits 25% of the crime in Delhi, CP has been directed to submit a note limiting the juvenile law to limit relief to those juvenile criminals who are criminals by accident of birth and circumstances only. Other juveniles who repeatedly indulge in crime should not have the protection of the juvenile law, a practice which is followed in some of the Western countries like the United States of America.

03.03.2011

111. Number of surprise checking by pickets should be stepped up. reak up of checking by fixed pickets and surprise pickets should also be given. *(Action: Jt. CPs/Ranges)*

112. A presentation may be given at the next meeting on number, natureand time of calls received in PCR on telephone number 100 and the response time of PCR Vans. *(Action: Jt. CP/Ops)*

113. Juvenile offenders involved in snatching, etc. Crimes should be given an opportunity to rehabilitate themselves by sending them to Industrial Training Institutes (it is) for industrial training. *(Action: Jt. CPs/Ranges)*

14.03.2011

114. Breach of security in the issue of pre-paid mobile cards in huge numbers, based on false and fake identity documents of applicants by service providers creates hurdles in the investigations of terrorist and other heinous crimes. There is need to tighten the identity norms that govern issue of prepaid mobile numbers. The Telecom Department needs to be addressed to make changes urgently.

115. Taking serious note of toxic fruits and vegetables sold in the open market, LG directed the CP to ensure that the serious issues impacting public health be taken up with Director, Food Adulteration Prevention, GNCT Delhi. Officials colluding with sellers of toxic goods and vegetables be dealt with under criminal laws of the country.

28.03.2011

116. priority in all areas specially in the areas of heinous investigation and commando training.

04.04.2011

117. LG renewed his instructions to ensure that the excise policy should have a clause making it mandatory for all liquor vendors including Govt. owned outlets to install CCTV cameras outside their vends with 30 days recording facility.

18.04.2011

118. CP will ensure that there are regular meetings with the different groups from the North East of India also known as Seven Sisters from time to time to ensure that their security and safety concerns are heard and measures taken to reduce the element of fear which possesses the people from the North East who live in Delhi and earn their livelihood.

119. De-addiction centres for providing care and treatment of drug addicts arrested on charges and then remanded to judicial custody need to be ensured. In the light of revelations that drug addict figures are escalating in Delhi, Delhi Police should play a stellar role in the functioning of more de-addiction centres in Delhi to rehabilitate as many drug addicts as possible.

21.04.2011

120. St. John Ambulance and Red Cross Society should be requested to supply illustrative leaflets to all PCR Vans regarding precautions to be taken for different types of injury. *(Action: Spl. CP/Operators and OSD to LG)*

25.04.2011

121. LG specified to the Principal Secretary (Home) that a liquor vending policy in this financial year should ensure the incorporation of rules and regulations mandating placement of CCTV cameras covering 50 meters outside all Govt. licensed liquor vends.

122. Issues which need to be settled on priority involving the Delhi Police and MCD, Delhi Police and the NDMC and Delhi Police and the DDA should be listed out and conveyed to the LG's Secretariat for follow up action. If required, a meeting across the board for immediate decision on a specific urgent or otherwise intractable issue could be organized.

123. The CP should obtain an assessment from the concerned administrative head in GNCT with respect to power and water situation during the summer of 201. This report will be useful to make preparations for anticipated law & order situations in pockets of Delhi where power and water situation may worsen in the summer of 2011 .

02.05.2011

124. On the report that public parks became hideouts for criminals between 3.00 am and 5.00 am in the morning, LG directed that PCR vans located near parks should conduct searching operations during these hours in the parks close to their location.

125. Keeping the public parks well lighted throughout the night is important to prevent crime as unlit parks provide an opportunity to criminals to commit crimes and take shelter there after crime. Member Engineering, DDA is already under instructions to ensure that all DDA parks are well lit. OSD(SS) was directed to follow up the pace of lighting of DDA controlled public parks with Member Engineering, DDA.

126. District level meeting with Member of Parliament presiding or in his absence the District Police Chief chairing the meeting with MLA of the area being present along with local representatives should take place once in two months. All points that are actionable may be acted upon expeditiously and participants informed of the action taken.

127. Pr. Secretary (Home) was directed to examine the possibility of incorporating rules allowing direct recruitment of Sub-Inspectors of Police in Delhi Police by the CP under the recruitment procedure that is in place in Delhi Police.

128. Jamia area being a sensitive area from the point of law & order, presence of criminal elements, high density population continued unauthorized encroachment/construction suffers from low standard of civic amenities and police presence etc. Delhi Police should make an effort to ensure improved living conditions, better civic amenities, better police presence by making

special efforts through regular interaction with representatives of residents living in Jamia Nagar area of Okhla.

09.05.2011

129. Drug addiction among juveniles and students belonging to the affluent classes in Delhi is becoming alarming. Crimes that take place following drug addiction require that adequate information about drug addiction among the students and juveniles in the affluent classes is collected by creating and tapping sources among principals and teachers in academic institutions, their relations and their parents and any other source deemed necessary.

130. Shriram Institute for Industrial Research, 19, University Road, Delhi-7 should be increasingly referred to for testing consumable food items seized from the market when suspected to be unfit for human consumption.

131. The Commissioner of Police conveyed that PCRs who are the first to reach a scene of crime will henceforth, physically fence and protect the entire scene of crime. Further, Jt. CP (Crime) will ensure that in investigation of crimes all Investigating Officers use DNA tests to fix identity of criminals. Additionally, in a bid to keep a check on bad characters and criminals, specified members of the beat staff will be assigned by name such hard core criminals to continuously monitor their criminal activity and log the same.

19.05.2011

132. Principal Secretary (Home) should examme the desirability, feasibility and modalities of registering and regulating placement agencies offering maids and domestic servants. Appropriate advertisements should also be issued on the subject. (Action: Ppi. Secy. *(Home) & Spl. CP/Crime)*

133. In view of reports of substantial increase in drug seizure, District Police Chiefs, and other officers on his instruction, should interact with principal and teachers in educational institutions under their jurisdiction to collect information of the students who are believed to be taking drugs. Rehabilitation measures thereafter should be taken to stop drugs intakes by such students. Sale of ice-cream/candy, etc outside school gates should be checked/watched to prevent their adulteration with addictive drugs. *(Action: Jt. CP/Ranges)*

30.05.2011

134. CP reported that Jamia Nagar continues to be a very sensitive area where disruption, violence, incidents with communal overtones can erupt. The LG directed that apart from police continuing to deal with all apprehensions, the SDM of the area should hold regular Darbars with residents to listen to the grievance and amileorate them. Installation of CCTV cameras around the Police Stations and other sensitive areas duly protected from damage should also be installed.

135. SDMs of Delhi have to be activated to ensure that they exercise their executive functions as assigned to them specifically in Chapter-X Criminal Procedure Code with due diligence and care. In this regard, already detailed orders have been issued by the Divisional Commissioner.

02.06.2011

136. Crime prone poorly lit street/roads by identified and concerned civic agencies be informed to provide and pay for the required street lights.

(Action: Jt. CP/Ranges)

04.07.2011

137. Under the Juvenile Act, all juveniles are protected from being treated as criminals when apprehended for crimes committed by them. Increasingly, adult criminals are using them for crimes and escaping action by the Police. The Police and the Social Welfare Department were directed to work together on schemes to wean away juveniles from criminal activities by ensuring that they are involved in education, training and other sporting etc. activities which are also simultaneously made remunerative by the Social Welfare Department.

21.07.2011

138. Beat Constables should be directed to note down registration numbers of parked vehicles with tinted glasses for appropriate legal action.

(Action: Jt. CPs/Ranges/Traffic)

139. The number of trained spotters should be substantially increased. Criminals like snatchers, bank robbers, terrorist planning bomb blats, stalkers etc. should be spotted and actioned before they are able to execute their plans.

(Action: Sp!. CP/Sp!. Cell)

25.07.2011

140. The movement of young males at late night hours including early morning in group in a SUV should invariably be checked and if the occupants look and behave suspiciously, they should be detained and allowed to go on ly after there is complete assurance about their movements.

141. Special efforts to develop contacts among educated classes in the minority community (muslims) shou ld be made by all ranks in Delhi Police to collect information and intelligence about possible criminals/terrorist activities known to them.

142. Quarterly meetings with MPs, with MLAs participating, should be regularly held by District Police Chiefs.

143. The number of trained observers (spotters) among Delhi Police personnel watching out for suspicious criminal behavior especially in vulnerable sites in Delhi should be accelerated.

01.08.2011

144. Security Agencies are required to ensure that those recruited by them for security guard duty are trained in the Training Centre notified by the Home Department and their antecedents verified by reference to the Police Station under whose jurisdiction they live. This exercise has not yet commenced and the LG desired that these directions may be implemented immediately.

22.09.2011

145. Registration of private security agencies should be an going process, not limited to the month of April every year. Draft training norms for private security guards should be hosted on the web-site of Home Deptt. for inviting comments. *(Action: Ppl. Secy. (Home)*

146. Police men on duty in PCR Vans should be alert to locate, identify and apprehend those whose suspicious behavior suggests that they may be planning a crime. Each PCR Van should carry a list of abnormal behavior patterns of potential criminals and watch out for their activities in the areas they patrol. (Action : Spl. Commissioner (PCR)

10.10.2011

147. The issue of extortionists and land mafia in collusion with the local police making demands on the common man has come to the attention of the hon'ble LG. Such criminals and their associates in Delhi Police should be identified and dealt with in the most tringent terms.

148. South Campus Delhi University women students and teachers should receive complete protection from harassment while in the Campus.

149. At night all areas in Delhi which are crime prone should be well lit. Delhi Police should identify such areas and direct the di scoms and the civic authorities, the MCD, NDMC, DDA, PWD etc. who ever be the land owning agency to have such areas well lit. That civic authority must take steps to immediately Carry out these directions as this concerns the security of Delhi and its residents.

13.10.2011

150. It should be examined whether a special corps of "Spotters" can be developed in Delhi Police and specially trained to keep a watch at Rai lway Stations, Bus Terminals, religious places, etc. The job of spotters will be to watch and detect suspicious movements and unnatural behviour showing furtiveness.

(Action: Spl.CP/Spl. Cell). /SI)

151. Commissioner, Transport should examine if driving licenses of the drivers convicted in criminal cases can be revoked or suspended.

(Action: Commissioner/Transport & Jt. CP/Traffic)

24.10.2011

152. LG pointed out that accident prone areas are (1) small gas cylinders bursting and (2) people mowed down by vehicles as they rest/leep on pavements/ verges. Delhi Police should take preventive measures.

28.10.2011

153. Ranges should keep a sharp look out for building Mafioso, who may indulge in property related crimes and extortion from businessman. Statutory provision under NSA, MCOCA etc. may be invoked against these persons. SHOs of the areas prone to such crimes may be asked about their requirements, in terms of additional men, transport and equipment, to effectively tackle such crimes.

(Action: Spl. CP/L &O & Jt. CPs/Ranges)

31.10.2011

154. On the issue of security in the Metro, CP was advised to ensure that DMRC installs CCTV cameras in all Metro coaches. Since DMRC is using TETRA communication network which is JAWA enabled, immediately a CCTV footage of any criminal on the Metro coach can be flashed and crime prevented/detected.

155. Co-ordination between Delhi Police and City Police in the NCR region should be regular and closely coordinated at the appropriate level. Possibility of unverified tenants and unverified servants in the NCR Region committing crimes including terrorist crime in Delhi is a possibility and close co-ordination to ensure such verification is essential.

156. LG reiterated need to ensure that there are adequate number of special spotters in Delhi Police. Their training has to be of the highest order and expert trainers may be appointed by engaging Consultives who can then train Delhi Police trainers who will in turn train the spotters.

11.11.2011

157. Delhi Police may share any information they have about Interstate gun running rackets/illicit manufacturing bases with MHA so that concerned states can be mandated to take proper action through Govt. of India also.

(Action: Spl. CP/Crime)

14.11.2011

158. Jamia Nagar area continues to be in the regular scanner of Delhi Police. SHO of Jamia Nagar is under instructions to identify trouble spots and take adequate measures to prevent any disorder. The CP complimented the SHO for his zeal and hard work in the trouble spots of Jamia Nagar.

21.11.2011

159. Fire resistant tentage of non-combustible material be made compulsory for use in all functions where there are fire hazards. Simultaneously, practices in other States in order to prevent fire on such occasions may also be ascertained and implemented.

160. The role of the SDM as a constituent of the Disaster Management Authority of Delhi of the area to prevent disaster where social functions take place, needs to be delineated. He should be in the loop whenever, functions, where there is presence of one thousand persons or more, take place. He will be made responsible to take all steps necessary to prevent any kind of disaster.

161. To meet security concerns, the Delhi Police should not wait for NOC from civic authority for cutting up road etc. After dong the needful like digging trenches, cutting up roads etc., the Delhi Police should also restore the area. Similarly for security reasons where DDA land is required for parking of vehicles, such vacant land should be appropriated for such use by Delhi Police under intimation to DDA and used for parking till DDA begins construction activity on the land.

24.11.2011

162. All SHOs may be directed to ensure effective control is kept on active and desperate criminals.

163. In crime prone areas like Seelampur, Mangolpuri, Bawana etc. high police visibility be ensured by rationalizing/increasing deployment.

(Action: Spl. CP/L &0 and Jt. CP/Ranges)

28.11.2011

164. CP explained in detail action that is being taken by the Crime Branch undetected.

165. LG instructed the CP to select important detections, investigations, prosecutions etc. for analytical case studies. Such researched ocumentation of crimes will serve to spread knowledge about methods of investigation, detection, prosecution handled by Delhi Police personnel.

05.12.2011

166. LG reiterated the need for installing anti-theft devices in all four wheelers by car manufacturing Industries in their factories before sale of these vehicles. Another letter in this connection wi11 be issued to the hon'ble Minister of Heavy Industries by the hon' ble LG.

05.01.2012

167. Constant watch be maintained to prevent possibility of anti-social elements

indulging in extortion particularly in the area of rural Police Stations.
(Action: Spl. CP/L&O & Jt. CPs/Ranges)

168. Sensitize field officers about the ruling of the Hon' ble Supreme Court of India regarding invalidity of immovable property transactions through Power of Attorney. *(Action: Spl. CPIL&O, Jt. CPs/Ranges)*

01.03.2012

169. Concerned electric power distribution companies be tasked to provide/ repair street lighting in crime prone poorly lit areas in a time bound manner under intimation to Hon'ble LG's office. *(Action: Jt. CP/Ranges)*

170. Surprise 'Nakas' by changing location/timings be set up. Staff should be briefed about suspicious behaviors etc. which should be spotted during such checking. *(Action: Spl. CPs/Ops., Law & Order & Jt. CPs/Ranges)*

171. Constant watch be maintained to prevent emergence of any budding Mafioso. *(Action: Jt. CPs/Ranges)*

172. Process for amending Delhi Shops and Establishments Rules, 1954 be initiated to incorporate rules mandating deployment of armed guards where shops/ establishments handling cash remain open after 09.00 PM.
(Action: Pr Secretary (Home)

173. Regular checking of guest houses be ensured. *(Action: Jt. CPs/Ranges)*

174. Whenever novice criminals indulging in offences like snatching etc. are apprehended, an endeavour be made to ascertain their reasons for joining the life crime. Assistance of a trained social psychologist should also be obtained for debriefing/counseling. Effort should be to reform such persons.
(Action: Spl. CP/Crime & Jt. CPs/Ranges)

15.03.2012

175. Watch be maintained on budding criminals in areas like Bawana, Narela, Najafgarh etc. *[Action: Jt. CP/Ranges]*

176. A review of bad characters registered with Police Stations may be periodically ensured. If a bad character seeks to explain his conduct, he should be heard by the DCP/Jt.CP and given a chance to explain why he should be de-listed as bad character. *[Action: Jt. CP (All Ranges)*

03.04.2012

177. During Inter-State Coordination meeting, concerned police agencies and concerned states be urged to take effective follow-up action on disclosures made by criminals arrested with illicit country-made firearms regarding location of illicit weapon manufacturing facilities in the adjoining states.
[Action : Spl.CP/Crime]

178. A note on acquittals in Arms Act cases be submitted to enable Chief Secretary, GNCTD to take up the issue with appropriate quarters.
[Action: Spl. CP/Spl. Cell].

179. Constant watch be maintained to prevent emergence of any budding Mafioso. *[Action: Jt. CPs/Ranges]*

180. MCD should issue an order directing all concerned to notify the local police station at least one week before excavation of any basement, to enable the local police to check whether requisite permissions have been obtained.
[Action: Commissioner, MCD and Spl. CP/L&o]

23.04.2012

181. Alert citizens of Delhi should be invited through messages on Delhi Police website, advertisements on the FM etc. to alert the nearest policemen, the Beat or the PCR or the Chowki or the Police Station or any senior officer as the case may be whenever they apprehend some heinous crime is likely to take place. Their identity need not be revealed.

182. Pr. Secretary (Home) was requested by the hon' ble LG to keep a close watch on the progress of the following proposals at SI.(a) and (b) from the LG sent to the Home Department and SI. (c) sent to the Ministry of Heavy Industry.

183. Deterrent action against sale of SIM cards by cellular cos. distributors without proper verification of the buyers.

184. Deterrent action against juveniles who repeatedly commit heinous cnmes.

185. Getting manufacturers of 4 wheeled cars to install secure anti-theft devices in the factory before marketing their products.

17.05.2012

186. How sensitive law and order situations have been handled should be documented as case studies for future reference and training. Suitable honorarium can be given to the police officers undertaking this task.

(Action: CP/Spl. Spl. CP/Intelligence, Crime and L&O)

187. Timelines for installation of street lights in Bawana be ascertained from DSIDC and thereafter adherence to the timelines be ensured.

(Action: Principal Secretary (Home)

21.05.2012

188. Complaints against management of number of placement agencies in Delhi have been reported. The Labour Department, GNCTD has taken steps to monitor the functioning of the placement agencies in Delhi. Pr. Secretary (Home) was directed to follow up the matter with Labour Department. CP may be apprised of the action being taken by the Labour Department so that Delhi Police may associate itself with this work of Labour Department.

189. The Mewati gangs of Haryana are active in Delhi committing thefts of vehicles and cattle. Delhi Police should have intelligence about the leaders of the Mewati gangs and proceed thereafter to initiate stringent legal action against these leaders to render them ineffective in Delhi.

28.05.2012

190. Pro Secretary (Home) informed the LG about the progress on the following areas :-

   (i) Amendments to the Juvenile Act on the lines suggested by the hon'ble LG.

   (ii) Installation of anti-theft devices in the 4 wheelers before they are sold to customers.

   (iii) Control over areas where Mewatis reside by stationing detachment from the Central Para-Military Forces in those areas.

11.06.2012

191. Servant's verification data should include the age of the servant so that there is a record available to check if required at any stage whether the servant employed was a minor or a major on the date of verification.

18.06.2012

192. LG advised Pro Secretary (Home) to take up the issue of construction of De-Addiction Centres Shelters for Women and Children who are victims of domestic violence, Shelters for children rescued from factories etc. where they are illegally employed or other runaway children who are rescued and have no homes, with the Social Welfare Department, GNCTD. Gram Sabha land will be made available for such Centres and corporate houses may be called upon by the Welfare Department to shoulder their social responsibility in this regard by accepting to construct and manage such Centres on Gram Sabha land.

25.06.2012

193. The issue of safety devices including masks, oxygen cylinders and other equipments for cleaning of sewerage, tanks, channels was discussed. Instances of toxic gases causing skin infection, loss of eye sight, respiratory disorder and death caused grave concern. They need to be prevented if not eliminated. Responsibility may be fixed when such instances are reported.

194. All Police Stations officers be cautioned that not resolving disputes will lead to crime. All disputes reported to the Police Station by complainants should be duly heard and resolved and not dismissed as nonpolice work.

02.08.2012

195. A detailed note may be sent to Principal Secretary (Home) indicating facilities required to be provided at the Transit Home, Lampur, Delhi for safe stay of foreigners against whom restriction orders have been issued pending their deportation. *(Action: Spl. CP/L&O)*

196. Criminals gangs repeatedly operating in Delhi may be booked under MCOCA. *(Action: Jt. CPs/Ranges)*

197. Intensive checking of hotels, guest houses and other places where any undesirable person can hide be ensured till Independence Day Arrangements are over. Beat officers be briefed to keep a sharp lookout in their areas. *(Action: Jt. CPs/Ranges)*

198. Approval for granting concurrent powers to ACsP/Sub- Divisions under section 133 (1)(b) Cr. PC may be issued on priority. *(Action: Principal Secretary (Home)*

199. Random checking of group of youngsters travelling on four wheelers, particularly SUVs, be ensured. *(Action: Jt. CPs/Ranges)*

200. Wherever road ownmg agencies have taken requisite steps to improve road safety, formal appreciation could be conveyed to them. *(Action : Jt. CP/Traffic)*

201. Area security be provided where vulnerable establishments like Banks, Jewellers are located. *(Action: Jt. CPs/Ranges)*

18.10.2012

202. The Hon'ble LG wanted that in order to have an overview of "hot spots" of snatchings, each district should draw up bar charts of areas where this crime takes place. *(Action: Jt. CPs/Ranges)*

203. Delhi Govt. buildings and MCD buildings need to be surveyed from the security point of view and gaps noticed to be conveyed to the Delhi Govt. and MCD with copy to LG office. *(Action: Sp!. CP/Spl. Cell)*

30.10.2012

204. With the marriage season at hand, the CP was advised to ensure that carriage-

ways are not blocked, noise of music is kept within restricted hours and dancing is not permitted so as to block vehicular movement by those who are participating in marriages.

13.12.2012

205. No laser shows should be permitted in the funnel area of the 1GI Airport. Requisite order U/S 133 (1) (b) Cr. PC could be issued after the conferment of such powers on police. *(Action: Spl. CP/L&O)*

206. No violations having law and order implications should be ignored and appropriate action should be taken to prevent their snow-balling into major problems. *(Action : Jt. CPs/Ranges)*

207. MCOCA should be applied in respect of persons belonging to criminal gangs. *(Action: Spl. CP/Crime, Spl. CP/Cell and Jt. CPs/Ranges)*

208. Maintenance of History Sheets of Bad Characters should be carefully monitored by District DCsP. In various cases of ternment, it has seen that history sheets need to be reviewed. The existing history sheets be reviewed at the level of DCP monitored by the Jt. CP of the range to ensure that only those criminals are retained as bad character with history sheets who are active in the are of crime. Those who are not active as criminals may be deleted from the history sheets of respective Police Station. *(Action: Jt. CP/Ranges)*

209. Hon'ble LG referred to the large number of motor cycle borne criminals creating panic in the city and wanted these incidents to be brought under firm control immediately. He stressed upon the need to properly brief/debrief the staff of the PCR. He wanted personnel with high motivation levels to be posted in the PCR and that unsuited personnel be identified and posted out. The LG also wanted Delhi Police to examine whether special pay can be given to those posted in PCR Units. *(Action : Jt. CPs/Ranges, Spl. CP/lnt.)*

10.01.2013

210. Concerned road maintenance authorities be informed that non functional street Lights must be rectified within 24 hours of being informed of the same. *[Action: Pro Secy. (Power) and all Jt. CP of Ranges]*

211. Assistance of willing retired govt. servants, ex-serviceman, Civil Defence volunteers could be obtained for joint patrolling in vulnerable areas. *[Action: Jt. CPs/Ranges]*

212. Night checking officers should visit police stations to prevent possibility of any delinquency on the part of police personnel. *[Action: Jt. CPs/Ranges]*

213. Unclaimed vehicles lying at police stations should be auctioned after giving due and adequate notice to owners and sale proceeds thereof deposited in govt. account. Whenever any rightful claimant comes forward, money realized during auction in respect of his vehicle can be given to him after adjusting admissible & reasonable changes. Wherever necessary, orders of the competent Court shold be obtained for early disposal of vehic1es lying at police stations as property. *[Action: Jt.CPs/Ranges]*

214. PCR Vans while on patrol duties should keep a sharp look out for suspected criminals and immediately alert the local police to check on them. *[Action: Spl. CPIPCR & Jt. CPs/Ranges]*

14.02.2013

215. Advance liaison with the organizers of protest programmes should be held to enlist their co-operation. Police personnel should be sensitized to behave patiently with the participants and not fall prey to any provocation. In particular, utmost respect and courtesy should be shown to women participants. Wherever organizers do not keep their commitment of staging a peaceful protest and preventive measures are taken, sensitive dealing with women protesters has to be invariably. *[Action: Spl. CP/L&O and Jt. CPs/lRanges]*

216. State Transport Authority may be advised that the GPS linked panic buttons in TSRs and other public transport vehicles should not only be linked with their Control Room but should also set off a loud siren to attract immediate help from people around. [Action: Spl. CP/Ops.]

217. Speedy verification of Public Service Vehicle (PSV) badge applicants may be ensured. *[Action: Spl.CP/Int.]*

218. All Police Stations should be visited by surprise at least three/four times a month by earmarked officers and the visit note should mention among other things how complainants, specially women and senior citizens are being treated by the Police Help Desk. *[Action: Jt. CP/Ranges, Spl. CP/Law and Order]*

4.3.2013

219. CP, Delhi was asked to consider issuing directions to ensure that equitable action to maintain Law & Order must ensure that the party mainly responsible for breach of peace is held to account. The practice of issuing a kalandra involving both parties should be an exception rather than the rule in such circumstances. Equitable action should mean justice for the victim who may have also breached the peace but has been compelled to do so on account of unwarranted and manipulated action by the opposite party.

14.03.2013

220. An application may be moved in the Hon' ble Supreme Court of India to implead MHA as a party in the matter regarding provision of security cover for protected persons. *[Action: Spl. CP/Security]*

221. Surprise checks be conducted to assess the alertness of PCR staff. *[Action: Spl.CP/Ops.]*

222. Local police should maintain a close look out for any budding Mafioso and take preventive action against such elements. *[Action: Jt. CPs/Ranges]*

11.4.2013

223. Broad classification of complaints against Police received during the Jan Sampark Programme be indicated. Particular attention should be paid to the complaints against police officers. *[Action: Spl. CP/Crime & Jt. CPs/Ranges}*

224. Continued watch be maintained on activities of criminals operating from Mewat region. *[Action: Spl. CP/Crime & Spl. CP/L&O]*

225. Periodic telephone contact be maintained with the office bearers of IFS Officers Housing Society, Mayur Vihar to see that Rickshaw parking etc do not cause them avoidable inconvenience. *[Action: Spl. CP/Traffic and Jt. CP/SER]*

226. Temple authorities be advised to make adequate security arrangements

including deployment of spotters during Navratras and other such festivals. *[Action: Spl. CP/L &0 and Jt. CPs/Ranges]*

227. Whenever any incident of illegal tree felling is reported, prompt legal action should be taken by PCR as well as local police. *[Action : Spl. CP/Ops and Spl. CP/L&O]*

228. Religious structures on public streets/parks, etc should not be permitted to encroach on public lands. *[Action: Spl. CP/Ops and Spl. CP/L&O]*

25.04.2013

229. Complaints of land grabbing, which are received during Jan Sampark Sabhas, should be viewed seriously. Information should also be given to concerned land owning agency with copy to OSD (RM) to Hon'ble LG, Delhi. *[Action: Jt. CPs/Ranges]*

230. Number of inputs received from public giving information about suspicious activities on the part of any individual/individuals indicating possible involvement in terrorist activity be indicated. *[Action: Spl. CP/Spl. Cell]*

231. A draft letter be put up for Hon'ble Union Telecom Minister from Hon'ble LG, Delhi to direct at mobile service providers to ensure installation of location based servers. *[Action: Spl. CP/Spl. Cell]*

232. Technology Tracking Cell should continuously monitor newer technologies relevant for policing and security of women/senior atizens etc. *[A ction: Spl. CP/Traffic]*

233. Feasibility of shifting of gas godowns around Jhandewalan Temple to some other location be urgently examined. *[Action: Jt. CP/CR & Principal Commissioner LD-DDA]*

09.05.2013

234. Complaints/issues relating to other Civic Bodies, raised by schools with PCR officials, be conveyed to OSD (RM) to Hon'ble LG to enable appropriate tasking of concerned agencies. *[Action: Spl. CP/Ops]*

235. Clarificationl Information sought by Delhi Police regarding black listed driving licensees may be provided on priority . *[Action: Commissioner Transport]*

236. IOC be asked to shift the gas godowns from Jhandewalan in a time bound manner and outcome reported to LG's office. *[Action: Jt. CP/CR]*

30.05.2013

237. The number of cases closed by EOW which were not to the satisfaction of the complainants and for which they continue to seek registration of FIRs may be indicated. *[Action: Spl. CP/Crime]*

238. Police to ensure close watch on the activities of criminals indulging in mafia like behaviour. If any police officer is found conniving with them or tolerating their activities, strict action should be taken.

Improving Security of Women

25.04.2008

1. Reception Hostels for women in distress may be established in each district of Delhi as transit accommodation for women in di stress.

   (Action- Sp!. CP/Admn)

15.10.2008

2. Complaints from women regarding stalking or harassment should be promptly looked into. *(Action: Jt. CPs/Ranges)*

05.02.2009

3. Lady Constables should be deployed in slums and areas lacking civic amenities. They should interact with women in slums and identify potential eve teasers/molesters. Appropriate preventive action should then be taken.

   (Action- Jt. CPs/Ranges)

19.02.2009

4. The Hon'ble LG appreciated the response to the newly started helplines put up by the Delhi Police and wanted additional information such as how many women had approached the police and the nature of their grievances, the action taken and whether the matter was finally sorted out satisfactorily.

   (Action- Jt. CPs/Crime, Ranges and Addl. CP/Ops)

05.03.2009

5. Women beat constables should maintain contact with girls/women in settlement colonies to forestall rape and molestation.

   (Action; Jt. CPs/Ranges)

19.03.2009

6. Lady Constable may be deployed in Sangam Vihar to prevent crime against women. *(Action- Jt. CP/SR)*

30.04.2009

7. Women Beat Constable may be deployed for preventive surveillance in areas prone to crime against women. *(Action- Jt. CP/Ranges)*

28.05.2009

8. Stem action should be taken against stalkers of women like binding them under bonds of good behaviour etc. *(Action: Jt.CPs/Ranges)*

11.06.2009

9. The ACR proforma for police officers should include a column regarding the officer's attitude towards women in distress. *(Action: Jt. CP/Hdqrs)*

20.08.2009

10. Parivartan Scheme may be introduced in the area under P.S Swaroop Nagar to prevent cases of molestation/rape etc. *(Action- It. CPINR)*

11. Patrolling by women constables/officers in slums and other congested areas for the safety of women should be intensified. *(Action - Jt. CPs/Ranges)*

22.10.2009

12. A letter should go from CP to Commissioner (Transport) firmly advising that antecedents of all drivers of public service vehicles such as Taxis, auto-rickshaws, cabs etc. must be got verified from the police and they should also carry biometric photo- i.d. cards while driving the vehicles. Permits be issued only after police verification. *(Action- CP)*

13. Success in controlling eve- teasing and molestation of women should be projected in the media. *(Action- Jt. CP/Crime)*

07.01.2010

14. The high incidents of rape registered at PS Neb Sarai and PS Jaitpur should be looked into for possible causes and steps should be initiated through schemes like Parivartan to reduce/eliminate crimes of rape in the jurisdiction of these two Police Stations. *(Action- Jt. CP/Ranges)*

15.04.2010

15. A public message may be given in the media for reporting stalking/shadowing cases. *(Action- CP)*

06.05.2010

16. An analysis of areas with high number of molestation of women cases, in buses and otherwise, should be presented at the next meeting. *(Action: Jt. CP/Crime)*

08.07.2010

17. Dr. Shyam Menon of B. R. Ambedkar University may be contacted to carry out an external audit of the working 0f the Crime Against Women and Children Cell of Delhi Police to ensure that all the directions issued in respect of handling of crimes against women and children are being followed and implemented. *(Action- Jt. CP/CAW)*

18. There should be an independent website of Crime Against Women and Children Cell of Delhi Police, in addition to the existing link in Delhi Police Website. (Action- Jt. CP/CA W)

02.12.2010

19. In the list of Do's and Don'ts issued to Beat Constable, suitable instructions to keep watch on habitual eve-teasers/stalkers and prevent molestation of women should be incorporated. *(Action- Jt. CPs/Ranges)*

23.12.2010

20. Implementation of directions issued to BPOs by Delhi Police regarding transportation of lay employees during night should be constantly monitored. Digital data of drivers on BPO cabs should be updated on a regular basis.
(Action- Jt. CPs/Ranges)

21. Posting of constables at bus stops instills a sense of security in female commuters and should , therefore be done, whenever feasible .
(Action- Jt. CPs/Ranges)

03.02.2011

22. A list of companies which are providing transport services to employees of BPOs/multinational companies should be made. The proprietors/mangers of these companies may be called to brief them about the security measures they are required to adopt. *(Action- SpI.CP/Crime)*

03.03.2011

23. Figures of women complaints contacting the helpline and break up of follow up action taken should be given at the next meeting. *(Action- Spl. CP/Crime)*

17.03.2011

24. An advertisement may be issued requesting female BPO employees to report at the specified numbers in case a BPO engaged vehicle drops them at a place other than their places of stay during odd hours. *(Action: Spl. CP/Crime)*

19.05.2011

25. A feedback should be given at the next meeting regarding number of women complainants approaching women help desk in Police Stations in North-West District category wise. *(Action- Jt. CP/NR & DCP/NWD)*

13.10.2011

26. SPUW &C should find out the procedure being followed in developed countries to deal with domestic violence. It should be found out if these countries have a system of publicly funded Reception Homes to accommodate the victims of domestic violence temporarily. *(Action- Jt. CP/SPUW &C)*

28.10.2011

27. All DTC Bus stops In North and South Campus be covered by police deployment. *(Action- Spl. CP/L&O, Jt. CsPlRanges & Jt. CP ITraffic)*

28. Accused - victim relationship in rape cases reported in Mumbai and Chennai may be obtained to compare our situation in this regard.
(Action- Spl. CP/Crime)

11.11.2011

29. A study may be undertaken, across all Police Stations over a given time period, number of women approaching Women Help Desks and feedback on their experience with their visits and assistance provided by the Desk. Sample statistics of calls received on Women Help Line during the period may also be compiled. *(Action- Spl. CP/Crime & Spl. CP/Ops)*

30. All bus stands at North & South Campus of Delhi University may be covered by police deployment. *(Action-Spl. CP/L&O & Jt. CPs/Ranges)*

20.11.2011

31. More emphasis needs to be given to 'Parivartan' scheme in areas affected by crime against women. *(Action- Jt. CP/Ranges)*

02.02.2012

32. Molestation of women cases be analyzed to identify incidents here (i) other offences were not mixed with the offence outraging the modesty of women (Section 354 IPC); (ii) other offences were mixed with the offence. The offences may be further classified into two categories (a) at public places and (b) in public transport. *(Action- Spl. CP/Crime)*

33. Cases of rape be analyzed to ascertain their incidence in slums and areas inhabited by persons belonging to lower economic strata. *(Action- Spl. CP/Crime)*

15.03.2012

34. Trial of rape cases be expedited by setting up a dedicated courts for trial of rape cases only. *(Action- Spl. CP/Crime)*

35. Number of women who have approached the PCR Van seeking safe passage when feeling vulnerable at isolated spots may be furni shed *(Action- Spl. CP/Operations)*

36. Establishments like BPOs be directed to drop their women employees at their residence after 8 P.M *(Action- Spl. CP (L&O)*

03.04.2012

37. Proposal for constitution of Special Courts for trial of rape cases be pursued appropriately with Delhi High Court. *(Action- Chief Secretary, GNCTD)*

04.06.2012

38. Incidents of rape be analyzed to identify cases where teenagers are the accused. *(Action- Spl. CP/Crime)*

39. Appropriate verification of antecedents be carried out of the staff of Call Centres who have been assigned the task of responding to "Women in distress" helpl ine calls. *(Action- Spl. CP/Ops)*

19.07.2012

40. Areas prone to rape incidents be covered by the ' Parivartan' initiative. *(Action- Jt.CPs/Ranges)*

23.08.2012

41. A four digit single help line number for women in distress be designated and publicized. *(Action- Spl. CP/Ops.)*

15.10.2012

42. All rape cases ending in acquittal in trial Courts should be carefully considered for fili ng an appeal. Any decision not to file an appeal will be put up for the perusal of the hon'ble LG.

01.11.2012

43. There is a need to check whether the 'Women Help Desks' in police stations are getting complaints regarding stalking. *(Action- Jt. CP/Ranges)*

44. In order to encourage complaints and publicize the Domestic Violence Act, the Hon'ble LG wanted Delhi Police to put out advertisements in newspapers and on FM radio to make complainants aware that complaints of eve teasing, lewd behavior and stalking will lead to stringent action by the Police. *(Action- Spl. CP/Crime)*

10.01.2013

45. The Law and Order Meeting discussed proactive steps to ensure zero tolerance towards deviant behavior towards women. On a report by Jt. CP Range that there is manifold increase in complaints being reported by women at the Women's Police desks in the Police Station it was ordered that a break-up of complaints lodged by women be collated suitably and analysed. This analysis be put up for LG's perusal. *[Action: Spl. CP/Crime and Jt. CPs/Ranges]*

46. Feedback be obtained from women NGOs and other respectable groups to ascertain public perception about the enhanced preventive measures taken for safety of women. The "Parivartan" scheme should be expended to all Police Districts. *[Action: Jt. CPs/Ranges]*

47. Instructions be issued to DTC and Commissioner, Transport that whenever any crime against a woman passenger is committed, the bus should be taken to the nearest PCR/Police Post/Police Station. They should also switch on the headlights in the daytime to alert police personnel. A suitable advertisement may also be issued. *[Action: OSD to Hon'ble LG and Spl. CP/Crime]*

48. SHO's of all police stations should keep track of youth displaying deviant Tendencies and through Parivartan and other schemes ensure that they do not indulge in sexual crimes. *[Action: Jt. CPs/Ranges]*

49. Police presence by way of PCR/motorcycle/foot patrols be organized around girls/ co-ed schools and colleges. *[Action: Jt. CPs/Ranges]*

50. Advisory be sent to all media houses and other employers to make security mangement on the lines of BPOs for safe return to their homes for their women staff leaving offices after 2130 hours. *[Action: Spl. CP/Crime]*

51. Patrolling by Women Constables/officers in slums and other congested areas for the safety of women should be intensified. *(Action: Jt. CPs/Ranges)*

52. Review of effective implementation of steps taken to enhance safety of women will henceforth be a permanent agenda item of the LG's Law & Order meetings. *[Action: Jt. CPs/Ranges]*

53. Police Trainees should undergo gender sensitization training modules by involving reputed NGOs. *[Action: Spl.CP/Training]*

54. All calls made by women to the cell headed by Spl.CP/Traffic, should be fo llowed up and a record kept of the calls and their proper disposal. *[Action: Spl. CP/Traffic]*

55. Feedback about the effectiveness of PCR vans deployed around girls schools/ colleges should be obtained from the concerned principals and periodically reported in the Law & Order Meetings. *[Action: Spl.CP/Operations]*

56. Eve teasing, use of uncivilized language and harassment of women will invite serious actions against the defaulting police officials. *[Action: Jt. CPs/Ranges]*

57. Traffic patrols should also keep girls schools/colJeges covered during opening/closing hours to check activities of miscreants. *[Action: Spl. CP/Traffic]*

58. Section 65 of Delhi Police Act should be used, wherever appropriate, against persons loitering around girl schools/colleges. *(Action: Jt.CPs/Ranges)*

28.01.2013

59. Those women volunteers who have so far offered to serve as volunteers to provide security and safety etc. of women be accredited by Delhi Police to serve in that capacity within the jurisdiction of the Police Station/Stations that are mentioned in the accredition card, that is issued to them by Delhi Police.

30.1.2013.

60. Review of effective implementation of steps taken to enhance safety of men will henceforth be a permanent agenda item of the LG's Law & Order.
[Action: Jt. CPs /Ranges]

04.02.2013

61. The offer of several Women Rights Groups and NGOs to submit details of such volunteers, if received may be acted upon expeditiously.

62. Addl. CP (Licensing) may take a meeting of arms license holders Police Station wise and ascertain their willingness to volunteer to patrol areas within the Police Station jurisdiction of their place of stay to protect and keep safe women in public spaces. Such volunteers may be designated special volunteer to patrol designated areas to keep women safe and secure in Delhi.

14.02.2013

63. Students of Girls Schools and Colleges need protection from sexual harassment including eve teasing, stalking, molestation at times when schools and colleges open and close. *[Action: Jt. CPs/Range]*

64. Surprise inspections of Police Stations should inter alia focus on general alertness of staff, cleanliness of surroundings, working of women help desks and handling of general complaints. *[Action: Spl.CP/L&O]*

65. Incidence of molestation of women in public transport be indicated in the next meeting. *[Action: Spl. CP/Crime]*

04.3.2013

66. All women volunteers may be issued accredition cards with their photographs giving them responsibilities to visit Police Stations to do a third party audit about ambience of the Police Station and the functioning of its Women Help Desk.

14.3.2013

67. Information about prompt solution of cases involving crimes against women be suitably placed in the public domain. *[Action: Spl. CP/L&O]*

28.3.2013

68. Control Room should have a digital data base of all women/co- ed. educational institutions which are required to be watched by PCR vans at the time opens and at the time it closes. *[Action: Spl. CP/Ops.}*

69. Charge sheet in rape cases should be filed expeditiously.
[Action: Jt. CPs/Ranges}

70. Break up of molestation cases at ' roads ' indicating profile of the criminals (age, socio-economic status etc) be indicated during the next meeting.
[Action: Spl. Cp/Crime]

71. A suitable advertisement be issued advising school/college Principals to immediately inform Delhi Police at a dedicated telephone number at PHQ if

the girl students face any harassment around their schools/colleges or along the routes to such institutions. *[Action: Spi. CP/Traffic & Spl. CP/L&O]*

72. Women NGOs be told to keep Delhi Police informed whenever any instance of misbehavior with a woman by any police personnel comes to their notice *[Action: Spl. CP/Traffic.]*

73. Examine the feasibility of declaring no parking zones around girls schools/ colleges. *[Action: Spl. CP/Traffic.]*

5.04.2013

74. Accused victim relationship in respect of incidents of rapes involving minor victims should also be indicated. *[Action: Spl. CP/Crime]*
75. Break-up of strangers/known persons/ family involved in molestation and eve teasing cases be indicated. Economic status break-up of such accused persons be indicated. *[Action: Spl. CP/Crime]*
76. Periodic contact should be maintained with Principals of co-ed schools-colleges by DCsP to obtain their feedback regarding safety of girl students.

Security of Senior Citizen and Children

19.5.2011

1. Beat Officers should be directed to be on the look-out for cottage industries employing minors as labour. *(Action: Jt. CPs/Ranges)*

11.11.2011

2. Local SHOs/Beat Officers be provided with telephone numbers of senior citizens residing in their jurisdiction. They should contact them at least once a month and also periodically elicit their opinion and suggestions about state of policing in their areas. *(Action : Spl. CP/L&O Jt. CPs/Ranges)*

14.11.2011

3. Senior citizens living alone will be required to be contacted on a regular basis by responsible officers in the Police Stations in whose jurisdiction they are located. The beat constables will personally contact the Senior citizens once every month.

24.11.2011

4. Calls of Senior Citizens received in Police Stations, which are important and require action, should be immediately acted upon by SHOs. *(Action: Jt. CPs/Ranges)*

05.01.2012

5. Regular contract with Senior Citizens, particularly eminent persons law and order in the areas of residence. *(Action: Jt. CPs/Ranges)*

30.5.2012

6. Joint CPs/Ranges should maintain contact with senior citizens in their areas. They should pro-actively contact a few of them from time to time and

seek their feedback about the law and order situation in their locality.

[Action: Jt. CP/Ranges]

23.08.2012

7. Gender distribution of missing children be indicated during the next meeting. Causative factors behind missing children be also depicted by a pie chart.

(Action: Spl. CP/Crime)

11.9.2012

8. Occasional calls should be made to senior citizens from Senior citizens cells at PHQ as well as districts/police stations to enquire about their welfare and suggestions. Their feedback may be mentioned during the next meeting.

(Action: Jt. CPs/Ranges)

18.10.2012

9. The Hon'ble LG desired that each distinct should draw up a chart of crime against senior citizens. *(Action: Jt. CPs/Ranges)*

Improvement in Traffic

25.04.2008

1. A constant publicity campaign should be mounted to educate members of public to keep carriageways clear by not parking vehicles on them unauthorizedly. *(Action: Jt. CP/Traffic)*

22.05.2008

2. Traffic police should take the initiative in removing advertisements which are blocking traffic signals. Citizens should be invited/encouraged to give their suggestions on improving traffic-management. Contract details of the Traffic Management Center should be advertised for information of the general public. *(Action: Jt. CP/Traffic)*

3. Traffic experts should be used as 'sounding boards' on issues like demarcating "no entry zones". Traffic Management Centre should have its own email id. *(Action: Jt. CP/Traffic)*

4. Pedestrians should be given priority right of way. *(Action: Jt. CP/ traffic)*

04.09.2008

5. More attention needs to be paid to provide safety to pedestrians while crossing the roads. *(Action: Jt. CP/Traffic)*

19.02.2009

6. The Hon'ble LG also desired that sufficient time be made available to pedestrians to cross the road, for which the timings of the signal may have to be adjusted. He also desired that advisory communications to the public regarding the rules of the 'right of way' be issued. *(Action :Jt. CP/Traffic)*

30.04.2009

7. No driver of any public carrier/commercial vehicle be allowed to drive on

the strength of receipts for seized driving licenses. This should be urgently examined in consultation with Commissioner (Transport).

(Action: Commissioner (Tpt.)/Jt. CPs/Traffic & Ranges)

28.05.2009

8. During the ensuing Safe Pedestrian Drive, videography at important traffic junctions be done. *(Action: Jt. CPs/Traffic)*

23.07.2009

9. Delhi Traffic Police may undertake a community participation programme as part of Safe Pedestrian drive in which labels can be distributed for di splay on vehicles showing concern for pedestrians, e.g. "I respect pedestrian", "I stop at Zebra Line" etc. *(Action : Joint CP (Traffic)*

06.08.2009

10. A pilot project for solar traffic light signals may be given to BEL on nomination basis. *(Action: Jt. CP/Traffic)*

20.08.2009

11. During the next Safe Pedestrian Week, some intersections may be designated as 'Zero Tolerance Area" for any pedestrian right violations and violators be acted against as per law. Vehicles of the Institute of Road Traffic Education (IRTE) (Shri Rohit Baluja, President) could also be displayed for videography at these intersections. Video clips of both violations and compliance be shown in cinema halls for raising public awareness, about the need to ensure safe pedestrian crossings. *(Action; Jt. CP/Tarffic)*

12. A simulator may be installed at Teen Murti Traffic Police Lines for testing the efficiency of errant drivers. *(Action: Jt. CP/Traffic)*

13. Whenever there is water logging in underpass due to rains, the time taken to pump out the water by the concerned authorities should be logged.

(Action: Jt. CP/Traffic)

26.11.2009

14. The best global practices for pedestrian safety should be studied and those which can be implemented effectively in NCT Delhi should be placed before the LG. *(Action: Spl. CP/Traffic)*

30.11.2009

15. LG directed that carriage-ways should not be permitted to be blocked or reduced in space by parking of cars of people attending the marriage or by their blocking road in dancing and making merry on the carriage-ways blocking all traffic. Advertisements discouraging this activity should be published.

08.12.2009

16. There is urgent necessity of installing Solar Traffic Signals in Delhi that should be trouble free was reiterated. The CP was directed to set up a Price Negotiation Committee for installing Solar Traffic Signal. The expenditure incurred on installation of Solar Traffic Signals by BEL in Bangalore should be ascertained. An agreement with BEL at competitive rate to commence installing of Solar Traffic Signals at the earliest should then be carefully considered.

10.12.2009

17. A major media campaign may be launched for educating Delhi's drivers and pedestrians to improve pedestrian safety. *(Action: Spl. CP/Traffic)*

18. Errant heavy goods vehicle drivers may be asked to take special driving lessons at the Upper India Automobile Association's Institutional Area. *(Action: Spl. CP/Traffic)*

11.01.2010

19. The present Dhaula Kaun Bus Stop is an adhoc one where there are neither proper parking bays nor is it well lighted. The LG reiterated the need for proper bus parking areas and proper lighting. The CS has agreed that the PWD should take a hand in this and complete the entire operation of construction of parking bays and ensuring proper lighting within next 4 months. LG re iterated the need for completing the PWD road in the Okhla area. This road will serve also to prevent encroachment on Jamuna land. This is a repeat direction, the earlier ones having issued on 13.10.09 and 26. 10.09.

21.01.2010

20. In order to ensure free movement of emergency vehicles, a public education campaign for motorists and other road users should be launched. *(Action: Spl. CP/Traffic)*

25.02.2010

21. A review of the panel of lawyers for Motor Accident Compensation Tribunal may be carried out. *(Action: Secy. Home)*

22. Adequate publicity be arranged to educate members of public to vacate the extreme right lane whenever an emergency vehicle is on the move and blows the Seren. *(Action: Spl. CP/Traffic)*

01.04.2010

23. The blockage of carriageways by spillover of worshippers at places of worship is to be controlled/minimized in consultation with heads of such places of worship. Availability of land for construction of places of worship may be identified in consultation with DDA so that worshippers can avail of the facility of prayers/worship close to their place of residence. *(Action: Jt.CPs/Ranges)*

15.04.2010

24. For pedestrian safety at zebra crossings, traffic place should regulate pedestrian movement and support the needy i.e. disabled and old age pensions. At the next meeting, lists of crossings where Pelican signals are in proper working condition, and the crossings where these are not, should be brought. *(Action: Spl. CP/Traffic)*

25. Traffic Police may engage a creative communication advisor to develop a message for road users to bring about a change in their behaviour. The same may be sponsored by some corporate house for telecast and broadcasting purposes. *(Action: Spl. CP/Traffic)*

06.05.2010

26. Delhi Traffic Police should have its own unit to demarcate parking areas so that the main carriage-ways are not blocked by parked vehicles. *(Action: Spl. CP/Traffic)*

24.05.2010

27. LG has directed that Traffic Police should ensure that once an ambulance siren or fi re engine siren is heard, the entire traffic on the road should vacate the extreme right of the road to enable the ambulance or the fire engine to proceed to the destination without any hindrance from the on-going traffic.

24.06.2010

28. Educative advertisements should be published to the effect that mamage processions should not block public carriage - ways. *(Action : Jt. CP/Ranges)*

08.07.2010

29. Proper record of water logging affecting traffic should bemaintained the concerned agencies may be asked to give some incentives to pump operators. *(Action: S. CP/Traffic)*

30. MCD should bear the cost of restoration of damaged Traffic signals uprooted during street scaping. *(Action: Spl. CP/Traffic/Commissioner MCD)*

09.09.2010

31. The Traffic police may prepare a list of areas where debris has still ot been removed from carriage ways. Thereafter a meeting may take place between the Traffic Police, PWD, MCD, NDMC and DDA etc. to ensure removal. *(Action: Spl. Commissioner, Traffic)*

11.10.2010

32. LG took note of reports of traffic violations by motor-cycle riding youngsters at night on the Tilak Nagar Road and directed that such hooligans have to be curbed firmly and culprits be severely dealt with.

33. LG directed that the Traffic Police should create a Traffic Safety Unit within its existing strength. This Unit should carry out exercises to locate and identify where existing features are a risk to on-going traffic. The recommendation of the Safety Unit should then be reported to the UTTIPEC for necessary directions to eliminate such features on carriage way to ensure safe and secure traffic movements.

1.10.2010

34. Regular exercises should be conducted to train citizens to give the right of 11) to emergency vehicles. *(Action : Spl. CP/Traffic)*

15.11.2010

35. CP has initiated measures to implement the intelligence Traffic System in Delhi. He has introduced schemes for compliance of all existing regulations on uaffic by officers of Delhi Traffic Police. He expects to reduce corrupt practices in !he future. In past cases action will follow on complaints he assured the LG.

02.12.2010

36. Signages to enforce lane driving should be ensured on the roads which have been selected as special corridors for smooth flow of traffic. Lanes for different type 0: traffic should be earmarked and conspicuously displayed on these roads at the liest. *(Action: Spl. CP/Traffic)*

37. Preferred sites for installation of 60 number of PTZ cameras so as to get 360 degree view of Delhi may be indicated by Delhi Police to information Technology Department, GNCTD. *(Action: Spl. CP/Traffic)*

38. A detailed letter may be written to Commissioner Transport pointing ou the, "iolations being committed by Gramin Sewa and requesting for strict implementation of permit conditions. *(Action: Jt. CP/Traffic)*

39. The traffic in front of Metro Stations, especially Mayur Vihar Metro station where rickshaws often crow upon passengers and block carriageways, should be properly controlled. Rickshaw stands with proper signage and permissible numbers should be earmarked opposite Metro Stations where rickshaws await passengers; any of these arrangements should be sternly dealt with arrested. *(Action: Spl. CP/Traffic.)*

40. Traffic Police may carry out a study of the parking requirement during State functions at Raj Niwas and available options for the same including the plot at 8, Rajpur Road. *(Action: Spl. CP/Traffic)*

23.12.2010

41. There are many areas where illegal parking is taking place at the instance of mafia and muscle men. Such areas are not authorized by the land owning exercies. The parking sites proposed by MCD may be jointly inspected with them decision of Delhi Police regarding grant of NOC to these sites expedited. *(Action: Spl. CP Admn)*

10.01.2011

42. An advertisement may be issued by Traffic Police glvmg details of prosecutions for use of tinted films in the vehicles. *(Action: Jt. CP/Traffic)*

3.02.2011

43. Need to notify early that vehicles should give way to ambulances and police\ ehic1es proceeding on emergent law & order and relief duties by keeping the exueme right lane free for them. *(Action: Spl. CP/Tarffic)*

17.02.2011

44. The website of Delhi Traffic Police should extend an invitation to interested hools for registering with them for receiving study material and lectures on road safery. A roster of registered schools should be maintained to impart such training. *(Action; Jt. CP/Traffic)*

3.03.2011

45. An advertisements should be issued by Traffic Police advising the citizens the penal provisions against driving vehicles without silencers. *(Action: Jt. CP/Traffic)*

08.04.2011

46. MCD should issue a public that authorized Motels and Farm Houses should sure that all vehicles are accommodated within the comud of Motel/ Farm House. It sould be advised that stringent action will be taken against the defaulting OleL 'Farm House, including sealing and cancelling the permission. *(Action: Commr, MCD)*

47. Information about Traffic prosecutions and penalties should be given wide publicity including display on the electric boards on various intersections. *(Action: Jt. CP/Traffic)*

21.04.2011

48. St. John Ambulance and Red Cross Society should be requested to supply substantive leaflets to all PCR Vans regarding precautions to be taken for different of injury. *(Action: Spl. CP/Operators and OSD to LG)*

48[A]. There should be more emphasis on providing safe pedestrian crossmgs. suitable advertisements should also be issued. *(Action: Jt CP/Traffic)*

49. Traffic Police may examine, in consultation with MCD, desirability of 'ring a

road repair unit of their own to attend to emergent situations.
(Action: Spl. CP/Traffic)

22.09.2011

50. To ensure safety of pillion women riders on two wheelers GNCT Delhi should examine a proposal for making it mandatory as far as possible for such pillion drivers also to wear helmets. *(Action: Ppl. Secy. (Home)*

51. Traffic Police Delhi should take up effective measures to ensure safe crossing of roads by pedestrians at designated places/Zebra crossings on roads in Delhi. *(Action: Spl. Commissioner (Traffic)*

13.10.2011

52. Traffic Police should urgently install blinking lights on masts at accident places. Motorists should be advised to slow down whenever they see such blinking lights. *(Action ; Jt. CP/Traffic)*

53. Commissioner, Transport should examine if driving licenses of the drivers concected in criminal cases can be revoked or suspended.
(Action : Commissioner/Transport & Jt CP/Traffic)

54. In consultation with Local Bodies and agencies maintaining major roads, mapping of all National Highways, major roads in NCT of Delhi shall done to identify accident prone areas, and additional measures to be taken to and smooth flow of vehicular traffic and pedestrians on these roads.
(Action: Spl. CP/Traffic)

24: 11.2011

55. Traffic Police Delhi should enhance their presence for conducting checks etc. bus stops than the three hundred buss stops where they are undertaking this.Road owning authorities including NHAI be asked to provide speed calming responsbility at present. Civil Society Volunteers could be deployed as honorary T Wardens at such bus stops. *(Action: Spl. CP/Traffic)*

56. Traffic Police should intensify the safe pedestrian drive. All roads with breadth more than 60′ should have warning signs and textured surface at a distance of 25 before pedestrian crossings. *(Action: Spl. CP/Traffic)*

57. Traffic Police should identify vacant pieces of public land in areas afflicted with the problem of encroachment of pavements by vendors. These vendors can be on these plots temporarily. *(Action: Jt. CP/Traffic)*

58. Delhi Police (Traffic) should ensure that all main roads/carriage ways are not for parking vehicles as far as possible. Vacant land even if allotted for construction should actively be used for parking vehicles till the construction does begin. Jt. CP (Traffic) should locate such vacant land wherever available and get them allotted temporarily for parking vehicles. Roads/carriage ways will be better available for moving traffic .

01.3.2012

59. Road owning authorities including NHAI be asked to provide speed calming coupled with signages for enhancing pedestrian safety. Their attention be drawn to their potential liability for criminal negligence in case of failure to provide facilities. Copies of those advisories be sent to Hon'ble LG's Office.
(Action: Spl. CP/Traffic & Jt. CP/Traffic)

60. Delhi Police may temporarily use vacant govt. land for parking of rickshaw/three wheelers etc. to prevent blockage of carriageway lanes.
(Action: Spl. CP/Law & Order and It. CP/Traffic)

61. Streets in poor state of repairs are the cause of many traffic accidents. Delhi Police will, therefore, contact the road engineers concerned and make them to carry repairs promptly wherever it apprehends that the road condition will lead to accidents.

17.05.2012

62. Cab management system at the Indira Gandhi International Airport be suitably simplified to enable its early implementation.

(Action: Spl. CP/Traffic)

63. Caution signages be installed well ahead of speed calming strips. Time bound installation be ensured by effective liaison with concerned road maintenance.

(Action: Spl. CP/Traffic)

21.06.2012

64. Facilities available at AAUI could be used to conduct driving competence check.

Action : Spl. CP/Traffic and Jt. CP/Traffic)

19.02.2012

65. Revised traffic circulation plan be tried out at Old Delhi Railway Station in with Northern Railways authorities to enable buses to drop/pick up passengers within station premises. *(Action: Spl. CP/Traffic)*

18.10 .2012

66. During discussions about traffic, the Hon'ble LG has desired the following:-

   - Advertisements regarding advisability of wearing of helmets by ladies needs put out to create gradual awareness.
   - Lane changing habits of drivers in the city needs improvement and steps be towards this.
   - There is need to bring home the message that emergency vehicles have the right of way. This could be done through inforcement.
   - An analysis be carried out regarding the number of jay-walkers who have lost lives in road accidents and based on this analysis, the traffic police should put out advertisements to educate the general public.
   - The Traffic Unit was also asked to examine desirable locations of zebra crossings and signals on NH-1, and other major carriageways in accident prone areas.

     "Calming measures" be introduced to reign in high speed vehicles.
   - There is need to advertise all aspects of "safe driving" over newspapers and channels. *(Action: Spl. CP/Traffic)*

30.10.2012

67. With the marriage season at hand, the CP was advised to ensure that carriages not blocked, noise of music is kept within restricted hours and dancing is permitted so as to block vehicular movement by those who are participating in marriages.

01.11.2012

68. Hon'ble LG also observed that in many market areas the shop owners tend to take away parking space meant for customers. This issue needs to be addressed and owners should be directed to park their vehicles in places away from the Traffic police could help out in locating such alternative areas.

(Action: Spl. CP/Traffic and Jt. CP/Ranges)

29.11.2012

69. Congested markets/public places, which can be declared pedestrian shopping areas, be identified. *(Action: Spl. CP/Traffic)*

70. Lane discipline during night hours, when trucks are permitted to ply, be enforced. *(Action: Spl. CP/Traffic)*

71. Traffic unit should organize renewed publicity for its SMS alert service.

72. Concerned road maintenance authorities be informed that non functional street lights must be rectified within 24 hours of being informed of the same. *[Action: Pro Secy. (Power) and all Jt. CPs of Ranges to follow up}*

73. Drivers of public carriers must have public service badges. Apart from active enforcement, suitable advertisements should be issued in this behalf. *[Action. Spl. CP/Traffic}*

30.01.2013

74. Officers bearers of TSR unions be called and urged to educate their members to observe traffic norms. Those responding positively should be publicly felicitated to ovate others to emulate them. *[Action: Spl.CP/Training]*

75. Traffic patrols should also keep girls schools/colleges covered during opening closing hours to check activities of miscreants. *[Action: Spl. CP/Traffic}*

76. Spl. CP/Traffic may write to Chief Secretary to cancel registration certificates - Vehicles prosecuted for plying without requisite permit. *[Action: Spl. CP/Traffic}*

77. Unclaimed vehicles lying at police stations should be auctioned after giving and adequate notice to owners and sale proceeds there of deposited in govt. account. Whenever any rightful claimant comes forward, money realized during auction in respect of his vehicle can be given to him after adjusting admissible & reasonble changes. Wherever necessary, orders of the competent Court should be obtained for early disposal of vehicles lying at police stations as case property. *[Action: Jt. CPs/Ranges}*

78. State Transport Authority may be advised that the GPS linked panic buttons and other public transport vehicles should not only be linked with their Control Room but should also set off a loud siren to attract immediate help from people around. *[Action: Spl. CP/Cps.]*

79. Speedy verification of Public Service Vehicle (PSV) badge applicants may beensured. *[Action: Spl.CP/Int.]*

80. Traffic patrols should intercede immediately if any crime/misdemeanor on the streets comes to their notice. *[Action: Spl. CP/Traffic]*

81. An advertisement be issued to educate motorists to shun lane weaving and to change their lane only after giving a proper light signal. *[Action: Spl. CP/Traffic]*

14.03.2013

82. A comprehensive policy be framed for regulation of battery operated rickshaws in consultation with Traffic unit of Delhi Police. *[Action: Commissioner Transport and Spl. CP/Traffic]*

83. A copy be provided to OSD to Hon'ble LG, Delhi of the order issued by DM, Kanjhawala permitting operations of tractors in violation of the notification

issued by the Transport Department, GNCT, Delhi.

[Action: Addl. CP/Tarffic]

84. A Definite timeline be prescribed by Traffic Police for installation of traffic safety features by road owning agencies. *[A ction: Addl. CP/Traffic]*

85. Shopping Areas be identified where pedestrian shopping zones can be notified. Similarly places where vending zones and parking zones can be located should be identified. *[Action. Spl. CP Traffic, GNCTD]*

1.04.2013

86. There is need to mentor Traffic police men so that they do not enter into altercation when they accost a citizen who has violated a traffic regulation, rule no matter what the provocation. Public spats between the Delhi Traffic Police and the members of the public has to be avoided.

11.04.2013

87. Issues concerning Gramin Sewa be identified and discussions held with their operators to discipline its operations.

[Action: Commissioner Transport and Spl. CP/Trafic]

88. A public notice be issued mandating all farm houses and motels having banqueting facilities to ensure in house parking. If any violations are noticed, proceedings for sealing the delinquent premises be initiated.

89. Road owing agencies be advised to ensure time bound installation of suggested road safety measures lest any vicarious criminal liability is attracted due to their tardiness. *[Action: Addl. CP/Trafic]*

90. Clarification/Information sought by Delhi Police regarding black listed driving licensees may be provided on priority.

[Action: Commissioner Transport]

Prevention of Terrorism

18.09.2008

1. Improvement on the mode and methods of intelligence gathering to prevent such occurrences.
2. To seek wide participation of public through greater alertness and provision of inputs regarding suspicious factors for improving the security environment.
(Action: Spl. CP/Intelligence)
3. Creation of anti-terrorism awareness amongst the public should remain high on the police agenda. *(Action: Jt. CP/Crime & Range)*

26.12.2008

4. Sensitive Locations may be declared as no hawking/vending zones to reduce congestion in view of the terrorist threat. Instances of levying excessive charges by authorized parking vehicles vendors to be checked by MCD and NDMC in their respective jurisdictions.
(Action: Jt. CP/Ranges/Commissioner, MCD, Chairman, NDMC)

20.04.2009

5. Delhi Police is alert to terrorist activities as information has been received that explosive may be stored in garbage bins and some LET operations have been planned during the days before election.
6. Mobile phone numbers of Anti-Terrorist Officers (ATOs) in each Police Station will be made available to members of the SIS who are working as confidential intelligent operators under the overall guidance of OS D(RM).
7. Consequent to the information that toilets in Hospitals, Nursing Homes etc. will be targeted for implanting explosives etc. by terrorists, LG ordered CP to circulate this information to all Supdts. of all such Hospitals that are in the NCT Delhi. Similarly, this information should be shared by CP with Medical

Supdts. Administrators of all big Nursing Homes in NCT Delhi. They should be directed to take measures to prevent such an eventuality.

8. Use of Ambassador Cars with fake star emblems as police vehicles and wearing of police uniforms by unauthorized persons should be checked and prevented in NCT Delhi by CP.

08.06.2009

9. With immediate effect the CP will ensure that at the barriers set up by Police, checking of ID of individuals whose movement arouse suspicion is thoroughly carried out. Those who do not have ID they should be persuaded to proceed to the nearest point where they should be photographed and their ID details recorded for a thorough check.

10. In order to strengthen security, Delhi Police will initiate steps to have helipads constructed in two convenient locations within Delhi Police control on Delhi Police land.

23.06.09

11. LG emphasized that Anti-Terrorist Officers (ATOs) in each Police Station should be among the best Inspectors in Delhi Police. They should be extra alert in all matters that relate to security in their jurisdiction. The CP assured that they were under watch and also being changed if they were not found upto the mark.

28.05.2009

12. Earmarking of Anti Terrorism officers (ATOs) in each PS and Quick Response Team(QRTs) had a salutary effect on security scenario. The same should be continued and further strengthened. *(Action: CP)*

13. Surprise and unobtrusive inspections should be carried out to check the alertness of private security agency staff deployed at malls, cinema houses, hotels etc. *(Action: Jt. CP/Ranges)*

23.07.2009

14. Proper checks on people coming to buy chemicals which can be used for explosives should be undertaken. *(Action: All concerned)*

06.08.2009

15. Guest houses owners may be asked to install CCTV cameras and they can also have cable links of the CCTV camera in Police Stations. Other places having high footfall, such as Shopping Malls, may also be asked for installation of CCTV Cameras. *(Action: Jt. CPs/Ranges)*

16. Intensive checking of Guest Houses, Cyber Cafes, etc need to be carried out and managers of Guest Houses need to be properly screened. *(Action: Jt. CPs/Ranges)*

17. The data base of Guest House owners should be shared by Adl. Police Commissioner/Licensing with Jt. CP/Special Cell. *(Action: Addl. CP/Lic.)*

20.08.2009

18. Bank Branches where usually large cash transactions take place should be identified and kept under surveillance. *(Action: Jt. CP/Crime)*

19. A proposal for providing a gypsy for all A TOs to improve their mobility and effectiveness may be submitted by CP to Hon'ble LG for moving the Home Ministry. *(Action: Jt. CP/GA)*

08.10.2009

20. There should be no let up in counter terrorist measures particularly in view of the ensuing festival season. Spotters should be activated at religious places. *(Action: CPs/Ranges)*

21. Naxalite presence in Delhi has surfaced in the wake of apprehension and errogation of a 'Maoist Politburo Member". A sharp and vigilant look out should be maintained for such Naxalite activities in Delhi. *(Action: Jt. CP/Special Cell)*

22. Regulations for installations of mandatory security surveillance gadgets and employment of manpower by private establishments with heavy footfalls, including guest houses, should be drafted and submitted expeditiously. *(Action: Addl. CP/Licensing)*

23. Greater surveillance on sensitive Embassies under threat be maintained. *(Action: CPs/Ranges)*

07.01.2010

24. Intelligence inputs regarding attempts at revival of militancy by Sikh militant groups should also be carefully tracked for necessary action. *(Action: Jt. CP/Special Cell)*

25. In sensitive mixed-population localities, a close watch needs to be maintained for any anti-national activity. Permanent presence of MCD building staff to keep a close watch on unauthorized construction activities should be ensured. Externment proceedings under section 48 of Delhi Police Act be imitated against those fomenting trouble in this regard. *(Action: Jt. CP/Special Cell)*

21.01.2010

26. The requirement to remain alert at vulnerable public places with high footfall and the need to tone up the response mechanism by security personnel posted at such locations was emphasized. In order to ensure a more effective response in case of any exigency, private security personnel at these locations also need to be sensitized. *(Action: Jt. CPs/Ranges)*

25.02.2010

27. Arms License may be issued to five star hotels which meet all licensing requirements for enhancing their internal security preparedness. *(Action: Addl. CP/Licensing)*

11.03.2010

28. Private security guards posted at vulnerable places should be screened by Police for suitability and written advisories in their behalf issued to management of these vulnerable places. *(Action: Joint CPs/Ranges)*

01.04.2010

29. Surprise checking by putting barricades at strategic locations may be carried out. *(Action: Jt. CPs/Ranges)*

30. An exercise to ascertain installation of the minimum security equipment by owners/managers of the identified 459 installations in the City may be undertaken. *(Action: Jt. CP/Spl. Cell)*

15.04.2010

31. A review of market places in the list of 461 identified vulnerable sites in Delhi may be undertaken to see how many of these have installed the minimum security equipment as prescribed by police in the wake of intelligence inputs

of possible terrorist strikes in these markets. A report in this regard should be submitted at the next law and order meeting. *(Action: Jt. CP/Spl. Cell)*

32. Delhi Police should build up a cadre of "Spotters" to be deployed at market places and other areas with considerable footfalls so that potential mischief makers can be spotted and removed from the area. *(Action: Jt. CP/Spl. Cell)*

33. Delhi Police should obtain collapsible barricades and deploy them without prior notice in areas of Delhi for checking at random vehicles/motor cycles and pedestrians. The feedback of these surprises checking carried out with the help of barricades should be obtained and necessary action to ensure security and safety of Delhi be undertaken. Feedback on surprise checking done at pickets and other points may be given at the next law and order meeting. *(Action: Jt. CP/Ranges)*

06.05.2010

34. Spotters in plain clothes will be posted at all modes of entry into the city (Railway Stations, Bus Terminals, Border Check Posts, etc.) to keep an eye on suspicious persons/movements. *(Action: Jt. CP/Spl. Cell & Distt. ATe)*

35. An exercise should be undertaken to brief shop-keepers from time to time regarding steps to be taken keep their shops and premises secure and safe. *(Action: Jt. CP/Ranges)*

4.06.2010

36. The problem arising out of issue of arms licenses in Doda District (J & K) to non-residents has a bearing on Law & order in Delhi. Chief Secretary, Delhi was requested by the LG to write to Chief Secretary (J & K) on this issue. MHA should be kept informed. Jt. CP, Special Cell will send details to the Chief Secretary, Delhi - enable him to write to Chief Secretary (J & K). *(Action: Jt. CP, Special Cell)*

1. 11.2010

37. Cargo scanner to check trucks coming from North side should be installed at an appropriate location on the Singhu Border. *(Action: Jt. CP/GA)*

02.11.2010

38. Special Commissioner of Police, Special Cell to keep track through contacts wilh his counterparts in other states of movements to Delhi from these States of surrendered militants. Their whereabouts in Delhi should be in the knowledge of the Special Cell who should keep a constant watch on their activities in Delhi. *(Action: Spl. Commr, Special Cell)*

39. Preferred sites for installation of 60 number of PTZ cameras so as to get 360 degree view of Delhi may be indicated by Delhi Police to information Technology Department, GNCTD. *(Action: Spl. CP/Traffic)*

15.11.2010

40. LG briefed the CP regarding the proposal of establishing a secure surveillance system in Delhi which is under consideration of the Union Home Ministry.

06. 01.2011

41. Close surveillance of vulnerable and iconic places should be maintained. Status of installation of the prescribed security gadgets in iconic buildings should be reported once a month. *(Action: Special CP, Special Cell)*

03. 3.2011

42. DJB sites should be checked at random to check the level and dedication of private security guards deployed there. *(Action: Spl. CP/Spl. Cell & Jt. CPs/Ranges)*

08.10.11

43. Surveillance on the trucks coming to Azad Pur Mandi should continue.
(Action: Jt.CP/NR)

05.5.11

44. Anti - terrorist measures should continue.
(Action: Jt. CPs/Ranges & Sp!. Cell)

30.05.2011

45. The CP reported developments pursuant to the crude Bomb Blast in front of Delhi High Court on 25.05.2011. Previous unsolved blast cases have been re-opened and meticulous follow up of clues has been initiated in respect of all such blasts not only in Delhi but also in the neighboring States.

46. CP reported that Jamia Nagar continues to be a very sensitive area where disruption. violence, incidents with communal overtones can erupt. The LG directed apart from police continuing to deal with all apprehensions, the SDM of the area should hold regular Darbars with residents to listen to the grievancs and amileorate them. CCTV cameras around the Police Stations and other sensitive areas duly protected from damage should be installed.

02.6.2011

47. Principal Secretary (Home) may write to DTC for procurement of Hand Held metal Detectors (HHMDs) for DTC Buses. These be used by conductors to scan luggage carriage by passengers. DTC should be requested to also install CCTV Camera in Buses. *(Action: Principal Secretary. (Home)*

48. Efforts be made to gather intelligence whether anyone in Delhi is indulging in making of IEDs. *(Action: Spl. CP/Sp!. Cell & Jt. CP/Ranges)*

28.06.2011

49. Inspectors, ATOs (Ante-Terrorist-Officers) should regularly submit reports about security gaps in vital installation and identified vulnerable locations. Information regarding Delhi Govt. Installation must be sent to Ppl. Secy. (Home) for further necessary action.
(Action: Spl. CP/Spl. Cell & Ppl. Secy (Home) GNCTD)

50. LG directed Special Cell Delhi Police to keep a strict watch over activities of emerging group, known as "Popular Front of India", which is believed to be an offshoot of the banned organizations SIMI and said to be active in UP. A close liaison may be maintained with UP and other State's authorities for regular exchange Intelligence on activities of the Group. Any activity impinging on the security of Delhi should be thwarted.
(Action: Spl. Commissioner (Spl. Cell)

18.07.2011

51. Anti-Terrorist Officers (ATOs) in each of the 155 Police Stations have been tasked to continuously monitor terrorist preventive measures in the vulnerable sites comprising 486 sites. They have been provided with vehicles and force to ensure that this exercise is meticulous and full proof.

21.07.2011

52. The number of trained spotters should be substantially increased. Criminals like snatchers, bank robbers, terrorist planning bomb blats, stalkers etc. should be spotted and action taken before they are able to execute their plans.
(Action: Spl. CP/Spl. Cell)

09.09.2011

53. All vital installations and iconic locations may be surveyed once again and

shortcomings may be notified to GNCTD and MHA for buildings under their control. Green colour coding should be given to a building only if the access to the building is also brought under surveillance. *(Action: Spl.CP/Spl. Cell)*

54. Temporary CCTV systems may be got installed on hire in important markets which are presently not covered. *(Action: Jt. CPs /Ranges)*

55. DMRC and CISF may be advised to expedite installation of CCTV Cameras to cover entrances and approach areas of Metro Stations. *(Action: Spl. CP/Crimes)*

56. A letter may be written to Chairman Railway Board requesting him for installation of CCTV cameras at important railways stations in Delhi. *(Action: Spl. CP/Crime)*

57. Approaches to all district courts be brought under surveillance by installing CCTVs on hire basis. MHA may be requested to expedite sanction of pending proposals relating to manpower for strengthening security of various courts. *(Action: Jt. CP/ Hdqrs)*

58. It may be examined whether shopkeepers with turnover above a suitable limit can be asked under the provisions of the DP Act to install CCTV cameras at entrances to their shops. *(Action: Jt. CP/PHQ)*

59. DTC should install CCTV cameras with recording facility in all new buses. A letter may be issued by Delhi Police to CMD/ IDTC in this regard. *(Action: Spl.CP/Spl. Cell)*

60. Use of National Security Act be considered against carriers of illicit arms apprehended by Delhi Police. *(Action:Jt. CP/Ranges & Sp/'CPI)*

61. Registration of private security agencies should be an going process, not limited to the month of April every year. Draft training norms for private security guards should be hosted on the website of Home Deptt. for inviting comments. *(Action: Ppl. Secy. (Home)*

03.10.2011

62. It should be examined whether a special corps of "Spotters" can be developed in Delhi Police and specially trained to keep a watch at Railway Stations, Bus Terminals, religious places, etc. The job of spotters will be to watch and detect suspicious movements and unnatural behaviour. *(Action: Spl.CP/Spl.Cell)*

19.10.2011

63. Organization known as Popular Front of India has established Hdqrs. in Delhi. The Special Branch, Delhi Police should continue to closely monitor their activities report for action any concrete information suggesting terrorist related activity by then.

64. Principal Secretary (Home) will give necessary direction to Directorate of Presention so that in terrorist cases resulting in acquittals, a copy of judgment is simultaneously sent to the Police, as has already been requested by the CP to CS. *(Action: Ppl. Secy. (Home)*

65. Delhi Police may share any information they have about Interstate gun running rackets/ill icit manufacturing bases with MHA so that concerned states can be mandated to take proper action through Govt. of India also. *(Action: Spl. CP/Crime)*

66. Regular checking of guest houses be ensured. *(Action: Jt. CPs/Ranes)*

13.10.2011

67. LG viewed seriously rampant issue of mobile phones by mobile vendors on fake identity cards. In order to stamp out this crime, the CP will ensure that the matter is taken up with the Union of India, Home Ministry by the LG.

68. Global best practices have to be adopted by Delhi Police to secure equipments for putting them in place in Delhi to prevent terrorist attempts in Delhi. The Delhi Police will secure advice from independent security experts before placing such equpments in place and also ensure that such equipments are taken on wet lease so as to ensure annual maintenance and continuous updating of the security equpment minimizing obsolescence.

69. India Gate and Rajpath are protected areas and considered vulnerable to possible terrorist strikes. During summer, late into the night, huge crowd congregate here. Anti-Terrorist Section of the Tilak Marg PS should be alert to prevent terrorist strikes specially when the area has huge footfalls. Special attention has to be paid to proper parking and removal of unauthorized vendors.

21.5.2011

70. Intensive checking of hotels, guest houses and other places where any desirable person can hide be ensired till Independence Day Arrangements are over. Beat officers be briefed to keep a sharp lookout in their areas. *(Action: Jt. CPs/Ranges)*

71. Installation of CCTV be made mandatory for Arms dealers. License conditions should mandate digital video recording of all transactions related to sale purchase of arms and ammunition. *(Action: Addl. CP/Licensing)*

72. Delhi Govt. buildings and MCD buildings need to be surveyed from the security points of view and gaps noticed to be conveyed to the Delhi Govt. and MCD copy to LG office. *(Action: Spl. CP/Spl. Cell)*

73. An advisory be issued to DDA and MCD to mandate CCTV coverage whenever any permission/licence is granted for holding wedding, receptions etc. at public places/parks. *[Action: Spl. CP/L&O]*

74. The security measures and access control at Police Complexes may be beefed up in view of the fidayeen attack in Srinagar. *(Action: Spl. CP/Crime, L&O,Traffic, Ops., AP, Int., Security and Spl. Cell]*

25.03.2011

75. Police will carry out a thorough check for unlicensed guest houses specily in the districts where terrorists belonging to the 1M Group and other foreign sponsored groups like to take rooms to stay in Delhi possibly for organizing their terrorist activ ities in Delhi.

76. Photographs of all residents who take rooms as residents/guests in guests in guest houses/hotels or as paying guests in residential areas to be obtained by those offering accomodation. These photographs should be pasted on the guest house register for visiters/residents.

77. Facility to check luggage of residents/visitors in all guest houses/hotels etc. to detect existence of arms explosive and ammunitions must be ensured by amending license conditions.

    25.04.2013

78. Number of inputs received from public giving information about suspicious activities on the part of any individual/individuals indicating possible involvement in terrorist activity be indicated.

    [Action: Spl. CP/Spl. Cell]

Community Policing

01.07.2008

1. Proactive community policing may be resorted to as a preventive crime control measure in JJ Colonies and highly crime prone areas.

(Action: Jt. CP/Ranges)

08.02.2010

2. Thana Level Committees and District Level Committees should regularly be called to meet at the designated place of their meeting. Minutes of the meeting should be sent for the perusal of the hon'ble LG.

11.02.2010

3. As already directed Thana Level Committee meetings will be held every two months and minutes of the meetings sent to the LG office.

(Action: Jt. CPs/Ranges)

11.03.2010.

4. The Annual report of Delhi Police should have a chapter on "Cooperative interface with Citizens". *(Action: Spl. CP/Admn.)*

12.04.2010

5. Points raised in Thana Level Committee meetings should also be followed up by the LG's Secretariat with the departments of the Govt. of National Capital Territory to which they relate.

23.12.2010

6. As a crime prevention measure, in order to reduce/prevent crime, it is necessary that healthy sports activities are organized for the youth who are idle and at a loose end. Delhi Police Officers should look for public land, especially in areas of Police Stations where crimes take place by youths, and recommend construction of sports grounds on the patterns of SOCCO-S. DDA will then be advised to take follow up action. *(Action: Spl. CP Crime/VC DDA)*

7. Pro-active action in the form of Parivartan and similar schemes should be taken in areas where incidence of rape is relatively higher.
(Action: Jt. CPs/Ranges)
8. Delhi Police may formulate and manage a skill development programme as a rehabilitation measure for habitual juvenile offenders.
06.01.2011
9. Senior Officers of Districts and Ranges should obtain regular feedback from people who file complaints at Police Stations under their jurisdiction to find their satisfaction level. *(Action: Jt. CPs/Ranges)*

17.02.2011

10. Hon'ble LG mentioned that he was considering to recommend inclusion of Community Policing as an agenda item at the ensuring Conference of Governors. This was supported by Commissioner of Police, Delhi Police would furnish the necessary background material. *(Action: Spl. CP/Crime)*
11. Senior officers should maintain a record of calls made by them to senior retired bureaucrats etc. to get a feedback about the Law and Order situation and then follow up action taken after these calls. *(Action: Jt. CPs/Ranges)*
12. The website of Delhi Traffic Police should extend an invitation to interested schools for registering with them for receiving study material and lectures on road safety. A roster of registered schools should be maintained to impart such training. *(Action; Jt. CP/Traffic)*

21.02.2011

13. CP should send for the perusal of the LG a short one page note on Community Policing in Delhi.

03.03.2011

14. Instructions have been issued to DDA to provide sports infrastructure at the sites elected by Delhi Police. Delhi Police should take follow up action to ensure that these sites become operational early.
(Action: SpJ. CP/Crime/Jt. CPs/Ranges)
15. Juvenile offenders involved in snatching, etc. crimes should be given an opportunity to rehabilitate themselves by sending them to Industrial Training Institutes for industrial training. *(Action: Jt. CPs/Ranges)*

08.03.2011

16. The Thana Level and District Level Committees should continue to function in accordance with the guidelines already issued. Minutes of these meeting should be promptly sent for the perusal of the hon'ble LG.

02.05.2011

17. District level meeting with Member of Parliament presiding or in his absence the District Police Chief chairing the meeting with MLA of the area being present along with local representatives should take place once in two months. All points that are actionable may be acted upon expeditiously and participants informed of the action taken.

25.07.2011

18. Quarterly meetings with MPs, with MLAs participating, should be regularly held by District Police Chiefs.

19.10.2011

19. Thana level and District level meetings should take place in accordance with orders issued regarding the periodicity of such meetings.

2.10.2011

20. List of senior prominent citizens and retired police and other senior government officers should be maintained by district officers. Periodic telephonic contact should be made with them to ascertain the status of policing in their areas, and state their suggestions, if any. *(Action: Spl. CP/L&O & Jt. CPs/Ranges)*

11.11.2011

21. Annual report of Delhi Police should include a chapter on various initiatives taken by Delhi Police on Community Policing. *(Action: Spl. CP/Crime.)*

24.11.2011

22. Engineers India Ltd. be contacted for organizmg vocational training for persons completing de-addiction programmes run by Tihar Jail and various NGOs as a part of their Corporate Social Responsibility initiatives. *(Action: OSD (RM) to LG)*

08.12.2011

23. Spl. CPlLaw & order should ensure that proper follow up action is taken on the issues raised in District Level & Thana Level meetings. *(Action: Spl. CP/L & 0)*

24. Spl. CP/Crime should highlight a few important suggestions received in the District Level and Thana Level Committee meetings and the follow up action taken thereon. *(Action: Spl. CP/Crime.)*

09.04.2012

25. CP was directed to ascertain and report if Community Service is a punishment within the Penal Codes of India.

04.06.2012

26. Youths participating in propgrammes being run by Delhi Police be asked about their vocational skill preference. There is pressing need to organize skill deyelopment programmes for them with the help of NGOs and Corporates. *(Action: SpI. CP/Crime and Jt. CPs/Ranges)*

21.06.2012

27. Vocational Training could be organized for youths opposite Gagan Cinema. Stipend could be given through Banking Channels. Funds could be raised by donations from leading Corporates. *(Action: Spl. CP/Crime)*

19.07.2012

28. Assistance of vocational teachers of Department of Education could be enlisted to impart vocational training to youth attending 'YUVA' programmes. Appropriate honorarium could be paid with the help of willing NGOs/ Corporates. *(Action: Jt. CPs/Ranges)*

29. SHOs be advised to ascertain career goals of chi ldren participating in 'YUVA' programmes to see what guidancel/help can be rendered to them. *(Action: Jt. CPs/Ranges)*

11.09.2012

30. Proper maintenance of playgrounds to be handed over by DDA to Delhi Police. be ensured.

3l. The Hon 'ble LG indicated that

a. Vocational teachers, whose residences are near the various grounds which have been handed over to the Delhi Police, could be asked to help in training youth under the "Yuva" Programme. These teachers could be given suitable honorarium for their efforts from the "Street Children's Welfare Fund".

b. All districts need to have the proper data-base of the youth who have been trained under the Yuva Programme, so that there is scope for immediate retrieval and when the need arises. *(Action: Spl. CP/L & 0 and Jt. CPs/Ranges)*

32. Services of vocational teachers of GNCT of Delhi could be utilized for 'Yuya', *(Action: Jt. CPs/Ranges)*

33. A Standing order could be issued for maintenance of a 'Street Children welfare Fund'. Donation received could be used to pay a small stipend to those attending 'YUVA' programme. *(Action: Spl. CP/Crime and Spl. CP/L&O)*

34. Services of vocational teachers of GNCT Delhi could be utilized for 'YUVA'. *(Action: Jt. CPs/Ranges)*

35. An executive sheet of trainees, who are offered employment under' YUVA', be maintained.

15.11.2012

36. 'Yuva' disseminated.

29.11.2012

37. Streat children may also be involved in ' Yuva' activities. *(Action: Jt. CPs/Ranges)*

13.12.2012

38. Information about youth who have been assisted in getting employment under the 'Yuva' initiative be put up on the website of Delhi Police. *(Action : Spl. CP/Crime)*

39. Detailed SOPs for internal administration, including financial management of 'YUVA' Society be devised. *(Action: Spl. CP/Crime and Spl. CP/L&O)*

40. Range Jt. CsP should maintain a list of civil society persons to be contacted pro-actively on phone. This could also include persons from the media. *(Action: Jt. CP/Ranges)*

41. Feedback be obtained from women NGOs and other respectable groups to ascertaing public perception about the enhanced preventive measures taken for safety of women. The "Parivartan" scheme should be expended to all Police Districts. *[Action: Jt. CPs/Ranges]*

42. SHOs of all police stations should keep track of youth displaying deviant tendencies and through Parivartan and other schemes ensure that they do not indulge in sexual crimes. *[Action: Jt. CPs/Ranges]*

21.01.2013

43. LG made enquries regarding the functioning of Yuva. Delhi Police has ongoing measures like Parivartan, Pehchan, Aap Ki Date, Operation Majnu etc. which help in enforcing law & order. Results achieved by these measures may be periodically reported in the crime Analysis report received from PHQ,

14.02.2013

44. Advance liaison with the organizers of protest programmes should be held to enlist their co-operation. Police personnel should be sensitized to behave patiently with the participants and not fall prey to any provocation. In particular, utmost respect and courtesy should be shown to women participants. Wherever organizers do not keep their commitment of staging a peaceful protest and preventive measures are taken, sensitive dealing with women protesters has to be invariably done. *[Action: Spl. CP/L&O and Jt.CPs/Ranges]*

28.02.2013

45. Data of youth trained and those provided employment under 'YUVA' be given to OSD to Hon' ble LG. *[Action: Spl. CP/Crime)*

46. Yuva Delhi Police should consider ways and means to increase numbers of vocational trained street children who are a part of the Yuva programme. Help of vocational teachers from all sources should, therefore, be tapped.

14.03.2013

47. Sector-wise and gender-wise breakup of youths provided employment under `Yuva' be indicated at the next meeting. *(Action: Spl. CP/Crime)*

11.04.2013

48. Minutes of meeting of Thana Level Committees should be issued to all concerned within 3 days of holding of the meeting. *[Action: Jt. CPs/Ranges]*

30.05.2013

49. An appraisal system for trainees under 'Yuva' be evolved. Trainees can be given an appropriate testimonial on satisfactory completion of their vocational training. *[Action: Spl. CP/L&O and Jt. CPs/Ranges)*

50. Joint CPs/Ranges should maintain contact with senior cirizens in their areas. They should pro-actively contact a few of them from time to time and seek their feedback about the law and order situation in their locality. *[Action: Jt CPs'Ranges]*

Prevention of Encroachment of Land

03.04.2008

1. While noting that SHO has a responsibility in informing the land owning agency of an unauthorized construction in his area, the LG has directed that the SHO henceforth should immediately not only inform the designated officer in the MCO, NOMC, OOA as the case may be put but also communicate to the Listening Post in the Raj Niwas at No. 155355.

01.07.2008

2. Carriageways In Jamia area should be kept clear for movement of ambulances, fire brigades, and other emergency vehicles.

05.03.2009

3. For removal of encroachments from the carriage-ways, public parks etc. the SDMs should be suitably empowered under the DMC Act and NDMC Act.

(Action: Commissioner MCD/Pr. Secy. UO)

11.06.2009

4. Action against unscrupulous property dealers should be kept up.

(Action : Jt. CPs/Ranges)

21.06.2009

5. The Screening Committee on religious structures also includes a representative from Delhi Police. This officer should be fortified with reports from the Special Branch in respect of removal of the particular religious structures proposed for removal and is under consideration. His views in the matter should be reported in the recommendations made for orders of the LG. It was also directed that before actual removal, Special Branch report should be again obtained if there is a gap between the orders of the LG and action of delay of more than one month may be considered as a gap. The hon 'ble LG should be invariably apprised of the day when action will be taken to remove the religious structure.

10.09.2009

6. Jt. CP Southern Range pointed out that presently none of the civic agencies had any presence on the ground in Jamia Nagar. Hon'ble Lt. Governor directed that the action should be initiated to hold an open house at least once a month by MCD, DIB, Power department and the Revenue Dy. Commissioner with residents of Jamia Nagar during which local problems could be sorted out. Principal Secretary (Home) may write to these agencies in this regard.

26.10.2009

7. LG issued directions that in 30 days, the Yamuna River bed adjacent to Batla House which has been encroached upon should be cleared of encroachment. The incomplete PWD road on Yamuna River bed connecting the ground below the DND Flyaway to Batla House and beyond should then be completed in accordance with the original PWD plans. It will also serve as the boundary to prevent further encroachment.

30.11.2009

8. LG directed that carriage-ways should not be permitted to be blocked or reduced in space by parking of cars of people attending the marriage or by their blocking road in dancing & making merry on the carriage-ways blocking all traffic. Advertisements discouraging this activity should be published.

08.12.2009

9. On the issue of removal of encroachments, LG has directed in cases where it is proposed to provide shelter to those who are evicted, an exercise to obtain full identity of such individuals by way of obtaining their Bio-metric data should be carried out wherever possible. They should then be listed for allotment of low cost flats which are planned to be constructed in Delhi.

24.05.2010

10. Delhi Police should take note of public land from which encroachment has been removed by its assistance by the land owning agency to ensure that the land owning agency fences the land and puts a proper board claiming ownership of the land. Thereafter any effort by trespasser to re-encroach should not be allowed and also reported to the land owning agency to reinforce the fencing that may have been breached.

11. LG directed the CP to take note of the Supreme Court judgement that no public land should be allowed to be encroached by any religious institution. Advertisements should be issued in the Hindi and Urdu press widely circulating the orders of the hon'ble Supreme Court prohibiting encroachment on public land by construction of religious structure.

21.06.2010

12. LG reiterated the need to ensure that public land freed from encroachment is properly fenced and protected by the land owning agency and in cases where such protection has not been provided, Delhi Police should immediately report the matter to the competent authority for corrective action.

24.06.2010

13. Wherever colonies are mushrooming on agricultural land and complaints are sent by SDMs and MCD to Delhi Police, prompt action has to be taken. All land mining agencies should send specific complaints regarding such encroachments on agricultural land. Copy of communications to Delhi Police should also be sent to Divisional Commissioner and OSD (PG) to LG.

(Action: Jt. CP Ranges/Divisional Commissioner GNCT)

02.08.2010

14. 3DGIS map of the Jamia Nagar area establishes considerable encroachment on public property after 2007. The CP was directed to give the hon 'ble LG a feed back about the role of civic agencies in this matter.

09.08.2010

15. Mr. Bhure Lal of the Monitoring Committee has informed the LG of illegal/ unauthorized/unabated constructions in Yamuna Bed area of Jamia Nagar. It is reported that all the units facing roads sides have been converted into commercial establishments defying the existing norms of construction. The CP will look into this report. This situation will be on daily scanner of the CP for corrective action.

31.08.2010

16. LG reviewed the Jamia Nagar situation and directed CS to ensure that the writ of administration is established inside the Jamia Nagar area. SDM of the area may be stationed under secured premises inside the Jamia Nagar area. If necessary, a separate (28th) sub-division be established for Jamia Nagar.

15.11.2010

17. CP took note of LG's orders that land owning agencies will file complaints with the PS of the area in all cases of unauthorized and illegal encroachments on public land. All these FIRs will be regularly monitored at competent levels in the PHQ.

18.11.2010

18. A proper system of keeping a watch on illegal construction and reporting the same on real time basis should be worked out on priority.*(Action : Jt. CP/NDR)*

29.11.2010

19. Existence of unsafe buildings in Delhi reveal that there is general non compliance of people to laws and instructions issued regarding construction of safe buildings. That generally there is non-compliance to laws has to be curbed by Delhi Police by taking action against those who break the law.

02.12.2010

20. Unauthorized construction should invariably be booked under the Delhi Police Act. *(Action: Jt. CP/Ranges)*

23.12.2010

21. Whenever Delhi Police participates in removing vendors from public land at the instance of a land owning agency, it should be ensured, to the extent possible, that some alternative place for vendors is assigned by the land owning agency.

(Action: Jt.CP Ranges/Commissioner MCDI VC DDA/ Divisional Commissioner)

22. There are many areas where illegal parking is taking place at the instance of the mafia and muscle men. Such areas are not authorized by the land owning agencies. The parking sites proposed by MCD may be jointly inspected with them and decision of Delhi Police regarding grant of NOC to these sites expedited. *(Action: Spl. CP Admn)*

21.12.2010

23. Encroachment on public land is an obstacle to secure law and order and hence continuous removal of unauthorized encroachment should be the target of

Delhi Police and all land owning agencies. Once encroachment is removed, no re-encroachment should be permitted by the land owning agencies who should report the re-encroachment instantly to Delhi Police and ensure the removal of all encroached and re-encroached land. The SHO of the area should be alert to detect cases of re-encroachment and along with the land owning agencies take steps to remove the encroachment/re-encroachment.

27.12.2010

24. The Special Task Force of Delhi Police should be revamped. It should be organized as a multi task force comprising all departments tasked with the responsibility of ending encroachment on public land. The CP will draw up the standard Operating Procedures (SOP) for this multi task group. LG expects this force operative by 15th January, 2011.

10.01.2011

25. Any unauthorized encroachment/unauthorized construction in any part of Delhi now will be immediately taken note of and action taken to prevent it.

1.01.2011 & 24.01.2011

26. Unauthorized encroachments and constructions in the Batla House area was reviewed. It was reiterated that the initial step in declaring unauthorized constructions unsafe in the Batla House area will be by the Executive Magistrate i.e. the SDM under the authority and powers vested in him by the Criminal Procedure Code. Violations and infringements of his order will be immediately reported to the nearest Police Station to book the culprits under the provisions of the Indian Penal Code.

27. LG suggested that the Home Department may consider issuing public notices to the effect that unauthorized constructions in Delhi will not be permitted.

08.03.2011

28. The task force to be created by Divisional Commissioner, Delhi to deal with unauthorized constructions and illegal encroachments on public land has to go into operation. Hon'ble LG reminded the CS that the decision to create one was taken on 4th January, 20 11.

14.02.2011

29. Action against unauthorized construction and unauthorized encroachment on public land should be reviewed from time to time to ensure that such illegal activities which have bearing on law & order and security of Delhi are minimized.

21.02.2011

30. Lack of co-ordination between the civic agencies and the police in respect of ercise to remove unauthorized constructions needs to be avoided to ensure o::aennined action in cases of unauthorized constructions. Decision to ensure executive action by Sub-Divisional Magistrates in respect of all unauthorized constructions in Delhi decided upon in early January, 2011 has yet to be implemented this should receive immediate attention .

04.4.2011

31. The removal of unauthorized constructions in sensitive areas in Delhi should be done by land owning agencies i.e. MCD, DDA, NDMC after following the guidelines, rules and regulations issued in this regard from time to time and the police presence to prevent a law & order situation will be effective only if all procedural regulations are meticulously followed by the land owning agencies for removal of the anauthorized constructions/encroachments.

08.04.2011

32. MCD should issue a public notice that authorized Motels and Farm Houses should ensure that all vehicles are accommodated within the comud of MotellFarm House. It should be advised that stringent action will be taken against the defaulting Motel/Farm House, including sealing & cancelling the permission.

(Action: Commr, MCD)

11.04.2011

33. In accordance with the direction of the Monitoring Committee, unauthorized constructions after February, 2007 have to be removed. This will be done under due process of law. A notice to the occupant/owner of the unauthorized construction will be issued to remove the unauthorized construction. Failing, the premises will be sealed. Thereafter, if the unauthorized construction remains demolition will take place. The District Police shall be given copy of notice issued and details of sealing prior to land owning agencies i.e. MCD, DDA, PWD, NDMC etc. seeking force for demolition.

34. Jamia area being a sensitive area from the point of law & order, presence of criminal elements, high density population continued unauthorized encroachchment/construction suffers from low standard of civic amenities and police presence etc. Delhi Police should make an effort to ensure improved living conditions better civic amenities, better police presence by making special efforts through regular interaction with representatives of residents living in Jamia Nagar of Okhla .

01.08.2011

35. Land owning agencies may declare areas as no vending zones and declare hours and areas where no loading or unloading will be permitted to enable Delhi Police to effectively implement their directions in both these areas.

24.10.2011

36. SHOs of Police Stations should be alert to potential property disputes within their jurisdiction and take preemptive steps so as not to allow any breach of peace. *(Action: Jt. CP/Ranges)*

14.11.2011

37. lamia Nagar area continues to be in the regular scanner of Delhi Police. SHO of Jamia Nagar is under instructions to identify trouble spots and take adequate measures to prevent any disorder. The CP complimented the SHO for his zeal and work in the trouble spots of Jamia Nagar.

13.03.2012

38. Illegal vendors have been mushrooming in important market places notably areas like Nehru Place. The CP agreed that continuous operations along with land owning agencies can be done to ensure that such places are free from illegal encroachment as continuous encroachment by illegal/unauthorized vendors is a security hazard. *(Action: CP)*

39. lamia agar area is a sensitive area where security concerns of Delhi Police area very High. Areas that have not been encroached and belong to DDA should be immediately fenced by DDA to prevent encroachment in future. Security Forces including Army, if necessary, will help in ensuring the fencing. LG's intervention may be obtained by DDA for assistance of the security forces.

(Action DDA)

27.02.2012

40. Construction activity permitted by the SDM in their Sub-Divisional area cannot be prevented by jurisdictional Police Stations. If any construction is considered unauthorized, the PS of the jurisdiction is competent to intimate such unauthorized construction to the MCD and the STF and only on receipt of requests from them to demolish such construction provide police assistance. There is no suoauthority with Police Stations to prevent unauthorized construction unless specifically mandated by Court orders .

09.04.2012

41. Unauthorized dangerous constructions continue to be the cause of injuries and deaths to members of the public. Despite powers vested in MCD officers, Executive Magistrates and Delhi Police officers to prevent and even stop dangerous constructions they continue. Use of powers by the Executive Magistrates under the Cr.PC, by MCD officers under the MCD Act and Delhi Police promptly, starting investigations on complaints of dangerous constructions will reduce such incidents. Those who fail to do will invite criminal and disciplinary action.

42. Regarding encroachment on Govt. land, LG referred to section 100 of Delhi Poli e Act where any trespass on Govt. property has to be dealt with by Delhi Police. In this light, directions were issued that beat constables in future will report any trespass on Govt. land that comes to their notice in their beat and the same will be immediately reported to a nodal officer under the Divisional Commissioner, Delhi. The Divisional Commissioner, Delhi has been directed by LG to appoint such a nodal officer and inform the CPo.

43. Encroachment by a masjid and a temple next to the Fire Temple of Parsis on Bhadurshah Zafar Marg will be examined by the CP and a report sent for the perusal of the hon 'ble LG.

44. CP confirmed that instructions have been issued to all Delhi Police Beats to report encroachment on Govt. land for conveying the same to the Nodal Officer appointed for this purpose by the Divisional Commissioner, Delhi.

45. LG reiterated that all SHOs should ensure that no basement is constructed in the walled city or in crowded residential/market areas of Delhi without approved plans of civic agency concerned.

46. Keep a stringent watch on land deals where land mafia, lower formation of the police and land revenue staff collude at the cost of the unwary property owner. *(Action Jt.CP Ranges)*

16.07.1012

47. The PWD road in Jamia Nagar forming a bandh between the populated area and the Yamuna is free from encroachment. However, malba etc. is being thrown should be prevented by speedily marking the alignment of the proposed road. *(Action PWD)*

48. In Jamia Nagar area since narrow roads and cheek by jowl construction make demolition of unauthorized construction, hazardous sealing of such construction in a combined operation of the police and the land owning agency should be first resorted .

06.08. 2012

49. There was detailed and intensive discussion on the Law & Order situation

in Jamia Nagar. There is a situation where lawlessness in Jamia Nagar as evidenced by massive unauthorized construction & repeated encroachment on Govt. land. The situation will require that pickets be maintained round the clock to ensure that construction material believed for use of unauthorized construction or encroachment on public land/Govt. land will be prevented from entering Jamia Nagar area.

21.08. 2012

50. L.G. directed that as the Supreme Court by an order in February, 2011 has prohibited encroachment in the shape of a religious structure on a public land, the Delhi Police should act upon this directive of the highest Court of the land to remove such encrochments on public land.

51. PWD has placed markers at every 100 ft. on the proposed linking road in Jamia Nagar which will also protect the '0' Zone from constructional activities while a new communication link to residents of Jamia Nagar. The proposed road should have more markers at every 25 ft., and Delhi Police should ensure that the makers are not disturbed. *(Action: Jt. CP/Range)*

11.09. 2012

52. Land and tenant disputes should be treated as civil matters by all police stations in Delhi, Criminal action should be initiated only where goons forcibly try to help the parties.

(Action: Jt. CPs/Ranges)

25.04. 2013

53. A public notice be issued mandating all farm houses and motels having banqueting facilities to ensure in house parking. If any violations are noticed, proceeding for sealing the delinquent premises be initiated.

[Action: Spl.CPtraffic, Jt. CPs Ranges,
Commissioners of MCD North. South & East]

Publicity

22.05.2008

1. More publicity on 'Eyes & Ear' Scheme indicating its positive results may be issued. *(Action: Jt. CP/Crime)*

01.07.2008

2. An icon may be added on the Delhi Police website for reporting crimes by members of Public. *(Action: Jt. CP/Crime)*

3. To create better public awareness home security devices may be exhibited in residential colonies by using an exhibition van and also at the Traffic Management Centre or any other suitable location. *(Action: Jt. CP/Crime & Jt. CP/Traffic)*

24.07.2008

4. The number of hits on Delhi Police website every month should be reported along with figures of information received in connection with crime. *(Action: Jt. CP/Crime)*

24.07.2008

5. Audio visual presentation on Parivartan programme should be put on Delhi Police Website. *(Action: Jt. CP/Crime)*

07.08.2008

6. Delhi Police advisories to citizens should be widely published in the media and be posted on its website as well, particularly the ones on thefts.

04.09.2008

7. Improvements made on the website of Delhi Police may be displayed at the next meeting alongwith an analysis of Public response. *(Action: Jt. CP/Crime)*

8. An advertisement advising people not to carry huge amounts of cash on their person without proper security may be released. *(Action: Jt. CP/Crime)*

03.10.2008

9. The steps needed to increase the security awareness of common people must continue. Co-operation of moderate elements of various communities should be elicited. *(Action: Jt. CPs/Ranges)*

30.10.2008

10. Posters, banners and buntings put up at unauthorized locations by political groups should be removed by special teams of MCD besides legal action by local police. *(Action: DC/MCD)*

11.05.2009.

11. An advisory to be issued by Delhi Police directing all concerns to desist from using fire crackers during marriage functions.

22.10.2009

12. Success controlling eve-teasing and molestation of women should be projected in the media. *(Action : Joint CP/Crime)*

26.11.2009

13. Press advertisements may be brought out to encourage action by civil society against eve-teasers. *(Action: Jt. CP/Crime)*

11.03.2010

14. Efforts be made to use slots offered by private TV Channels for regularly informing and educating members of public on security and traffic related aspects at least on a weekly basis. *(Action: Joint CPs/Crime)*

15. The annual report of Delhi Police should have a chapter on "Cooperative interface with Citizens". *(Action: Spl. CP/Admn)*

01.04.2010

16. A multimedia publicity campaigaing for bringing about road users behavioral change may be launched in the run up to the Games. *(Action: Spl. CP/Traffic)*

15.04.2010

17. A public message may be given in the media for reporting stalking/ shadowing cases. *(Action: CP)*

24. 6.2010

18. Advertisements should be released to newspapers, including vernacular newspapers, to the effect that all religious institutions using loudspeakers must ensure that the volume is always kept at tolerable levels. *(Action: Jt. CP/Ranges)*

23.12.2010

19. An advertisement carrying a list of property dealers being investigated by police may be hosted on Delhi Police and Delhi Govt. website warning citizens against having any dealings with them. *(Action: Spl. CP/Crimes)*

8.01.2011

20. An advertisement may be issued by Traffic Police giving details of prosecutions for use of tinted films in the vehicles. *(Action : Jt. CP/Traffic)*

8.4.2011

21. Information about Traffic prosecutions and penalties should be given wide publicity including display on the electric boards on various intersections. *(Action: Jt. CP/Traffic)*

18.4.2011

22. Delhi Police news letter should be published once a month and should also be uploaded on the Delhi Police website.

19.05.2011

23. An advertisement may be issued advising jewelers, banks, and other high value retailers to install CCTV Cameras in their premises.

    (Action: Spl. CP/Crime)

24. Citizens may be educated about anti-burglary devices available in the market. A suitable advertisements may be issued.

    (Action: Spl. CP/Crime & Jt. CPs/Ranges)

12.09.11

25. All bus stops should carry messages alerting the public waiting for buses to look for suspicious objects, baggages etc. and initiate steps to have them spotted and removed by the Police.

28.10.11

26. Public notice be issued asking farm house owners to notify full details of ocupancy status (self or tenanted) to local police.

    (Action: Spl. CP/L&O & Jt. CPs/Ranges)

24.11.2011

27. Placement agencies involved in placement of women staff such as maids be directed to infom local police stations about their functioning. An advertisement cautioning public about fly by night placement agencies may be issued. *(Action: Spl. CP/L&O & Jt. CPs/Ranges & OSD to LG)*

19.03.2012

28. The aspect of negative publicity by the electronic media and the print media faced by Delhi Police was analyzed by the hon'ble LG. The negative publicity can be minimized, the hon'ble LG felt, if those who manage the media in Delhi Police are able to prevent the negative publicity by anticipating the area of negative publicity and then channelizing information and facts that will establish that the news proposed to be given out is not based on correct assimilation of the ground situation that Delhi Police is confornted with. The CP was requested to seek expert guidance in the matter so that Delhi Police media managers act to prevent negative publicity in such areas where if the ground situation is correctly channelized to the media the proposed negative reports by both, print and electronic media will be aborted.

11. 12.12

29. Information about the Nursing Homes/Hospitals, which have extended the facility of free health check for police personnel be provided on Delhi Police website to similarly motivate other health service providers.

    Action: Spl. CP/Genl. & Admn)

30. An advertisement be issued to inform all senior citizens about the registration scheme launched by Delhi Police. *(Action: Spl. CP/Crime)*

27.09.2012

31. Suitable publicity be organized to motivate non-sikh women pillion riders to voluntarily wear helmets. *(Action: Spl. CP/Crime)*

32. A reference be made to Press Council of India about the motivated report

published in *Times of India* regarding the harassment of a woman reporter by a TSR driver. *[Action: Spl. CP/Operations)*

33. A suitable advertisement be issued to educate public that those rushing any injured person to hospital will not be asked to disclose their identity etc. and become witness unless they express their willingness in this behalf. *[Action: Spl. CP/Crime)*

34. Advisory be sent to all media houses and other employers to make security arrangements on the lines of BPOs for safe return to their homes for their women staff leaving offices after 2130 hours. *[Action: Spl. CP/Crime)*

35. Suitably designed advertisements be issued to dissuade men from indulging in domestic violence. *[Action: Spl. CP/ Traffic)*

36. An advisory be issued to DDA and MCs to mandate CCTV coverage whenever any permission/licence is granted for holding wedding, receptions etc. at public places/Park. *[Action: Spl. CP/L&O)*

37. Advertisement be issued to educate motorists to shun lane weaving and to change their lane only after giving a proper light signal. *[Action: Spl CP/Traffic]*

11.04 .2013

38. A suitable advertisement be issued advising school lcollege Principals to irmmediately inform Delhi Police at a dedicated telephone number at PHQ if the girl srudents face any harassment around their schools/colleges or along the routes to such institutions. *[Action: Spl. CP/Traffic & Spl. CP/L&O]*

25. 4.2013

39. A public notice be issued mandating all farm houses and motels having banqueting facilities to ensure in-house parking. If any violations are noticed, proceeding for sealing the delinquent premises be initiated. *[Action: Spl.CP/ Traffic, Jt. CPs/Ranges, Commissioners of MCD/North, South & East]*

Prosecution

13.09.2010

I. Absence of accommodation to Public Prosecutors in court premises shall be examined by Pr Secretary (Home) who will in consultation with the Director of Prosecution and the Registrar of High Court, Delhi takes steps to ensure that Delhi Police Public Prosecutors have appropriate accommodation to discharge their functions as Public Prosecutors in the courts where they are posted.

02.12.2010

2. Detailed instructions about shortcomings pointed out by the Law department. GNCTD should be issued on priority to all Investigating Officers for strict compliance. *(Action: Spl. CP/Crime)*

3. Public Prosecutors should function under supervision of Law Department, Govt. of NCT of Delhi. *(Action: Principal Secy. Home), GNCTD)*

17.02.2011

4. Home Department to refer to all cases in which there is a difference of opinion with the CP regarding filing of criminal appeals against acquittals to Hon' ble LG for final decision. *(Action: Ppl. Secy. (Home), GNCTD)*

21.02.2011

5. LG reviewed the performance of Forensic Laboratory, Delhi & found in its output & productivity scope for considerable improvement. The Pr. Secretary (Home) has been requested to review the performance of Forensic Laboratory, Delhi.

14.03.2011

6. Delhi Forensic Lab. has a huge pendency list. This is inhibiting criminal

investigations by Delhi Police. LG has ordered a full audit of the Delhi Forensic Lab. within the next 3 months.

28.06.2011

7. All cases in which there is a difference of opinion between Law Department, GNCTD & Delhi Police in the matter of filing of appeals, should be referred by the Home Department to Hon'ble LG for final decision as already decided at the Law & Order Meeting held on 17.02.2011.

   (Action: Ppl. Secy. (Home), GNCTD)

11.11.2011

8. Principal Secretary (Home) will give necessary direction to Directorate of Prosecution so that in terrorist cases resulting in acquittals, a copy of judgment is simultaneously sent to Police, as has already been requested by the CP to CS.

   (Action: Ppl. Secy. (Home)

17.05.2012

9. Capacity to carry out DNA testing at FSL/Delhi should be enhanced to clear pendency and enable FSL to take up fresh cases expeditiously.

04.06.2012

10. A public prosecutor will be linked with each Police Station to enable discussion of cases under investigation and scrutinize the draft charge sheets. *(Action: Principal Secretary (Home), Spl. CP/L & 0 and Director of Prosecution)*

11. Districts DCsP should hold monthly meeting with Public Prosecutors attached to their districts. *(Action: Jt. CPs/Ranges)*

23.08.2012

12. Proposal for hiring of additional legal consultants to strengthen Legal Cell of PHQ and to advise District DCsP be submitted. Meanwhile, Public Prosecutors should continue to vet replies prepared by various Districts & Units to legal notices etc.

    (Action: Jt. CPs/Hdqrs/Hqrs, Ranges, Crime & EWO and Director of Prosecution)

30.10.2012

13. On the advice of the Standing Counsel (Crl.), it was decided that whenever the Hon'ble High Court is informed that a particular parole appeal has been rejected on orders of the Hon'ble LG, the speaking order in entirely of the Hon'ble LG is conveyed to the Standing Counsel (Crl.)

10.06.2013

14. The serious flaws in investigation and prosecution in a murder that took place on 22.04.2010 at D-2, Vivek Vihar, New Delhi was discussed with the CP. It was decided, every heinous case charge-sheeted in a district will be filed only after the District DCP has signed the charge-sheet. This will be done only after he approves the investigation done and is satisfied that the material collected is sufficient evidence to sustain the charge-sheet.

Police Administration

03.04.2008

1. An evaluation of candidates be done at the time of interview for the posts of SI to assess their commitment levels and values.

2. The creation of a mechanism to prevent frittering away of resources, specially the manpower deployed for pairvi of cases in courts.

25.04.2008

3. Latest explosive detection system, which can detect plastic explosives also, should be identified for procurement and deployment during sensitive arrangements. *(Action: Jt. CP/PL)*

4. Pro-active action may be taken by the local police to prevent minor disputes escalating into serious crimes. *(Action: Jt. CP/Ranges)*

5. A database on the success of the 'Eyes & Ears' scheme may be created at PHQ level. *(Action: Jt. CP/ Crime)*

24.07.2008

6. Copies of all complaints received against police personnel on Delhi Police Website should be sent to the Vigilance Branch. (Action: Jt. CP/Crime)

7. District wise and Police Station-wise analysis of total daily diary enteries as against cases registered may be prepared for the month of July, 2008. *(Jt. CPs/Ranges)*

8. In cases of murder and attempt to murder, an analysis of incidents in which prior intimation to police was given be made. *(Action: Jt. CPs/Crime, Ranges)*

07.08.2008

9. Visibility of police in public places should be kept up. Senior officers should also be seen in the field. *(Action: Jt. CPs/Ranges, Crime)*

05.02.2009

10. During servant verification, an experienced police officer should interact with the employee concerned. If anything amiss is noted, the employer can be sounded to take precaution. *(Action: Jt. CPs/Ranges)*

05.03.2009

11. Use of technology enabled security enhancement systems should be augumeated across the city. *(Action: Jt. CP/GA)*

12. Those incharge of vital installations should be impressed upon to make good the deficiencies in security arrangements and report of progress achieved submitted to the Hon'ble LG, through CP, every month. *(Action: Jt. CPs/Ranges)*

13. A presentation on PCR calls received every fortnight and their content wise break up should be made giving details of calls on senior citizen help line and women helpline etc. *(Spl. CP. CP/Inl. & Ops.)*

14. Proper anti-sabotage and access control arrangements should be put by organizers/Police during public rallies, public meetings etc. *(Action: Jt. CPs/Ranges & Security)*

19.03.2009

15. Monthly meetings may be held under Spl. CP/Sec with Jt. CPINR and other tech savy officers so that appropriate technology upgrades can be recommended for Delhi Police. *(Action: Spl. CP/Sec, Jt. CP/NR, DCP/P&L, Addl. DCP (U)/Central)*

16.04.2009

16. CP may issue/reiterate instructions to all DCPs for spending fifteen minutes every day with Beat Constables, to get a feedback on the realistic security situation. *(Action: Joint CP, Southern Range/Commissioner of Police)*

30.04.2009

17. A scheme should be worked out wherein all employees of subordinate ranks of Delhi Police are subjected to regular annual periodic medical checkups. *(Action: Jt. CP/GA)*

28.05.2009

18. During night patrolling, PCR Vans should check suspicious vehicles moving around residential colonies. *(Action: Spl. CP[/Int. & Ops.)*

19. Appropriate briefing should given to PCRs so that they are on watch even while stationary. *(Action: Spl. CP[/Int. & Ops.)*

01.06.2009

20. CP will undertake an exercise on the quality of ethics, domain competence, and the ability to perform without supervision in case of all Inspectors in Delhi Police. This report will be submitted to LG within two months.

11.06.2009

21. Possibility of taking some ex-servicemen drivers for PCR vehicles on contract basis may be examined. *(Action: Jt. CP/Hqrs.)*

22. Accredited hospitals under Delhi Health Mission should be approached for Annual Health Check up of Police Personnel through GNCT of Delhi. A scheme may be prepared indicating the annual financial implications thereof. *(Action: Jt. CP/PHQ)*

25.06.2009

23. A proposal for extra pay for policemen on night duty may be considered. *(Action: Jt. CP/Hqrs.)*

24. When a team of policemen is deployed on law and order duty, it should be properly briefed. *(Action : Jt. CPs/Ranges)*

25. One to one interaction between district DCsP and AcsP with constabulary should take place to get a better appreciation of ground realities. *(Action: Jt. CPs/Ranges)*

20.08.2009

26. Explanation of SHO concerned in whose area the crime statistics show an increase be obtained. The same may be reviewed by CP alongwith ther DCP concerned and put up for perusal of Hon'ble LG. *(Action: CP)*

27. A proposal for providing a gypsy for all ATOs to improve their mobility and effectiveness may be submitted by CP to Hon'ble LG for moving the Home Ministry. *(Jt. CP/GA)*

05.10.2009

28. Public Grievances Commission dealing with Police cases should report to LG of important recommendations made to the Commissioner of Police in respect of grievances dealt by them as an ongoing process. Pro Sec. to LG was requested to write to the Chairman of the Public Grievances Commission in this connection.

18.01.2010

29. LG referred to information received by him from responsible quarters of corruption among the SHOs of Police Stations in Delhi Police. While there are reports of corruption, the CP informed the LG of action taken by him to deal with corrupt officers at the SHO level. LG has asked the CP to furnish a detailed note in this regard so that he is fully briefed on the subject.

25.02.2010

30. LG reiterated the need for creating a Case Study Cell in Police Hdqrs. Under the CPo This cell should function as a knowledge centre where material can be archived and retrieved concerning successful handling of security/law/ adverse situations and lessons learnt. *(Action: Spl. CP/P&L)*

31. NCC cadets may be included in the 'Eyes & Ears' scheme. *(Action: Jt. CP/PHQ)*

32. The definition of 'ex-servicemen' in Delhi Police rules may be reviewed in consultation with Rajya Sainik Board, Delhi. *(Action: Spl. CP/Admn.)*

01.04.2010

33. The ethical commitment and domain competence of every police officer should be carefully assessed. *(Action: All Jt. CPs & DCPs)*

06.05.2010

34. In Delhi large number of persons are listed as Civil Defence volunteers. Only those who are serious about discharging responsibilities should be retained on the list. Once in a quarter volunteers of the area should be summoned on rotational basis for duty at the Civil Defence Warden Post. Those who come forward should be listed for retention and the rest eased out. *(Action: Jt. CP/Ranges)*

10.06.2010

35. Beat Constables should regularly enquire from owners of restaurants, liquor vending shops etc. about instances of affray, drunker brawls, etc. and give their and other important contact numbers to them for immediate reporting of any such instance. *(Action: Jt. CP/Ranges)*

36. Independent Public feedback on performance of SHOs may be collected regularly for taking remedial measures. *(Action: Jt. CP/Ranges)*

24.06.2010

37. ACP level officers should work on the principle of 'Management by Walking' to regularly check mushrooming of Guest Houses and hotels in residential areas within their jurisdiction. *(Action: Jt. CP/Ranges)*

08.07.2010

38. Dr. Shyam Menon of B. R. Ambedkar University may be contacted to carry out an external audit of the working of the Crimes Against Women and Children Cell of Delhi Police to ensure that all the directions issued in respect of handling of crimes against women and children are being followed and implemented. *(Action: Jt. CP/CA W)*

39. There should be an independent website of Crime Against Women and Children Cell of Delhi Police, in addition to the existing link in Delhi Police WebSite. *(Action: Jt. CP/CA W.)*

22.07.2010

40. The CP will ensure that integrity and domain competence are the major considerations for posting officers as SHOs in the Police Stations. *(Action: CP.)*

31.08.2010

41. Commissioner of Police was directed to appralse all Sub-Inspectors and Inspectors in Delhi Police in accordance with (a) their ethical standard (b) domain competence and (c) ability to function autonomously.

21.10.2010

42. Adherence to ethical standards by all police personnel must be given the highest priority. *(Action: Jt. CPs/Ranges)*

43. LG reiterated that high ethics and professional competence is something that he looks for in all police officers and men. He observed that a "chain is as strong as its weakest link". Civilized behavior in all Police Stations is essential and must be ensured. *(Action: Jt. CPs/Ranges)*

04.11.2010

44. Get their feedback on ground level policing. *(Action: Jt. CPs/Ranges)*

18.11.2010

45. Necessary software to enable Delhi Police to utilize the data available with Survey of India under the Delhi Geo- Spatial Project may be purchased by Navyug and paid for by Delhi Police. *(Action: Jt. CP/NR)*

46. Senior police officers of the range should contact retired senior civil and police officers staying in their jurisdiction telephonically to obtain their feedback on the crime situation, interface between the police and public and measures required to further improve law and order and crime containment in Delhi. *(Action: Jt. CP/Ranges)*

02.12.2010

47. In the list of Do's and Don'ts issued to Beat Constables, suitable instructions to keep watch on habitual eve-teasers/stalkers and prevent molestation of women should be incorporated. *(Action: Jt. CPs/Ranges)*

48. Modalities of providing tea and some snacks to PCR staff on night duty to ensure their efficient functioning may be examined. *(Action: Spl. CP/Traffic)*

23.12.2010

49. Long pending departmental enquiries against police officers/men should be settled wherever possible by summoning the officers/men before a group of four senior officers. They will, after ascertaining the delinquent's explanation and seeing the result of enquiry, take a decision on the action to be taken against the police officer concerned and end the long pending DE. *(Spl. CP/Admn)*

50. A feed-back should be obtained from field officers of PSs where the incidence of heinous crime is consistently high. *(Spl. CP/Crimes & Jt. CPs/Ranges)*

51. A citizen's contact list comprising retired senior bureaucrats and service officers should be maintained in all districts. DCsP should get in touch with them periodically to obtain their feedback regarding the crime & law and order situations in their areas. *(Jt. Ranges)*

52. A four digit single helpline number for women in distress be designated and publicized. *(Action: Spl. CP/Ops.)*

03.02.2011

53. Spl. CPIVigilance should find out the number of cases in which complaints received on LG's listening post have been substantiated against police officers. *(Action: Spl. CP/Vigilance)*

17.02.2011

54. Delhi Police should set a target of about 15 months for construction of PS buildings for the Police Stations which are not working from proper buildings. *(Action: Jt. CP/P & I)*

21.02.2011

55. Annual health check of all police personnel in Delhi should henceforth be made compulsory.

28.02.2011

56. The issue of recruiting sports men in the Delhi Police force with the aim to ensure that sport activities is a method to prevent criminal activity on part of the idle mind among juveniles and among teens was discussed. CP agreed to have a fresh look at the question of revising Recruitment Rules to provide a sports quota for recruitment of Constables in Delhi Police.

03.03.2011

57. It may be examined if retired gazetted police officers can be employed as Consultants in Delhi Police on the lines of CBI and Other CPOs. *(Action: Jt. CP/Hqrs.)*

58. All fields units should be instructed to report back the action taken by them on the complaints referred to them by the Vigilance WinglHQ. *(Action: Spl. CP/Vigilance)*

08 .03.2011

59. LG instructed the CP to create a data base of Sub-Inspectors and Inspectors in Delhi Police on their domain competence, on their standard of integrity and on the level of responsibility they can discharge without supervision.

08.04.2011

60. Delhi Police should adopt a standard plan for Police Station buildings. Once the plan has been approved by DDA the same plan should be implemented in other places without getting the plan approved in each and every case. *(Action: Jt. CP/P & I and VC, DDA)*

25.04.2011

61. Database of all Senior officers in Delhi Police should be shared with the Home Department, Govt. of NCT, Delhi.

13.06.2011

62. The issue of Vigilance Investigation Unit at the PHQ for non-gazetted officers of Delhi Police was also discussed at length and after due clarification from the CP, the hon' ble LG agreed that internal investigations by the Delhi Police for nongazetted officers and below may be allowed to be carried out in addition to the cases being taken up by the Anti-Corruption Bureau of GNCT, as the same will in no way reduce the jurisdiction or compromise with the powers already vested in the ACB.

28.06.2011

63. Delhi Police should examine whether Police Housing satisfaction can be expeditiously enhanced by using pre-fab construction technology in suitable cases. *(Action: Jt. CP/P & I)*

21.07.2011

64. The practice of calling up retired bureaucrats living in Delhi and ascertaining from their views on policing in their area should continue at the level of Jt. CP of Ranges and District Police Chiefs. *(Action: Jt. CP/Ranges)*

08. 08.2011

65. In all cases of out of tum promotion, the Incentive Committee while making a recommendation should spell out the exact nature of work which the person individually has done to merit an out of turn promotion.

9.09.2011

66. Govt. of NCT of Delhi may examme if a police officer of appropriate seniority can be posted as Spl. Secy'/Addl. Secy. (Home) in GNCTD for better coordination. *(Action: Chief Secy./Ppl. Secy. (Home) GNCTD)*

21.09.2011

67. Ppl. Secy. (Home) should follow up proposals of Delhi Police ending with MHA. *(Action: Ppl. Secy. (Home)*

68. All SHOs should have a system for maintaining a record of all the calls received in their office. They should also return all the telephone calls received in their absence to improve relationships with the community. *(Action: Jt. CPs/Ranges)*

26.09.2011

69. Crime committed by Head Constable Ajay Tomar is a matter of grave concern. While appreciating the quick response of Head Constable Surinder Tyagi, hon'ble LG directed all citizens of Delhi should be informed that they should report all instances of extortions etc. on the part of Delhi Police functionaries to the CP directly.

70. Rogue elements within Delhi Police apprehended on the spot committing crime or caught red handed should be dealt with stringently including considered for immediate dismissal under Constitutional provisions.

71. Hon' ble LG reiterated the need to judge Delhi Police personnel who have on duty close interface with members of the public like Beat staff by regularly assessing them for their suitability.

13.10.2011

72. Spl. CP Vigilance should monitor if some police officers are repeatedly figuring in public complaints of harass ment, etc. A close watch should be kept on such police officers.

(Action: Spl. CP/Vigilance)

28. 10.2011

73. Pending Department Enquiries may be reviewed by the Vigilance Unit in consultation with Ranges and Headquarters. Minor cases, such as misdemeanor, etc. may be closed within a stipulated period of time by taking an undertaking from the concerned official or by issuing censure/warning. Departmental Enquiries be conducted only when allegations are serious in nature. *(Action: Spl. CP/Vigilance)*

11.11.2011

74. Infomation on nature of complaints received against policemen and enquired into by Vigilance Wing may be complied by dividing them in appropriate categories. Similarly, nature of allegations where complaints were substantiated during vigilance enquiry may also be complied.

(Action: Spl. CP Vigilance)

75. Updates on progress vis a vis projects connected with police welfare and police housing be given at the fortnightly meetings.

(Action: Jt. CP/Hdqrs. & Jt. CP/P & I)

76. A slide incorporating photo of a Beat Officer with beat officer's ann band be included in the next presentation. *(Action: Spl. CP/Crime)*

21.11.2011

77. To meet security concerns, the Delhi Police should not wait for NOC from civic authority for cutting up road etc. After doing the needful like digging trenches, cutting up roads etc., the Delhi Police should also restore the area. Similarly for security reasons where DDA land is required for parking of vehicles, such vacant land should be appropriated for such use by Delhi Police under intimation to DDA and used for parking till DDA begins construction activity on the land.

24.11.2011

78. Leading insurance agencies be consulted for formulating a comprehensive proposal for special insurance coverage of Delhi Police personnel.

(Action: Jt. CP/GA)

79. Adherence to time by the agencies executing police housing projects should be ensured. 1*(Action: Jt. CP/P & I)*

80. Information about percentage of complaints against Delhi Police Personnel substantiated during enquiries made by the Public Grievance Commission (PGC) during the last five years may be complied and presented for information of Hon'ble LG. *(Action: Special CP Vigilance)*

81. A slide depicting total number of DEs pending as on December, 201/along

with figures of the corresponding period of 2010 be included in the next presentation. *(Action: Spl. CP Vigilance)*

08.12.2011

82. DDA should expedite allotment of land for sports activities of Delhi Police Public School at Safdarjung Enclave. *(Action: VC/DDA.)*

83. To meet the shortage of residential/office accommodation, Delhi Police should again request Shirkey Constructions to take up prefab constructions on behalf of Delhi Police, before they take up assignment of prefab construction on behalf of any other department/authority, even if the requirement of Delhi Police does not match their minimum construction requirement. *(Action: Special CP (Admn.)*

05.01.2012

84. Foot Beat patrolling should be at the minimum in pairs. *(Action: Spl. CP/L & O, Jt. CPs/Ranges)*

85 PWD norms regarding maintenance ofresidentialloffice buildings be obtained to seek adequate funds for proper maintenance of police housing/police stations. *(Action: Jt. CP/G.A. & Jt. CP/P & I)*

86. Time Taken to complete DEs be collated and presented. *(Action: Spl. CP/Vigilance)*

1.01.2012

87. Assistance of willing retired govt. servants, ex- servicemen, Civil Defence volunteers could be obtained for joint patrolling in vulnerable areas. *(Action: Jt. CPs/Ranges)*

88. Night checking officers should visit police stations to prevent possibility of any delinquency on the part of police personnel. *(Action: Jt. CPs/Ranges)*

89. The ACR proforma for police officers should include a column regarding the officers anitude towards women. *(Action: Jt. CP/Hdqr)*

90. Examine feasibility of assigning night duty for two/three lady police officials viding accommodation to such women police officers near their place of duty, If necessary be taking houses on rent for them. *(Action: Add!. CP/HQ)*

19.1.2012

91. Expeditious action be ensured for early handling over/taking over of land identified by DDA for allotment to Delhi Police for Police Stations and other Police Complexes. *(Action: VC/DDA and CP/Delhi.)*

92. PCR staff should be selected keeping in view the need for their high alertness and rapid response requirements. *(Action: Jt. CP/Headquarter)*

02.02.2012

93. Gist of citizen feedback received under 'Know Your Police Stations hosted on Delhi Police web-site, be presented at the next fortnightly meeting. *(Action: Spl. CP/Crime)*

94. In future, public perception by way of feedback from RWAs etc should also be taken into account while selecting the best Police Station. *(Action: Spl. CP/L & 0)*

27.02.2012

95. Associate Finance in Police Hdqrs. may be expeditiously created and LG's orders obtained on the staffing.

96. LG reiterated the need to allow police officers on duty and in uniform to travel on public transport without payment as they by their presence ensure safety and security to other passengers.

97. Complainants dis-satisfied by the action taken on their complaints reported to Police Stations should meet the ACP/DCP who should be available during fixed hours to hear such aggrieved complainants. CP was directed to ensure by way of advertisements on FM channels and else where that ear-marked ACP and District OCP will be available to the public for hearing their grievances at fixed hours which will be mentioned in the advertisements.

1.03.2012

98. In the feedback statement for Know Your Police Station a third column indicating action taken on feedback received be added. A suitable advertisement may be used to make people aware about K.Y.P.S. facility.
(Action: Spl. CP/Crime)

15.03.2012

99. DDA should be asked to fence lands being offered to Police for sports and pmes. More such play grounds be identified particularly in other congested areas. Feasibility of organizing vocational training for children, who are coming to play games could also be examined. For this purpose a small porta-cabin could be erected and those attending such training could be given a monetary incentive. *(Action : Spl. CP/Crime and Jt. CP/SER)*

100. Delhi Police could consult MHA to evaluate the desirability of forming a Street Children Welfare Fund. Funding could be by donations from Corporate entities. Proper and transparent SOP and audit systems could be devised.
(Action: Spl. CP/Crime)

03.04.2012

101. Modalities for arranging regular annual health check-ups of all Delhi Policemen be explored by taking assistance of agencies like Delhi Red Cross etc. *(Action: Spl. CP/Admn)*

102. MHA may be consulted regarding the feasibility of taking a group insurance cover at government cost for Delhi Police personnel. *(Action: Spl. CP/Admn.)*

103. Dheerpur Police Housing project be monitored closely for expeditious execution. *(Action : Jt. CP/P & I)*

104. MCD should issue an order directing all concerned to notify the local police sration at least one week before excavation of any basement, to enable the local police to check whether requisite permissions have been obtained.
(Action : Commissioner, MCD and Spl. CP/L & O)

1 .05.2012

105. PCR Van staff be selected keeping in view their capacity to effectively respond to emergent situations. *(Action : Spl. CP/Operation and Jt. CP/Hdqrs.)*

106. Within the jurisdiction of their Police Stations, police officers may be directed to apply" Management by Walking" as a tool to keep tabs on the pulse of me area. *(Action: Jt. CPs/Ranges)*

1.06.2012

107. CP will frame guidelines for promotions in the out of turn category under Rule 19 (ii) of Delhi Police (Promotion & Confirmation) Rules, 1980.

108. CP offered to make available police officers on deputation to the Anti-Corruption Branch, GNCTD as and when requests for services of Delhi Police officers in all ranks are placed.

21.06.2012

109. Regular briefing and debriefing of Beat Officers be ensured. *(Action : Jt. CPs/Ranges)*

110. Meeting be held with Commissioner (Planning), DDA to identify land which can be allotted to Delhi Police. *(Action: Spl. CP Vigilance and Jt. CP/P & I)*

02.07.2012

111. Ensure better care to welfare of Delhi Police personnel by organizing their regular health check ups and enhancing their residential accommodation pool. This is a welfare measure directed by hon 'ble LG.

19.07.2012

112. A proposal for changing FAR use be sent to Shri S. P. Bansal, Commissioner Planning-III DDA so that land allotted for police complexes could accommodate more residential units. *(Action: Spl. CP/Amn.)*

113. Feedback given by public during Jan Saampark Abhiyan of Delhi Police and ations taken thereupon be indicated during next meeting. *(Action: Jt. CP/NR)*

02.08.2012

114. Assistance of Prof. Emeritus C.R.Babu of University of Delhi, who has been associated with development of Yamuna and Aravali Biodiversity Parks of DDA, could be obtained for developing green areas of Dheerpur project and other police Complexes. *(Action : Jt. CP/P & T)*

115. Health monitoring of police personnel could be done keeping in view their age group, which can be from 25-35, 35-45 & 45- 60 Years.) *(Action: Jt. CPs/Ranges)*

10.2012

116. Reverting to a reported case of suicide by a Delhi Police SI, LG directed that need to constantly monitor stress levels of Delhi Police officials of all ranks be determined with the assistance of Institute of Human Behaviour & Allied Sciences, Dilshad Garden, Shahadara, Delhi.

117. LG desired that Pr. Secretary (Home) should up date him with respect to the status of authorizing Delhi Police officers to issue orders U/S 133 Cr.PC and other Cr.PC provisions and also regarding authorizing Inspectors posted in the Vigilance Investigating Unit to investigate cases under the Prevention of Corruption Act.

118. Hon'ble LG said that all police personnel including PCR staff, including those in PHQ Control Rom need to be mandated to behave courteously with the Public. Any deviation from this norm should result in corrective action and those who are incorrigible should be severely dealt with. *(Action: Spl. CP/Ops.)*

119. LG instructed that all personnel in Security Units should undergo physical tests regularly. *(Spl. CP/Security)*

120. Spl. CPVigilance to review complaints received in PHQ Vigilance and give a presentation on action taken on complaints registered in the Listening Post, vis-a-vis the nature of complaints, action taken on them etc. *(Action: Spl. CP Vigilance)*

121. Departmental Enquires where herrings have concluded should be disposed off by the 10th of December. *(Action: Spl. CP Vigilance)*

122. Complaints against Field Police Personnel under the category of "inaction" be analysed to ascertain the number of cases where the allegations were found to have been justified. Conclusions be indicated in the next meeting. *(Action: Spl. CP Vigilance)*

123. Disciplinary authorities may be advised to generally initiate DEs in cases of serious misdemeanors. Minor infringement can be settled by "Orderly Room" proceedings. *(Action: Special. CP/Vigilance)*

124. Delhi Police personnel be constantly sensitized to behave in a civilized manner during their interactions with the public. *(Action: Jt. CPs/Ranges)*

21.11.2012

125. Pol ice personnel, identified with ailments requiring advanced treatment, could be accommodated in lighter jobs. Record of preventive health check ups be kept up for future reference. *(Action: Spi. CP/Genl.Admn. and Jt. CP/Hdqrs.)*

126. Police Helpline numbers be replaced with more user friendly numbers. *(Action: Spl. CP/Hqs)*

29.11.2012

127. DDA be told to immediately start construction of a Community Hall at Village Kotla PS Pandav Nagar. *(Action: Jt. CP/SER)*

128. Perfab technology may be used for Police Housing on experimental basis. *(Action: Spl. CP/Gen Admn)*

13.12.2012

129. Where proper PS buildings are not available and nearby Gram Sabha land can be allotted, proposals should be sent for such allotment to the concerned Revenueauthorities with a copy of Hon'ble LG's Secretariat. *(Action: Jt. CPs/Ranges and Jt. CP/P & I)*

Technology, Infrastructural Development and Case Studies for better Delhi Policing

08.05.2008

1. The possibility of creation of an Engineering Cell for undertaking urgent remedial action in case of the need of minor engineering repairs on carriageway in Traffic Unit should be explored.

   (Action: Jt. CP/Traffic)

05.06.2008

2. A database on engineering innovations done by the Traffic Police should be prepared. *(Action: Jt. CP/Traffic)*

3. An emergency road repair cell be opened in the Traffic Unit. This should be equipped with the latest equipment/technology to take contingent measures for easing traffic congestion.

   (Action: Jt. CP/Traffic)

19.06.2008

4. Using the services of experts from DRDO, CSIR etc for assisting in procurement of technology related systems/products may be considered.

   (Action: Jt. CP/P &L)

5. Hon'ble LG endorsed the Delhi Police initiative of installing GPS system on a trial basis in some of their Patrol vehicles.

6. Technology enabled system to provide security cover to the elderly by

providing connectivity of their homes with police stations, may be looked into and a pilot project initiated. *(Action: Jt. CP/Crime)*

01.07.2008

7. Engineering Cell of the Traffic Police should be strengthened to quickly implement minor Engineering solutions on the ground. *(Action: Jt. CP/Traffic)*

18.09.2008

8. A Delhi Police Research Unit may be created within Delhi Police to continuously identify and analyse important issues connected with public security and safety and suggest measures to meet the new challenges posed by phenomena like terrorism, organized crime etc.

9. Delhi Police should upgrade its consultation with experts in this field. *(Action: Spl. CP/Admn)*

03.10.2008

10. A traffic engineering Unit may be created which can attend to pressing road repairs of a minor nature. *(Action: Jt. CP/Traffic)*

16.10.2008

11. A Traffic Engineering Cell consisting of trained and qualified staff with standard operating procedures should be created within the Traffic Unit to attend urgent road safety engineering requirements. *(Action: Jt. CP/Traffic)*

12. Creation of a Strategic Media Cell within the Delhi Police may be considered. *(Action: Spl. CP/Crime)*

26.12.2008

13. A Hotline between Police Control and Command Room & Raj Niwas may be installed. *(Action: Jt. CP/Operations)*

22.01.2009

14. The Delhi Police Research Unit (DPRU) should obtain the details of tenancy laws pertaining to senior citizens from Bangkok. *(Action: Spl. CP/DPRU)*

05.02.2009

15. A Small Communication Research Unit may be created to continuously explore ideas and methodology to educate public on issues of security. College of Art, who have a course on media art/animation could among others be contacted to seek expert advice. *(Action: Jt. CP/Crime)*

17.05.2009

16. How sensitive law and order situations have been handled should be documented as case studies for future reference and training. Suitable honorarium can be given to the police officers undertaking this task. *(Action: CP/ Spl. CPs/ Intelligence, Crime and L & 0)*

08.06.2009

17. In order to strengthen security, Delhi Police will initiate steps to have helipads constructed in two convenient locations within Delhi Police control on Delhi Police land.

25.06.2009

18. DPRU should constantly work on innovative technological solutions to the

problems of security and its suggestions be kept in a log book and, after CP has approved, implemented and LG apprised.

(Action : Spl. CP/DPRU, Jt. CP Spl. & Jt.CP Ranges)

30.11.2009

19. LG has also asked the CP to explore the possibility of using satellite facility of Googles for security related information without breach of essentials of confidentiality .

01.08.2010

20. Wireless handsets may be taken on lease from Motorola by Delhi Police to supplement the existing numbers to meet the requirements of Delhi Police till TETRA communication network provides reliable and continuous connectivity.

15.11.2010

21. The TETRA communication network is not functional in Delhi Police. In security operations a functional TETRA Communication Service is vital. LG has desired to be regularly updated on its performance.

22. All police Stations are required to be fitted with CCTV cameras and it has to be ensured that these CCTV cameras keep a week's record of their footage.

07.12.2010

23. CP should create a police technology evaluation cell where assignees should scan all facilities to collect information on all available knowledge to improve the use oftechnology at the ground level by Delhi Police personnel.

21.12.2010

24. Wherever CCTV cameras are installed and will be installed in future they should have a recording provision of 30 days. CP may ensure that this directive is implemented through necessary notifications/directives etc.

06.01.2011

25. A technology research unit should be established to find out details of the latest techniques being adopted by leading police forces all over the world.

(Action: Spl. CP/Crime)

16.05.2011

26. The use of TETRA sets by Delhi Police is reportedly inadequate. The CP reported that the communication channel provided by TETRA needs falls far short of acceptable norms. The service providers HCL and MOTOROLA have to considerably improve their services by the end of June, 2011 if TETRA is to be extensively used by Delhi Police as replacement to their present mode of communication. CP has spoken to MD HCL at LG's instance and the steps to improve the channel has been initiated.

27. The TETRA sets presently not under use will be made available to the existing Beats of Delhi Police with immediate effect.

19.05.2011

28. Delhi Police should examine if prefab construction technique can be adopted for urgently increasing the housing stock in Delhi Police.

(Action: Jt. CP/P & I)

23.05.2011

29. PCR personnel on duty in the New Delhi area should be provided night Vision binoculars. They should be stationed on machans wherever possible to

enable them to survey larger areas and thereby detect troubled spots well in time.

04.07.2011

30. LG directed that in the next 18 months all Police Stations must become infrastructurally functional.

11.07.2011

31. The TETRA communication system is a secured communication network. Delhi Police has been directed to adopt this secured communication system in the present context of security concerns of the State. However, the existing system may also continue simultaneously till this secured communication network is fully viable and can be wholly depended upon.

21.07.2011

32. Spl. CP Law & Order should get the design and material of machans' standardized. A 'rate contract' be entered, following due codal formalities, so that machans could be quickly erected, wherever required.

(Action: Spl. CP/Law & Order)

13.10.2011

33. There should be a Technology Tracking Cell in Delhi Police to find out details of latest security and surveillance devoices available in other countries. Efforts should be made to find out details of devices being provided to vulnerable sections lime senior citizens, etc. to alert the local police in case of any emergency.

(Action: Spl. CP/Crime)

24.10.2011

34. Police Station need to be connected electronically in Delhi similar to Police Stations in Gujarat and Andhra. CP may initiate steps to that effect.

24.11.2011

35. Use of prefab technology may be considered to implement police housing projects in a shorter time- frame. *(Action: Jt. CP/P & I)*

05.01.2012

36. Murder cases having genesis in ' disputes' be analyzed to see whether any could have been prevented. *(Action: SCP/Crimes)*

19. 1.1012

37. All incidents of murders should also be reviewed by supervisory officers to see whether these could have been prevented.

(Action: Spl. CP/L&O and Jt. Ranges)

38. Area around Karbala in Jorbagh may be suitably photographed/video-graphed for the purpose of record. *(Action: Jt. CP/SR)*

02.02.2012

39. A Technology Tracking Cell may be established by Crime Branch to explore and evaluate availab le technologies that can be adopted for improving police efficiency/efficiency. *(Action, Spl. CP/Crime)*

40. An Archive of case studies of management of important law and order events ealing with major crimes should be built up for posterity. Incentives can be officers documenting such case studies.

(Spl. CP/Crime & Spl. CP/L & 0)

41. Best practices adopted by other countries to protect traffic personnel from

vehicular emissions and Suspended Particulate Master (SPM) be studied to identify appropriate mitigating methodologies.

(Action : Jt. CP/Traffic)

42. Jawa enabled TETRA sets should be made available to the Beat staff. This enable them to transfer the footage of the crime taking place before their eyes to their immediate authority for corrective action. Risk to their person will thus be avoided when they are ill equipped to prevent the crime.

01.3.2012

43. Murder cases be analyzed to see whether the incidents could have been prevented. *(Action: Jt. CPs/Ranges)*

05.3.2012

44. The CP has mentioned that technological expansion of Delhi Police is essential. He is interacting on regular basis with Home Secretary, GOI to install gadgets for improved functioning by Delhi Police. These efforts of the CP were endorsed by the LG.

45. All Police Stations were required to be fitted with CCTV cameras and ensure that these CCTV cameras keep a week's record of their footage. This be looked into.

13.03.2012

46. Housing for the subordinate police formations is essential for keeping high their morale in the fight against crime. CP was instructed to consolidate the housing requirements for Delhi Police subordinate ranks and initiate steps to build prefab structures with an order of 5000 houses and above as early as possible.

15.03.2012

47. Use of Pre- fab technology be carefully considered to accelerate pace of constructing Police Housing. *(Action: Jt. CP (P & I)*

21.06.2012

48. Dr. R. K. Khandal, Director, Shri Ram Centre for Industrial Research be contacted to know what can be done to ensure better quality assurance of the Dheerpur Police Housing Project. *(Action: Jt. CPs/P & I)*

49. GPS be installed on QRTs and ERVs. *(Action: Spl. CP/Ops.)*

25.06.2012

50. Special Commissioner (Law & Order) will call for and obtain archival studies of law and order situations successfully resolved by adopting methods that are out of the book.

02.08.2012

51. Proper documentation and monitoring of self PCR calls be ensured.

(Action: Spl. CP/Ops)

30.10.2012

52. CP was directed to issue instructions to Senior officers to locate Govt. owned land near Police Stations which can be acquired for Delhi Police to construct residential and other ancillary units for better and more efficient functioning of the Police Stations to which this land will be attached.

29.11.2012

53. Archival record of important cases be kept at CP's office. Suitable honorarium be paid to officers undertaking such studies.

(Action: Spl. CP/Crime)

13.12.2012

53. An Archival Unit be set up at PHQ to maintain Case Studies of important cases/situations handled. Suitable honorarium could be paid to officers writing the case studies. *(Action: Spl. CP/Crime)*

54. Feasibility of installation of GPS bases navigation devices in PCR Vans be explored. *(Action: Spl. CP/Ops)*

55. The possibility of enlisting the services of a trained Physiognomist for crime prevention may be explored. *(Action: Spl. CP/Crime)*

14.01.2013

56. Technical Devices Tracking Cell may be created by the Commissioner of Police to list out such devices that can be effectively used by women who are stalked or accosted.

Improving Training

01.07.2008

1. Interactive training modules may be organized on a regular basis for all levels of the Police force in different areas of policing. *(Action: Jt. CP/Training)*

03.10.2008

2. All PCR staff should be trained in first- aid and handling of accident victims. *(Action: Jt. CP/Ops.)*

17.05.2009

3. Special CP/Security and Special CP/Training should meet Shri Praveen Swami, Member, Security Commission, to obtain his suggestions to improve training of police personnel. *(Action: Spl. CP/Security/Security & Spl. CP/Training)*

10.12.2009

4. Police Training curriculum should include combating terrorism. Resource persons on terrorism from reputed security organizations like Olive Group may be invited to address trainees. *(Action: Jt.CP/Trg.)*

08.02.2010

5. Training motivation and coordinate efforts acting as a force multiplier to improve output and performance was mentioned in some detail by the Hon'ble LG. He directed the CP to make a presentation on training imparted, the quality of trainers & whether outside trainers and foreign expert have been considered for impartingtraining to police officers. This presentation has been ordered on 11.02.2010.

11.02.2010

6. Action being taken to prevent theft of motor vehicles may be ascertained from Chennai to adopt best practices. *(Action: Spl. CP/Traffic)*

7. The syllabus of the Police University proposed to be set up by Govt. Of Gujarat may be obtained. *(Action: Jt. CP/Training)*

8. Proposals may be put up to revise the rates of honorarium for guest lectures at Police Training College, enchantment of budget provision for the same as well as increase in the number of post of trainers. A digital data base of each individual member of Delhi Police containing details of training undergone by him during his career should also be created. Persons undergone training should be asked to give a feedback on the contents of the training programme. They should also be invited to indicate their area of interest in undergoing specific training.

9. Training of trainers of Delhi Police Training College and schools may be further strengthened through cooperation arrangements with Police Forces offriendly countries viz. U. K., France, etc. *(Action: Jt. CP/Training)*

02.03.2010

10. The CP to create a Training Audit Cell to elicit the quality of training imparted to police officers who are being continuously sent to courses for specialized trainings in different places in Delhi Police training centres which are separate from PTC and Police Training School.

06.05.2010

11. First-Aid training of PCR staff to be also got done through Delhi Branch of Indian Red Cross. *(Action: Spl. CP/Ops)*

12. Principal Secretary (Home) should finalize, on priority, guidelines for training of staff of private security agencies. *(Action: Principal Secy . (Home)*

10.06.2010

13. Information on different types of training imparted in a month in terms of contents, man-drop etc. should be reported to PHQ. Total number of man days of training, duration of training, levels of persons trained, etc. be prepared at the next meeting. *(Action: Jt. CP/Trg.)*

08.07.2010

14. Police Training sessions should be more interactive and the target group should not be more than 25 people. An audit of quality of traning programme may be got done by Army authorities.

(Action: Spl. CP/Ops.)

22.07.2010

15. Training of 'Spotters' should be organized.

(Action: Spl. CP/Spl. Cell)

02.12.2010

16. Security, guidelines for training of staff of private security agencies be put up. *(Action: Principal Secy. (Home)*

17. Judicial Officers and other legal experts should be invited to deliver lectures to IOs. A specially designed course for Investigating Officers may be organized in Delhi Judicial Academy or Union Territories Civil Services Training Institute. *(Action: Jt. CP/Training)*

18. Public Prosecutors may be sent on deputation for short periods to Police Training College for IOs. *(Action: Principal Secy. (Home), GNCTD)*

28.03.2011

19. Training to Delhi Police personnel must remain the top priority in all areas specially in the areas of heinous investigation and commando training.

11.4.2011

20. The Police Training Academy should introduce for Sub-Inspectors (Probationers) and IPS (Probationers) a course to make them aware of use of technology as a force multiplier in all areas of police functioning.

18.4.2011

21. Commando training for Delhi Police personnel will henceforth also include training for disaster management specially in the case of earth quakes.

23.05.2011

22. Accommodation to trainees in Delhi Police is inadequate and the existing infrastructure is below par and not commensurate with the high standard and difficult training which all police personnel are required to undergo. Accommodation to trainees is one welfare measure which has to be given the highest priority and will be taken up for frequent monitoring at both the Monday's meeting with the CP and the fortnightly Law & Order meeting. Progress in improvement of the accommodation infrastructure would therefore be required to be reported at these meetings.

21.04.2011

23. St. John Ambulance and Red Cross Society should be requested to supply illustrative leaflets to all PCR Vans regarding precautions to be taken for different types of injury. *(Action: Spl. CP/Operators and OSD to LG)*

19.09.2011

24. Training of Delhi Police officers assigned to intelligence collection work needs to be modelled on the lines imparted by the Intelligence Bureau, GOI to its various ranks who are assigned to intelligence collection work. LG directed the CP, Delhi to ensure that this is done by the Delhi Police Training Academy.

24.11.2011

25. Regular refresher training be ensured for Commandos.
(Action : Spl. CP.Security & Spl. CP/SpJ. Cell)

05.01.2012

26. Highlights of the inputs and lessons learnt during the training attended by Spl. CP/Law & Order and Spl. CP/Ops be presented during the next meeting.
(Action: Spl. CP/L & O & Spl. CP/Ops.)

1.05.2012

27. Regular feedback should be obtained from trainees as they undergo their training programmes. *(Action: Spl. CP/Training and Security)*

01.11.2012

28. While on the subject of training, Hon'ble LG desired to be apprised regarding progress in the area of development of infrastructure in the Police Training College, Spl. CP/Training should monitor this work closely.
(Spl. CP/Training)

15.11.2012

29. Trainees during the induction and refresher training be encouraged to take the initiative to articulate their training needs to acquire any specific skills. Feedback during and after the training be used to fine tune the training programme. *(Action: Spl CP/Security)*

29.11.2012

30. 'Chits In a bowl' methodology be used to Improve trainees' involvement/ receptivity. After a lecture, two-three chits could be taken out and the trainees so selected asked to briefly tell the class about what they have imbibed.

30.01.2013

31. Police Trainees should undergo gender sensitization training modules by involving reputed NGOs. *[Action: SplCP/Training]*
32. Training programme on picket checking should include a lecture onsensitizing trainees about what they should look out for. *[Action: SplCP/Training]*
33. Officers bearers of TSR unions be called and urged to educate their members to observe traffic norms. Those responding positively should be publicly felicitated to motivate others to emulate them. *(Action: Spl.CP/Training]*

Index